THE AMERICAN RETREAT

The Reagan Foreign and Defense Policy

Joseph Churba

REGNERY GATEWAY • CHICAGO

Published by Regnery Gateway, Inc.
360 West Superior Street
Chicago, Illinois 60610

Library of Congress Catalog Card Number: 84-42712
ISBN:0-89526-604-0

This book is dedicated to
MAX H. KARL
for unfailing support and encouragement.

CONTENTS

PREFACE

ˢThe current Soviet regime may well be the result of the First World War; the Allied victory in the Second consolidated the role of the Kremlin as a chief source of unrest and upheaval throughout the world. The fusion of its vast propaganda resources and the utopian longings of large strata of the intelligentsia everywhere has enabled the Soviets to attempt to realize the dreams generated by the desperate Bolshevik revolution almost seven decades ago.

From its inception the Soviet regime had ties with leftwing parties; by the early thirties it had established contact with most governments, both by the diplomatic channels of states and through a swift development of techniques of espionage and subversion via countless groups and individuals worldwide.

Early on the Kremlin penetrated the highest levels of the United States and British governments at this subterranean level. When President Franklin Roosevelt recognized the U.S.S.R. in the early thirties, it began a new and respectable career, enjoying the esteem not merely of its leftwing partisans but also of influential strata in the United States, Great Britain, France and many other countries.

It is routine for scholars, bureaucrats, journalists and students to take a big government seriously, to scrutinize it through its own documents. A state with a vast government apparatus, benefiting by the toil of hundreds of millions of people, and above all with *military power*, is often regarded as a mirror-image, only slightly distorted, of one's own government.

This has made it natural for U.S. administrations—Republican and Democratic alike—to be taken in by the image of normality presented to the world by the Soviet state. Even when the Kremlin acquired nuclear arms a generation ago and became a rival of the United States, Americans generally were not dismayed: they took it for granted that the Soviet government, like their own, was preoccupied with the conditions of its existence, with its national interests.

Nevertheless, the Soviet Union is not like other states. It is, rather, like an organization—the Communist Party—that owns a country. That organization numbers about 10 percent of the population—20 million plus. Representing nothing but itself, it co-opts its membership. It disposes of the labor of 235 million people: its decisions, at the topmost level, are reached by a handful of men who can confer in a small room. It can implement those decisions without reference to public opinion, mass media, or coalitions of other interests in the government. Decision-making is inherently simple; implementation depends only on the objective difficulties with which an action must contend.

The Soviet leadership has inherited from the earliest phase of its existence two elements: a monolithic structure, with total control of all media, which enables it to concentrate its decision-making process; and a cluster of slogans which it can flourish abroad in order to channel enthusiasm for social and economic change and by which it can present itself as the standard-bearer of progressive ideals.

These abilities enable the Kremlin to treat the whole world as a chessboard on which for the last several years it has worked toward a consistent and unmistakable goal: world hegemony. A fundamental strength in that campaign is the Soviet camouflage of appearing to be a normally functioning government of a normally functioning nation. While all of the U.S. administrations since the end of the Second World War have failed to understand this fundamental fact, the failure in this respect of the Carter Administration was especially egregious.

At first it seemed that Reagan's pre-election campaign rhetoric in 1980 justified the hope that his administration would embody a new realism in foreign policy, but nothing has survived except the rhetoric: That is the more serious because it creates the illusion that something is being done. In fact, the Reagan Administration is doing nothing but making provocative remarks at press conferences, frowning at Soviet arms dispatches, and—at best—talking about rearmament. It is, to reverse Roosevelt's phrase, speaking loudly and carrying a very small stick.

In the following pages we shall see the rationale for the Soviet campaign for world hegemony, the shape of the plan initiated in 1975 for its implementation, and the measures that must be taken to protect the interests of the United States and the rest of the free world.

We begin with a chapter showing the purpose—the internal necessity—and the time-constraints which the Soviets appear to have. Then there are four chapters, each detailing a major American policy failure in the face of Soviet assertiveness: in the Persian Gulf, against Israel, in Africa, and in Central America. It is no accident that the chapter on Israel is the most elaborate, for U.S. policy inadequacies there can be documented on nearly a day-to-day basis. It is not sufficiently recognized that Israel is our best and firmest ally, and the linchpin to security and stability in the whole of the Middle East.

There follows a triad of chapters on policy failures—NATO, the MX, and general armaments—in which the U.S. does not even have the excuse of failing to meet Soviet incursions. These are areas in which it is largely or wholly within our power to do whatever needs to be done, if we have but the will and foresight to do it. Our failures stem simply from the inability or unwillingness to take seriously the threat of Soviet hegemony.

Finally, there are three chapters which attempt to provide in outline form: a) the right way to conceptualize U.S. defense requirements—in short, how to think about defense; b) the policies which need to be undertaken at this moment—what is to be done; and c) a way of organizing and targeting our future defense efforts—what likely will be necessary in the future.

Such an analysis, with its accompanying recommendations, argues for a new and more serious national commitment to U.S. defense needs, including a substantial increase in defense spending, universal military service, and considerable limitations on the freedom of U.S. corporations to sell high technology materials abroad. Nothing less than such measures will be adequate to meet U.S. defense requirements and the concommitant military manpower needs.

This book, in effect, completes my trilogy on the foreign and defense policies of the United States in the last decade (*Politics of Defeat*, 1977, and *Retreat From Freedom*, 1980, being the other volumes). My readers will no doubt be relieved to learn that I do not intend to burden them with yet another volume chronicling America's retreat from power. Let us hope the saga has ended.

Washington, DC
April 1984

1

The Soviet Lunge
For The World

The current crisis in world politics entered a new phase in the summer of 1975.

At that time the Soviet state, for the first time in Russian history, undertook a military operation thousands of miles from the borders of Russia: it airlifted substantial amounts of heavy weaponry to Angola in West Africa—6,000 miles away—put them in the hands of Cuban soldiers, and set up a puppet government.

This operation was followed by similar seizures of strong-points throughout Africa and the Middle East (also carried out by Cuban proxies) and resulted in the establishment of puppet governments.

As the Soviet campaign fanned out east and southeast it became obvious that its ultimate goal was the encirclement of the Persian Gulf. In January 1980 the Soviets discarded all pretense and invaded Afghanistan with a massive combat force composed of its own troops.

At present, the Russian forces have in fact already encircled the Gulf. Their combat garrisons in Aden, Yemen and the island of Socotra are buttressed by friendly (Marxist) regimes in Mozambique and Ethiopia. Treaties of cooperation with Iraq and Syria and combat-ready troops in Afghanistan—separated from the Gulf only by the small, politically negligible area of Baluchistan—are evidently capable of ensuring the control of the area as a whole in case of need (such as a seizure of the Arabian oil wells by one of the many clients of the Kremlin).

We shall see in a moment the decisive role of the Kremlin in the installation of a Muslim "fundamentalist" regime in Iran, indispensable for the envelopment of the Gulf.

The interminable current discussion about nuclear arms control, which has been preoccupying American opinion-makers for the past three decades and which has reached a zenith of verbosity since the operation in Angola in 1975, must be seen against the background of this ramified Soviet campaign, carried out by ordinary troops, with ordinary weapons, in what would seem, compared with the high technology of nuclear arms, a remarkably primitive procedure.

The Russian sweep in Africa and the Middle East has been so grand that it obviates the need for the detailed analysis that generally obscures clear thought in the realm of international statecraft. A single detail, such as the preponderance achieved by the Soviet Navy in the Indian Ocean, independent of any domestic defense requirements, makes it obvious that the Russians have a *plan*.

The purpose of this widespread use of proxies is simply—camouflage. It was vital for the Soviet Executive to mask its intentions from the very beginning, and even though the scale of the vast pincers operation was unmistakable, not to say sensational, it was nevertheless possible for the KGB, with its countless channels of disinformation aided by genuine partisans scattered throughout the world media, to pretend effectively that in the first place there was *no* general campaign, and that in the second place the allegedly fragmented events in this enormous area were independent of each other. The unifying link of the Cuban proxies was simply regarded as a voluntary act of the allegedly sovereign government of Cuba. Andrew Young, Ambassador to the United Nations in the Carter Administration, made a strong impression by asking what was *wrong* with Cubans choosing to march in Ethiopia: "The Cubans are human beings, aren't they?"

Throughout this whole complex campaign, accordingly, it was vital for the Kremlin to seem absolutely inert. There was always a risk, after all, that if what was happening was clear, even an outmaneuvered, baffled U.S. administration might react—with incalculable consequences.

The current Kremlin scenario was conceived half a century after the Bolshevik revolution in 1917 precisely because the early Bolshevik fantasies about the lightning spread of *The Revolution*—guaranteed by Marxist doctrine—were instantly shattered by facts. The advanced industrial nations—Germany, Great Britain, France, America—were not living up to Marx's prophecies. Lenin's revolution itself, embarked on in a burst of understandable euphoria, was not consummated by a tidal wave of revolution in Germany. By 1923, after the collapse of a feeble upheaval in Germany, the Bolshevik leadership saw itself on its own. The Soviet revival of capitalism in 1921, desperately needed to help the parvenu state cope with a grim crisis, was swiftly replaced by the characteristic institutions of totalitarianism: a totally controlled press and a monolithic executive. The massacre of the Kulak farmers in the first years of the thirties, the murderous repressions of the rest of the decade, the straitjacketing of the population as a whole—the slaughter, in sum, of some 66 million people in the first three decades of Bolshevik rule—proved to be the reality rather than the raising of standards of a new society.

By the time the regime emerged—mutilated, battered, bleeding—from World War II, it could still manhandle its own population, but it could not remotely satisfy consumption, or even organize its agriculture in the teeth of peasant disaffection. Russia, historically a granary, was reduced to importing wheat regularly on a massive scale.

What kept the Soviet elite going for decades was the dream formulated by Stalin in the thirties—to "overtake and pass America." And it is true that for a time, after the Second World

War, the regime was able to draw abreast of European industry, and even, in arms, outstrip America. Yet it could do this only by keeping the consumption of goods and services for its citizens on a very low level.

But even the optimism that might have been generated by its ability to establish heavy industry, which reached its zenith during the seventies, was dealt a mortal blow by the vast upheaval that began shaping up at the end of the seventies—and is still with us. The technological revolution is superseding the nineteenth century world of heavy industry based on the internal combustion machine, plastics, and textiles, and replacing it with three phenomena that are now transforming the world at a breath-taking pace: telecommunications—based on the fusion of computers and electronics—robotics, and bioengineering.

This revolution was, as we shall see, triggered by the fifteen-fold rise in petroleum prices in two phases, 1973–74 and 1979–80. This rise, however, merely brought to a head and vastly accelerated trends that had been emerging. By the middle of the seventies, the Soviet regime saw itself in an increasingly desperate position—with no way out.

Thus the same technological forces rooted in the trio of innovations associated with telecommunications, robotics and bioengineering have made the Soviet economy, molded on nineteenth-century technology, even more old-fashioned than it had to be. The Soviet economy is grounded in the heavy industry it copied from Germany. That heavy industry, which throughout the century of the industrial revolution was based ultimately on cheap labor, cheap raw materials, and cheap energy, could not, even at the zenith of its development in the Soviet Union, satisfy the human needs of its population. And now it has been outclassed by the new high technology.

The Soviet intelligentsia, which except for the elite sectors dealing with arms production, is, like everything else in that country, still stifled by an elephantine bureaucracy. It will be incapable of solving its problems by the adaptation of telecommunications, robotics or bioengineering. It is, indeed, the least prepared of all industrial nations for the transition to the new technologies; it is far behind Europe and still further behind Japan.

Thus, toward the end of the seventies, the Kremlin was to find itself unable to manufacture enough for its people, unable to construct decent housing, unable to farm its land, unable to enliven its bloated bureaucracy. All it could still do was to manufacture arms and plot strategies.

And its most grandiose strategy was to pull itself out of its dead end by a daring leap—the control of the world.

Looking at the vast population of China, itself straitjacketed by a rival totalitarian regime, and at the mighty economy of America, the Russian rulers must have realized that there was only one way they could bypass its unsolvable problems. They must expand the area they could control by securing a "breathing spell" without the pressure of superior social systems like the industrial democracies on the one hand or the greater reservoir of labor like China on the other. This expansion over a controllable area—the world—must have seemed to the Soviet tyranny the only way to ensure the survival of their despotism.

The Kremlin strategists, cautious and painstaking by nature, were *forced* into boldness by their precarious position. The radical weaknesses of the Soviet economy obliged them to lunge for world hegemony.

The encirclement of the Persian Gulf would give the Kremlin decisive leverage in controlling at least the continent of Europe and also Japan itself, both entirely dependent on the Gulf for oil. Coupled with its control over political parties in Italy, France and Spain, and with substantial levers in Germany and even Great Britain, the Kremlin—through the encirclement of the Gulf and through the threat that its conquest of strong-points in Africa would enable it to pose to South Africa—would upset the current balance of power in its own favor.

The control of the Gulf oil supplies would subjugate Western Europe and put Japan in a vice. It would, at last, be possible for the United States to be shunted aside.

It is precisely against this world background that the expulsion of America influence from the Middle East, Africa and Europe, sharpens the point of the other set of operations being conducted against America in its own backyard—the escalation of hostilities in Central America.

The Soviet leadership, making use here too of its most flexible and versatile puppet, Cuba, has been systematically eroding the fragile structures of a number of Latin American states.

In the beginning was its victory over the Kennedy administration in the installation and maintenance of a powerful forward base in Cuba twenty-two years ago—a portentous fact uniformly glossed over, for different reasons, by hypocritical administrations and by gullible commentators. Then, five years ago, the Kremlin began building up its Cuban puppet. It quickly succeeded in installing a regime of urban Marxist guerrillas in Nicaragua, and has been penetrating and enveloping El Salvador, Honduras and Guatemala.

The lively discussion of these facts in media, on the campuses and in Washington has created a maelstrom of verbiage about a very simple situation: a hostile foreign government has created strong-points in the immediate vicinity of the American mainland. With contemporary missile technology, these strong-points can be converted into outposts from which an attack can be mounted against any point in the U.S. and can, at the very least, be used to distract the attention of the public from vital strategic theaters elsewhere.

The Monroe Doctrine, a perfectly reasonable projection of the self-conception of a great power, is so forgotten that a reference to it in any political forum would surely be greeted with stunned silence followed by jeers and catcalls. The efforts of the Reagan Administration during the past three years to focus attention on El Salvador alone, with the role played by Cuba and Russia in assisting Nicaragua dealt with in purely rhetorical statements, have been peculiarly futile, especially when juxtaposed with the Reagan statements about Poland in 1981–83. If America cannot protect its own backyard, what is the value of its moralizing about Soviet behavior in countries handed over to the Kremlin by Roosevelt and Churchill at Yalta?

The Soviet strategy may call for the establishment of bases around the perimeter of North America, or maybe it is merely exploiting the nuisance value of the persistent campaign in Central and South America to benumb, confuse and distract public opinion in Washington. In any case, the ability of the Kremlin, via its many puppets and agents, to focus endemic social conflicts and afflictions into the channel of its own aims has been amply demonstrated. Its purpose is surely to persuade American opinion-makers that withdrawal from the dynamic world centers—the Middle East and the Indian Ocean—is required by the evolution of contemporary social forces.

Thus, with America neutralized in Africa, the Middle East and Europe, and increasingly preoccupied with defending the American Heartland itself, Russia would be able to put China and its vast population under its yoke. The installation of a puppet regime in China, and the reduction of America to its own segment of the Western hemisphere, would make Russia the sole world power.

This is the scenario that can be deduced from the campaign that started in the summer of 1975 in Angola. It is a scenario that is in no sense rooted in psychology. The Russians are not "power-mad," paranoid, or anything similar. Nor is the scenario extravagant: the present state of technology enables a great state, once it can nullify its possible adversaries' ambitions, to reduce political conflict throughout the world to the level of a police operation. That the Bolsheviks have, for almost seventy years demonstrated the ability to manhandle an enormous population, slaughter millions, and still survive, is itself a model for the technical potentialities of the modern state.

In terms of global strategy, the Angola campaign in the summer of 1975 evidenced a specific strategy, based upon a specific concept and focused on a specific target. The timing, of course, is of cardinal significance, arising from the confluence of two factors. It is the consensus of experts that the Chinese can be expected to develop significant nuclear capabilities in roughly 10–15 years. America, although it has a formidable nuclear defense capability, has, for that very reason, allowed its conventional forces to lag seriously behind those of the Soviets. Hence the Soviet decision to launch a campaign aimed at the Persian Gulf was given its chronological outline by two considerations: China had to be nullified before it could add a nuclear capability to its mammoth population; America had to be outmaneuvered before it could restore its conventional capabilities.

These two factors together imposed a sort of deadline on the

Soviets: before China had nuclear arms, and before America *woke up*.

Specifically, the development of a nuclear capability could enable the Chinese government to turn its mammoth population into a weapon of strategic scope. China could gamble on the sacrifice of many millions of its own people as long as it could wipe out the Soviet population centers.

The psychological warfare campaign in America has been evident for decades. Successive administrations and the bulk of "enlightened" public opinion have been paralyzed by the horrors of nuclear war. The United States, which for years had a manifest superiority in nuclear weaponry, could assume that because of the "unthinkability" of a nuclear war—i.e., the doctrine of Mutual Assured Destruction (MAD)—there could be no real prospect of nuclear war between the superpowers.

It is this dovetailing of factors that accounts for a speech made in the spring of 1973 by the late Leonid Brezhnev to a secret meeting of Eastern European Communist Party heads:

> We are achieving with detente what our predecessors
> have been unable to achieve using the fist . . . By
> 1985 we shall be able to extend our will wherever
> we need to.

It must have been around 1973, accordingly, that the Soviet leadership decided to try to install a puppet regime in Angola. By the spring of 1975 it had become evident that American "public opinion," as reflected in the Congress and the Department of State, still dismayed by the Vietnam fiasco and vulnerable to the influences radiated by the vast KGB disinformation network, could be counted on to reject out of hand the idea of sending military assistance, let alone troops, to a "faraway" place like Angola.

Properly understood, the Angola operation is significant because it utterly destroys the recent and current concept of detente underlying the interminable "negotiations" dealing with nuclear weapons.

The Angola maneuver, followed by the controlled campaign of takeovers and subversions in Africa and the Middle East, makes it obvious that the Kremlin never took seriously what has nevertheless been the core of the "debate" with the United States on nuclear disarmament: the theory of Mutual Assured Destruction.

For decades Soviet policymakers have been discussing, quite objectively, the problems, prospects and strategies involved in the possibility of a nuclear war with the United States. At the same time, however, the public stance of the Soviet leadership has been a pretense of eventual accommodation with America. The policy of detente, the key concept of the past two decades has been that coexistence between the superpowers was at last possible.

Thus the Soviet regime had two policies, or rather, one policy and one tactic: The policy was to ensure that the Soviet Union could survive a nuclear collision with the United States; the tactic was to pretend that it was not inevitable, but had been staved off indefinitely by the potential of detente.

The Angola operation, in short, made it obvious that MAD was merely given lip service by the Soviet policymakers.

Because of this the Soviets, while gradually overtaking and finally outdistancing the nuclear capabilities of the United States, had simultaneously turned to the development of conventional arms and military strategies—very old-fashioned: machine guns, airplanes, non-nuclear missiles, artillery, etc. Thus, while American strategists were distracted by the speed of the Soviet shellgame, it was easy for the Kremlin to embark, by the end of the seventies, on a ramified, many-pronged thrust that has now moved Soviet power to the rim of the Persian Gulf.

Even when the U.S. nuclear complex was superior to that of the Russians, that superiority was irrelevant to practical politics, as opposed to the apocalyptic fantasies of journalists and strategists alike. If it is true that the Russians may have a definite edge on American nuclear arms, American defense forces may be able to defend America itself from a nuclear attack, and no doubt retaliate against the Soviet Union: but it can do nothing else.

It can do nothing else because the whole thrust of the Russian maneuver has undercut the nuclear umbrella on which the top American strategists are fixated. In their multiple marches throughout West and East Africa, the Arabian Peninsula, and the Persian Gulf areas as a whole, the Russians have simply been using ordinary weapons with ordinary troops. In view of the stakes involved, the combat forces have been astonishingly small: a few tens of thousands of young Cubans have repaid the Kremlin for its two-decade support of Cuba by securing Africa and in the near future, no doubt, the Persian Gulf itself.

At the same time the Soviet General Staff has integrated the armies of Syria and Iraq with its own operational centers. Its supporters, to some extent clandestine, within Iran are also ready to play their roles when the time comes.

It is plain that the Soviet leadership is bent on attaining world hegemony *without war*. Unlike American planners, it is not hypnotized by the model of the first two World Wars, in which two "sides" confronted each other in mortal combat and there was only one victor. The Soviet planners take the view that World War III has been going on since 1975 and is still going on.

But to achieve victory without war, an absolutely indispensable adjunct has been, precisely, its camouflage. The awakening of America had to be postponed as long as possible, so that when the administration *did* finally perceive what was obvious, it would simply be too late to do much about it in the conventional military sense, while public opinion was still too benumbed by the contemplation of the nuclear horrors dinned into it for decades to countenance any use of the inadequate nuclear capabilities at hand.

The Russian disinformation campaign enveloping the many-pronged advance throughout Africa and the Middle East was surely one of the amplest, the most subtle, the most ramified of psychological warfare campaigns in history, all aimed at driving home the vital psychological element of the campaign—that it did not exist.

Aside from the paralyzing effect of the wholly bogus dilemma—nuclear horrors *or* detente—the camouflage of the whole advance was effected, via countless channels in American media (themselves made receptive through the general climate of opinion) by a variety of propaganda lines put out by the Kremlin strategists and their numerous well-meaning dupes—the well-intentioned people Lenin called "useful idiots."

Russia, it has been said by hardheaded observers, is fundamentally inept. Russians can do *nothing*—look at their buildings, their

agriculture, their consumer industries, their topheavy bureaucracy. Taking this as a given—and of course it is true—they draw
the desired conclusion: the Russians, and especially not their aging
leadership!, would never dare to try anything.

And their problems! The birthrate of the Muslim minority is
soaring, the satellites are restive, Poland is a cauldron, the clumsy
bureaucracy is overextended, agriculture is unproductive, construction is mediocre, and domestic problems are endless.

On the philosophical plane, students of history wag their heads
wisely. How could these people rule the world? The endless variety
of unforeseeable events, the unfathomable complexity of dynamic
forces make world hegemony simply inconceivable. Anyone who
thinks it possible is a hopeless paranoid.

Thus, the real problems of Soviet society, which may well be
unsolvable, and the philosophical cliches of academics, are combined to make it axiomatic that the Kremlin has no plans *at all*.

Accordingly, since no plan is even conceivable to begin with,
and since the Kremlin and the 350 million people it controls are
entirely inept, what looks like a plan is, in reality, mere exploitation
of "targets of opportunity": timorous, defensive, confused and inept, the Russians are simply snatching at straws.

This last attitude has become an editorial staple of many influential media. Russia, they insist, is making one blunder after another. It is bogging down all over—in Angola, in Ethiopia, in
Zimbabwe, in South Yemen, in Namibia, in Iran, in Afghanistan,
in Cuba, in Nicaragua, in El Salvador, in Honduras, in Guatemala—everywhere!

Thus the notorious shortcomings of Soviet society are interpreted
to produce a conclusion that contradicts the glaring fact—that the
Russians have created a network of strong-points all over Africa,
the Middle East and Central America.

For these reasons the byplay around NATO, nuclear weapons
in Europe, and the MX-missile, among other things, must be seen
as a mere inert background to the outstanding fact of the past
decade—the shifting of Soviet strategy from a merely passive exploitation of trouble-spots around the world to an orchestrated,
carefully calibrated campaign aimed at the exclusion of America

and China from an international role, and their ultimate subordination, as Brezhnev put it to the will of the Kremlin.

But though the nuclear balance of the superpowers is a mere background to the current thrust of the Soviets, the possibility of a nuclear war is obviously a problem of paramount importance. It is, indeed, just because public opinion everywhere perceives that importance with such horror that the Kremlin can exploit it so effectively as it proceeds with its global advance.

The factors of the nuclear balance will be analyzed in a special chapter.

2

Encirclement of the Persian Gulf

The Middle East is now under direct attack by the Soviet Union. Soviet strong-points—notably in South Yemen and the island of Socotra, the deep Soviet involvement in the armies of Iraq and Syria, strategic support points in Ethiopia and the new Zimbabwe, outline the dimensions of the crisis.

The entire Middle East is now threatened by Soviet expansion. The very existence of the old-line, semi-feudal regimes around the Persian Gulf—Saudi Arabia, Kuwait, Bahrain, Oman, North Yemen, the Emirates—is at stake.

The imposition of any Soviet puppet upon these societies, in the form of the PLO or another auxiliary, would most likely mean the physical extinction of the ruling strata or, at best, their exile. Their kingdoms would be integrated into the Soviet imperial system. For those societies which are not directly dominated, the future promises client status, with the Soviet Union as patron.

The Middle East is where the Soviet Union's intrusion most dramatically affects the national security as well as the economic viability of the industrialized free world. The Soviet's two-pronged advance toward the major oil deposits of the Persian Gulf and a "breakout" into the Indian Ocean, if allowed to continue unopposed, would soon place the Soviet Union in a position to dictate the terms of any future accommodation with the United States, Europe and Japan. Yet, it is here, in the very area so vital to our interests, that the Western response has been subverted by selfish corporate concerns masquerading as national interests, which have in turn nurtured a remarkable set of illusions and delusions about the region, its political realities and its dynamics. Ironically, the failure of the United States and its allies to come to grips with the Middle East as it is, and *not as they imagine it to be*, has in itself contributed significantly to the relative ease of the Soviet advance into the area, and thus further fueled Soviet ambitions.

If we focus our gaze on the Persian Gulf, we can see that it is already entirely surrounded both by Soviet forces (as in Afghanistan) and by satellite regimes, such as South Yemen and Socotra, and the Marxist regime in Ethiopia.

South Yemen, which has strong ties with both Ethiopia and Libya (which latter will call for special comment), is simply part of the Soviet bloc. Its situation on the Gulf of Aden and its tribal-political pull on North Yemen (Yemenite Arab Republic) give it crucial strategic and economic importance. Its capital, Aden, is a major port.

In 1980 South Yemen, officially known as the People's Republic of Yemen, signed a treaty of "friendship and cooperation" with the Soviet Union. All other groups which had surfaced after the country achieved its independence in 1967 were simply merged (April 20, 1980) into the Socialist Party of Yemen whose structure is modeled on that of the Communist Party of the Soviet Union.

South Yemen supports the "National Democratic Front" in North Yemen, which has been active since 1976. In 1979 South Yemen invaded North Yemen with the help of the National Democratic Front: a cease-fire was negotiated by the Arab League.

The Kremlin is, of course, active in both Yemens. Though North

Yemen is generally described as "Saudi-supported," it is the Soviet state which supplies and trains eleven out of twelve brigades of the North Yemen Army. The North Yemen regime explains its heavy dependence on the Soviet Government as a part of its determination to assert its independence of the Saudis.

Though the United States has made heavy contributions to North Yemen—one of its brigades was trained by the U.S. using Saudi funds, while the Saudis under American direction financed an arms agreement to the tune of $390 million—the Kremlin is flexible enough to retain on-the-spot control, taking advantage of the help given North Yemen by Americans and Saudis, through its major construction projects as well as its training of the bulk of the North Yemen army. Thus, the Soviets constructed the Red Sea port of Hodeida, the San'a airport, a road between Hodeida and Taizz, and a cement plant at Bajil. In the past decade Moscow has shifted its assistance to the military; in 1979 it made an arms agreement with the North Yemen government, totaling $1–1½ billion, and including MIG and Sukhoi fighter jets, as well as tanks.

North Yemen is at the southern tip of the Arabian Peninsula. The crucial state north of the Persian Gulf is, of course, Iran. But though the silence of media on the affairs of the two Yemens may be explained by its lack of interest even for the educated public, the refusal of media to recognize the seminal role played by the Kremlin in the toppling of the Shah of Iran is stunning.

Iran was a dazzling triumph for the disinformation branch of the KGB, whose control of the events leading up to the ousting of the Shah was, for all practical purposes, disregarded by everyone. Media, overwhelmingly in the United States and very largely in Europe, swallowed the "explanations" and "analyses" carefully prepared for the public by the KGB. As a result, in the space of only a few years the Shah's regime, which beforehand had been given, rather routinely, favorable treatment throughout the world media, was entirely satanized, and the way prepared for a figurehead, Khomeini, to be presented to the world as the dictator of a fanatically reformist Muslim regime.

Until 1972 the Shah was given somewhat banal treatment in the world media as a glamorous monarch and, in addition, a well-meaning reformer.

The preparations for the execution of the Shah's lavish celebration of the 2,500th anniversary of the establishment of the Persian Empire were greeted with admiration. The Empire is regarded as having been founded by Cyrus the Great (559–529 B.C.), and though the Shah's Pahlevi family could not claim a direct genetic link with the early emperors, the celebrations at the ancient city of Persepolis, in 1972, were generally viewed with a mixture of awe and curiosity.

During these festivities the Shah's international prestige was at its height; the campaign to undermine the public standing of his person, his regime, his family and of Iran's infrastructure had not yet begun. Thus, the world press reported, with an undertone of respect, the arrival at Persepolis of representatives of many of the royal houses of the world, ranging from the Kingdom of Denmark to the Kingdom of Thailand.

Characteristic of opinions expressed at that time was a remark by Mr. David Lilienthal, founder of the Tennessee Valley Authority during Franklin Roosevelt's administration, who saw the Persepolis celebrations as a means of strengthening morale and self-esteem among the Iranian people. He said: "Pride motivates people to better themselves. You have to show them some glamour, and you have to show them what you're bringing them into the modern world for. . . ."

But shortly after the tremendous festivities at Persepolis in 1972 there was a switch in treatment throughout the world media. Abruptly, indeed, practically overnight, the Shah became notorious not merely as a reactionary beast, the strangler of Iranian society, but as a monster who personally tortured countless political prisoners in the cellars of Savak, the Iranian security police, which also became a household horror among people who barely knew where Iran was.

The satanization of the Shah took place so quickly that it was possible to dispense even with bogus documentation. People would simply say "everyone *knows* the Shah is a torturer," and since no one in fact knew anything about Iran to begin with, it was possible to turn this cliche of atrocity into a cliche that required no further evidence beyond its repetition.

The Soviet technique of defamation was applied with immense success. Even though it was obvious from the very beginning that, regardless of Soviet interests in Iran, only the KGB was technically capable of spreading disinformation throughout the length and breadth of media, experienced newspaper people were systematically hoodwinked.

Media were, in fact, flooded with fabrications: sensational demonstrations were held by "students" of one kind or another; charges of fantastic corruption were added to even more fantastic tales of torture; the wealth of the Shah's family was grotesquely exaggerated; countless organizations sporting a "human rights" label suddenly began signing letters, petitions and manifestos against the Shah.

Both in France, especially, and in the United States violent demonstrations by such "students" became commonplace. Conduits for anti-Shah propaganda included the Committee for the Intellectual and Artistic Freedom of Iran, the International League for Human Rights, and the Federation of Iranian Students. The Shah was accused by these and other bodies of supporting the Iranian secret service, the Savak, in a virulent suppression campaign. The numbers used in this propaganda drive tended to escalate. Thus, in February 1976, Amnesty International, the Paris daily *Le Monde* and the International League for Human Rights alleged that some 100,000 political prisoners were being held by the Teheran regime. Earlier, in a "Meet the Press" television interview with the Shah (May 18, 1975), questioners spoke of a reported 40,000 prisoners. The Shah replied that such allegations were "purely Communist propaganda," adding that only some 3,000 persons had been imprisoned for "terrorist" activity.

In the United States, one Iranian spokesman, Reza Baraheni, identified as a "poet and literary critic," was said to have spent 102 days in Iranian prisons. He had, of course, been released by the Teheran regime and permitted to immigrate to the United States—much in contrast to the fate of other individuals who, under the regime of Ayatollah Khomeini, were executed in wholesale numbers. Reza Baraheni, together with such U.S. writers as Arthur Miller, Kurt Vonnegut, Jr., and Muriel Rukeyser published an open letter (August 2, 1975) appealing to "freedom-loving people" everywhere to fight the "strangulation" of Iranian intellectual life.

Early in 1976, Fidel Castro met the leader of the outlawed Iranian Communist Party, Iraj Eskaneri, during the 25th Communist Party Congress in Moscow. This led Iran to break diplomatic relations with Cuba (April 27, 1976). That same month, Ayatollah Shamsabadi was assassinated in Iran, and his killer was identified as a supporter of the then little-known Ayatollah Khomeini.

In early 1977 there was a dramatic demonstration in New York, where six alleged students, members of the "American Revolutionary Students Brigade," chained themselves inside the crown of the Statue of Liberty in "protest against the fact of political prisoners in Iran." At the University of Michigan, hundreds of students protested against a motion picture contract between the university and Iran. Reza Baraheni's book, *The Crowned Cannibals*, was published in New York, and the International League of Human Rights protested to the Shah and U.S. Secretary of State Cyrus Vance on June 23 against the alleged activity of Savak agents in the United States.

The Department of State subsequently stated that such activity could not be documented. Five hundred demonstrators "against U.S. imperialism" sought to prevent Empress Farah from visiting the University of Southern California. The Empress received an Appeal of Conscience Award, in honor of her activity in improving the status of women in Iran. And when Empress Farah visited Mrs. Carter at the White House, 1,000 masked "students" demonstrated outside the presidential residence.

On the occasion of his birthday, the Shah gave amnesty to 279 prisoners, of whom 131 were identified as political prisoners. During a visit of the Shah to the United States, a bomb went off outside the offices of Iran Air, at 405 Madison Avenue. The anti-Shah campaign led to demonstrations the next day (November 15) outside the White House. When the *New York Times* carried a news dispatch which said that anti-terrorist demonstrations had taken place in Teheran, another "student" demonstration took place outside the *Times* offices. The orchestrated campaign extended to Rome, where still other "students" invaded the Iranian Embassy on December 10, burning documents and smashing windows and furniture.

1978 began with a visit by President and Mrs. Carter to Iran, while 200 Iranians identified as students demonstrated outside the White House. This was followed by similar demonstrations in New York, outside the hotel where Empress Farah was staying (she was visiting the Asia Society). Prime Minister Indira Gandhi received the Shah in New Delhi for discussions of economic cooperation early in February. Two weeks later, riots broke out in Tabriz, and in East Germany, police seized fourteen "students" who had occupied the Iranian Embassy.

Iranian officials claimed that "Islamic Marxists" were responsible for a fire in Abadan. The conflagration broke out in a theater, and 422 people were killed. The International League for Human Rights blamed the Shah's government for the incident. Chinese leader Hua Kuo-feng visited Teheran in August, on his way for a three-week tour of Romania and Yugoslavia. Press dispatches emphasized that Hua shared a "common suspicion of Moscow" with Iranian officials.

In September, yet another "student" demonstration broke out in Los Angeles; police arrested 100 members of the Federation of Iranian students for rock throwing and other acts of violence. Because of unrest at home, the Shah postponed a scheduled trip to East Germany. In October 1978, Khomeini, an elderly Muslim cleric, arrived in Paris from Iraq, where he had been in exile since 1963.

On November 19, 1978, Brezhnev warned the United States not to "intervene" in Iran. Ten days later Khomeini's spokesmen appealed for a general strike. In the United States, the anti-Shah campaign moved into high gear, with a denunciation by Ralph Schoenman, speaking for the Committee for Intellectual and Artistic Freedom of Iran. The ABC television network carried a program with the title "The Politics of Torture." In San Francisco, 2,000 "students" and their "supporters" blocked traffic outside the Iranian consulate and federal buildings.

During this period the Shah and his wife, evidently underestimating the scope and the source of the tidal wave of orchestrated hatred, were moving about quite normally.

From 1975 to 1978, the Shah and his family were received cordially in many parts of the world, and their visits were returned by western, third world and communist officials. In 1975, the Shah visited Austrian President Bruno Kreisky, then met French President Giscard d'Estaing in St. Moritz, Switzerland. Worldwide interest was aroused by plans for a cultural center in Teheran, Shahestan Pahlevi, to be erected at a cost of from $3 to 5 billion. A medical center was to be built in Teheran in cooperation with Columbia University. In March 1975, fifteen members of a "revolutionary Student Brigade" protested at Columbia: six of them were arrested when they locked themselves in the dean's office. None could be identified as *bona fide* students.

The Shah and his wife, Empress Farah, visited Washington and had talks with President Ford in May. The Shah's sister, Princess Ashraf Pahlevi, was welcomed in Peking and, even more remarkable, spent five days in North Korea at the invitation of Kim Il Sung. Later that year, in a perceptive speech, Empress Farah opened a symposium at Persepolis (September 15–19) on the theme "Iran: Past, Present and Future," in which she observed that Iranian society was being "traumatized by the conflicting winds of tradition and change."

Meanwhile the agitation against the Shah in Iran and abroad was stepped up. Khomeini held regular press conferences in which, despite his alleged French education, he said nothing to anyone. "Aides" distributed hand-outs couched in the most sweepingly authoritative language to all the media.

In Iran, the Shah, bewildered by the growing barrage of atrocity propaganda abroad and by the gathering opposition at home where the network of Soviet agents was immense, ramified and effective, appointed Shahpar Bakhtiar Prime Minister. This was the first step in a series of carefully controlled events which precisely a year later were to culminate in Khomeini's arrival in Teheran, founding a "revolutionary Islamic regime," whose outstanding feature was the presence of many open Marxists of various shades, and in a series of Marxist statements—of the humanitarian civil rights type—attributed to Khomeini himself.

In January 1979 the vast campaign initiated in Angola in the summer of 1975 seemed about to culminate in a stunning achievement—the control of the Persian Gulf. An alliance of Soviet agents, Soviet front-organizations, urban "radicals" and parochial Muslims overthrew the Shah.

Marxists of various shadings, sponsored in one way or another by the Soviet government, played a key role in steering this alliance. In view of the well-known fact that the Soviet Union controlled a huge network of open, semi-open and covert agents and institutions of all kinds in Iran between 1946 and 1978, including a massive KGB presence, this is hardly surprising.

Not only was the new regime supported by the Tudeh [Communist] Party but it was also the PLO, an open Soviet puppet, that helped install it. Yasir Arafat was, indeed, the first "guest of state" welcomed by the parvenu regime. The very first international action of the "Muslim fanatics" was to stop oil shipments to South Africa, a country absolutely irrelevant to any genuine Muslim preoccupation. The rhetoric of Khomeini's spokesmen, with its emphasis on the "oppression" of blacks and women in America, is the rhetoric of contemporary kitchen Marxism.

That Moscow was the principal catalyst in the Iranian hostage-taking was deliberately downplayed by the Carter Administration. *Photographic evidence of known KGB agents* involved in the takeover of our embassy and accurate disclosures of Soviet money, weapons and expert advice to both left-wing and ultra-Muslim factions in Iran, were suppressed. The State Department deliberately ignored the anti-American broadcasts, from inside southern Russia, that incited Iranians to riot against Americans. The State Department also ignored Soviet-PLO coordination of weapons to Iranian Leftists and the training of Iranian guerrillas in Palestinian camps in Lebanon.

Iran's destabilizing industrialization, its ethnic rivalries and its political problems facilitated moves by the Soviet Union to place its own partisans in positions of influence in Teheran so that the world's media, which docilely focused on the "Islamic" aspect of the Iranian upset, could be counted on by and large to ignore those aspects of the resolution that smile on Moscow.

If one links Khomeini's Iran with the Soviets' invasion of Af-

ghanistan early in 1980, it is plain that the Soviets are aiming at
the control of the warm waters of the Gulf and its oil. Thirty-five
years ago, when the Kremlin sponsored the Kurdish and other
separatist movements in Iran, it believed that, because of American
power, Iran could be subjugated only through direct action—a risk
the Soviets at that time did not want to take. Today, the actions
they take are hardly risks.

Events in the Gulf region have demonstrated that geography
remains a fundamental determinant in strategic planning. The factors U.S. strategic planners must take into account include: (a)
proximity of the region to the Soviet Union; (b) the importance of
the Suez Canal, the Turkish Straits and the Strait of Hormuz; (c)
the north-south land route to the Soviet Union; (d) the need to
secure the vast oil deposits for the West; and, (e) protection of
NATO's southern flank.

Thus a crucial consequence of the British withdrawal from Aden
(1968) and the Gulf (1971) now stands out in high relief. The difference today is that the Shah's role of developing a powerful
enough state to fill the vacuum created by that withdrawal has
been aborted: Russia now looms over the Gulf.

The vital interests of the West, perhaps its existence, are now
at stake.

A decade ago, Greece and Turkey were cooperating partners in
NATO, Lebanon was intact and pro-Western, Israeli forces at the
Suez Canal were denying the Russians access to the short Black
Sea-Red Sea water route and American military power was supreme. Since that time, Lebanon has all but disappeared as a
sovereign state, South Yemen and Ethiopia have shifted into the
Soviet orbit and Israeli ground power has been forced to contract
after a Soviet-sponsored war of aggression in October 1973. Iran
has succumbed to an insurrectionist regime, large parts of Turkey
are under martial law and Pakistan fears dismemberment if Afghanistan chooses to arouse the Baluchi secessionists on Pakistan's
western border. Afghanistan, a Soviet dependency even before
becoming an outright satellite in the coup of April 1978, was invaded in December 1979 by a full-dress Soviet army. Pakistan's
fear of the Soviets is now immediate.

The specter now hovering over Iran could hardly be more menacing. Under no circumstances can the United States, and the industrial democracies in general, countenance Soviet control of Iranian oil. Iran in the Soviet sphere would threaten to radicalize all of Arabia and portend the neutralization of Western Europe, the encirclement of China and ultimately the isolation of the United States. Soviet domination of Iran would shatter the structure of global politics.

On the two previous occasions in this century when Iran's sovereignty was extinquished by great power rivalries played out on its soil (1907, 1941–46), the rivalries of the powers were drastically limited by their local opportunities. In 1946, when the Soviet Union attempted to establish a proxy regime in Northwest Iran, it failed when the Truman Administration preemptorily ordered the Soviets to dismantle their puppet administration forthwith and the Soviet Union, without nuclear weapons and exhausted by the German war, was forced into impotence.

The situation has altered radically. Not only does the Soviet Union now have a nuclear panoply it can brandish as a deterrent to reactions from the United States but it also has evolved a formula, both dynamic and subtle, in the use of its surrogates, both open and covert. It has maximized its geographic advantages in the Middle East by acquiring strategic mobility and a wide-ranging, self-sufficient, quick-reaction force, which is a means of increasing Soviet diplomatic and military options in the third world. The growth of Soviet naval power in the eastern Mediterranean has, of course, marked the end of the exclusive domination of those waters by a single power—the United States. This has been the most conspicuous change in the region's strategic environment in the past twenty years. To preempt the U.S. and China—it's principal rivals—the Soviet Union also seeks to secure its strategic relationships with India.

Strategic military and political gains, in turn, require Moscow to extend its lines of communication through the Middle East, along the shores of the Red Sea and the Persian Gulf and into East Africa. Soviet influences in Iraq, Syria, South Yemen, Ethiopia and Mozambique complement the envelopment of Iran and Afghanistan, Turkey and Pakistan. To avoid exclusive dependence on the Black Sea-Red Sea route through the highly vulnerable Suez Canal, Soviet strategists emphasize the development of alternative land routes that lead south to the Indian Ocean. Given the immense maneuverability and independence of their Indian Ocean fleet, Moscow's capacity to control the flow of oil from there would be enormous.

While the Soviets have capitalized on their advantages in the Gulf area—geographic proximity, conventional military superiority, an infrastructure of airfields and naval bases in South Yemen, Ethiopia, Afghanistan, Libya and Iraq, and their Cuban surrogate troops—the United States has failed to secure the strategic geographic locations that we need to give flexibility to American power. Indeed, our flaccid response during the American embassy crisis in Teheran and during the sacking of embassies in Pakistan and Libya, and our bafflement in the face of the Soviet invasion of Afghanistan, testify to the erosion of America's military strength. Ambivalence, indecision and cowardice in response to Soviet threats is our established pattern of behavior.

The encirclement of the Gulf entails, very naturally, a major investment not only in the countries bordering the Gulf itself and the Arabian and Indian Oceans, but the whole of Africa. It will become evident that the seizure of Angola by a Cuban-backed puppet regime, the initial phase of the whole vast pincer movement aimed primarily at the Gulf but also at South Africa, was a vital precondition for the envelopment of the Gulf by pro-Soviet forces.

3

Mishandling the
Israeli Asset

Although the Arab-Israeli issue is far from being the most fundamental conflict in the Middle East, the controversy surrounding it has made it the thorniest. The fact remains, however, that our interest in securing access to Persian Gulf oil runs parallel with the national interest in preserving the security and strength of Israel. This enduring reality, to be sure, is rooted in moral considerations that go far beyond calculations of self-interest. Yet it also corresponds with our national security, since without a strong Israel, our position in the area would be much weaker and more vulnerable than it is today. Soviet leaders must constantly take into account the effectiveness of Israeli defense forces, especially the projection of power of the Israeli Air Force over critical land and sea corridors in the region. It is only with a full appreciation of the critical role played by Israel in U.S. strategy that we can shape the means for thwarting Moscow's designs on territories and resources vital to our security. Yet it is in the mishandling of the Israeli asset that the Reagan Administration has been particularly delinquent when faced with the challenge for a creative national security policy.

President Reagan, whose accession to the White House was greeted by many deeply discouraged with the sentimental, unrealistic, and conciliatory policies of his predecessor, quickly found himself taking a course that—except for the rhetoric—was identical with that of the Carter administration.

While as Candidate he made the usual promises and professions of support for Israel as all American presidents and presidential candidates, he later succumbed to the same influences which had determined Carter's policies. As a candidate he said (August 15, 1979, in the *Washington Post*) "The paramount American interest in the Middle East is to prevent the region from falling under the domination of the Soviet Union," and even argued that the endangering of Persian Gulf oil supplies might invite the neutralization of Western Europe and Japan. He also noted that Soviet plans were quite independent of Israel, and said firmly: "Our own position would be weaker without the political and military assets Israel provides." American policymakers, he said, "downgrade just those three attributes of Israel that are potentially beneficial to the West: its 'geopolitical importance as a stabilizing force,' its ability to serve as 'a deterrent to radical hegemony' and its capacity to be a 'military offset to the Soviet Union.' " In Reagan's words: "The fall of Iran has increased Israel's value as perhaps the only remaining strategic asset on which the U.S. can truly rely; other pro-Western states in the region, especially Saudi Arabia and the smaller Gulf kingdoms, are weak and vulnerable." He noted that Israel's unique value derived from its Western orientation and stable, democratic government, adding that Israel was endowed with "the democratic will, national cohesion, technological capacity and military fiber to stand forth as America's trusted ally." Reagan catalogued in specific terms what Israel had to offer the U.S.: cooperation with its intelligence services; maintenance of American equipment; and use of "facilities and air fields" as "secure point(s) of access if required at a moment of emergency." Soviet options, Reagan noted, were already constrained by Israel's air power. Candidate Reagan concluded by welcoming the security cooperation of Egypt (which he described as "friendly to us at a particular moment"), but stated that such Arab states were "secondary links" that "cannot substitute for a strong Israel." He warned against weakening Israel, calling it "foolhardy." American policies promoting a radical Palestinian state or providing insufficient military assistance would, he predicted, "enormously" ease the tasks of Soviet planners. "Only by full appreciation of the critical role the State of Israel plays in our strategic calculus can we build the foundation for thwarting Moscow's designs. . . ."

On March 19, 1980, in the *Near East Report* he again referred to the weakness of Saudi Arabia and the risks of relying upon it and "even on Egypt." Repeating an earlier call for U.S. bases in the Middle East," Reagan asserted that "Israel and the two excellent bases constructed in the Sinai desert should certainly be considered in the strategic planning of our military." On Middle East policy in general, Reagan said that "Israel must receive advanced U.S. military equipment and technology to protect its survival," and that "I would not provide advance weaponry to Arab nations opposing the Egyptian-Israeli peace treaty." He also warned that the U.S. should avoid a repetition of the Iranian debacle, when "our weapons" fell into the hands of an unfriendly regime. He said that he "would bring in (to peace negotiations) other Arab nations, particularly Jordan and Saudi Arabia, two countries dependent upon the United States for their security," and that Arab states which oppose the Egyptian-Israeli peace treaty are "obstacles to regional peace" and "indirectly promote Soviet interests in the region." Reagan opposed "dealing with the P.L.O." or "negotiations with that body of terrorists until it renounces terrorism, accepts UN Resolution 242, changes its charter and recognizes Israel's right to exist. I am strongly opposed to the numerous overtures the present administration has been making to the P.L.O." Reagan said Carter's Middle East policy could best be described by the term, "gross incompetence," and attacked Carter for, among other things, "putting into question on numerous occasions our commitments to Israel."

Yet from the moment President Reagan took office it became

evident that the very notion of Israel's primacy had been dropped. President Reagan, incapable, no doubt, of creating a conceptual infrastructure for the broad moralizing banalities he is fond of, found himself, like Carter before him—though without Carter's intellectual ability—a mere spokesman for sub rosa factions in his administration: Arabists in the State Department, those under the direct influence of the oil interests, and outright ignoramuses vulnerable ipso facto to both Arabists and oil people.

By the end of 1981 relations between the U.S. and Israel were strained. The Saudis, characterized by candidate Reagan as "weak and vulnerable," became the linchpin of a new strategy that gave primacy not to Israel as a lever of American policy, but to the feudal, ramshackle Saudi regime.

When Secretary of State Haig, for instance, made a tour of the Middle East in the spring of 1981, it was made apparent that his task was to secure strategic cooperation from various "friendly" regimes in the region against the Soviet Union. Announcing a "strategic consensus" from Pakistan to Egypt on March 19, the Secretary of State said that the Soviet threat overrode the Arab-Israeli conflict in importance.[1] On his arrival in Israel, however, despite repeated references to the role that Israel would play in a new U.S. strategy for the region, no mention was made of the United States assuming control of the Sinai bases which Israel was to vacate the following year. Yet on his return to the United States, the Secretary of State testified before the House Foreign Operations Subcommittee of the Committee on Appropriations that Israel was to play a vital role in the plans for an increased U.S. presence in the Middle East.

The confusion surrounding the exact role that Israel was to play in meeting the Russian threat in the Middle East increased after the Israeli attack on the Iraqi nuclear reactor at Osirak in late June. The Administration was so anxious to avoid being implicated in the raid that it postponed the delivery of F-16 aircraft to Israel, citing as an excuse Israel's breach of the Foreign Military Sales Act, and announced that the strategic dialogue with Israel had been put in the "deep-freeze." A Defense Department memorandum even went so far as to inform the White House that Israel "should not be allowed to dictate policy" and that a confrontation between the United States and Israel was in the offing.[2] On August 4, President Reagan spoke of convincing Arab states that the U.S. was not "biased" towards Israel, and demonstrated its goodwill by further delaying the shipment of F-16s to Israel, in the wake of her bombing of the P.L.O.'s headquarters in Beirut.[3]

After thus pandering to Arab susceptibilities during the summer of 1981, the Administration returned to its favorite theme of U.S.-Israeli cooperation—with Secretary of State Haig's "meat on the bones" speech on September 5.[4] Later that day, the State Department spelled out the areas for broad discussion that President Reagan had referred to in 1979. On September 30, Israeli Foreign Minister Shamir announced that discussions were in progress. Yet, even before word was out concerning the scheduled signing of the strategic Memorandum of Understanding (MOU) on November 30, Administration officials downplayed and reduced the dimensions of the agreement. The White House discouraged talk of extensive cooperation between Israel and the United States. When the Secretary of State announced on September 10 the areas that strategic cooperation would include (they were much the same as those in the final, limited MOU), he declared that the expanded relationship was "not a historic breakthrough"—a remarkable piece of hedging.[5] The next day, as Prime Minister Begin was being heavily criticized in Israel for offering the United States the use of Israeli air and naval bases, the Defense Department was saying that strategic cooperation was still in the "conceptual stage."[6] By the time this charade had ended, the American public was informed that the "strategic" relationship seemed to be limited to the pre-position of medical supplies.

While the Administration was busy repudiating the notion that any strategic agreement between the United States and Israel implied extensive cooperation, it was going out of its way to manifest an interest in the well-being of various Arab states. On September 23, in a message to King Hussein, the U.S. proclaimed its commitment to Jordan's security and its "enduring character" (the latter being an attempt to calm the Hashemite regime which is troubled by calls for Transjordan to be recognized as the Palestinian state that it really is). A similar motivation was at work when President Reagan asserted that only strong support for Saudi Arabia would avert its collapse.[7] When Israel expressed concern at the intended sale of AWACs to Saudi Arabia, it was stressed that far from being a threat to Israel's security, they would provide an effective defense for the whole region against the Soviet threat.

The Reagan Administration's refusal to enter into anything more than a limited agreement with Israel on strategic cooperation for fear of offending the Arabs, amounted to nothing less than a betrayal of its pledge to use Israel to counter Soviet aggression in the region. This policy continued during the remaining months of 1981. On November 16, there were press leaks that the United States was resisting Israeli "demands" and refusing to expand the scope of strategic cooperation.[8] On November 19, State Department officials explained the fear of Arab reaction as the rationale for the continued delay in establishing strategic cooperation. Two revealing public statements were made on November 22: Weinberger announced that the MOU would be limited, while Haig gave as the reason "the political constraints associated with our relationship with Israel and the maintenance of good relations with a number of moderate Arab regimes." Weinberger was at pains to describe the relationship defined by the MOU as *not* something new, but a mere continuation of past policies.[9] On November 26, there were additional statements from the Administration, all but rebuking Israel for having asked for (or offered) too much. A "senior U.S. official" again cited the possibility of "wrong interpretations by Arab nations." The MOU signing ceremony on November 30 was an embarrassment. No pictures of the event were allowed. A routine press briefing was cancelled. It was later reported that Weinberger had in fact opposed a written MOU. The Joint Chiefs of Staff were even more vocal, threatening to bypass the Secretary of Defense in order to protest directly to the President. Even after the MOU had been signed, the Joint Chiefs continued to exclude Israel from the list of possible host countries for the Rapid Deployment Force: an incredibly irresponsible decision if one assumes that the military was actually serious about a viable RDF force to operate in the region. The Sinai, in fact, was the logical location for major U.S. bases, enjoying security and logistical advantages unequalled in any area outside the continental United States. Bases there would serve the further purpose of securing the Egyptian-Israel accords, protecting Egypt, and advancing prospects for peace in the region. It was not to be; vetoed by our new friend—Egypt.

On December 5, there were additional leaks to the press explaining how the Administration had rejected ground exercises, reluctantly accepted air exercises, insisted that references to pre-positioning of material be left vague and excluded any mention of cooperation against "Soviet controlled forces from within the region." At the same time, Premier Begin and Defense Minister Sharon were under attack in the Knesset for their failure to have the MOU affirm a U.S. commitment to Israel's defense against Arab attack. Similarly, Begin and Sharon were assailed for having accepted a document that committed Israel, as not even the NATO treaties did, to oppose the USSR by name. The U.S. was silent while the Knesset debate raged, but Weinberger made a little-reported trip to Morocco to explain the limited impact of the MOU. Arab response was hostile from the time of the signing; citing this, State Department sources suggested on December 10 that Israel should feel grateful for what it got.

The very real disregard for strategic cooperation with Israel was apparent in the aftermath of Israel's extension of its civil law to the Golan Heights, the so-called "Golan annexation." Of course, one ally doesn't normally sanction another, yet—as in June with Israel's attack on Iraq's nuclear facility—the Joint Chiefs again called for sanctions against Israel.[10] On December 18, the MOU was suspended, despite the dubious legality of such a move. So were a range of negotiations to implement strategic cooperation, including those aimed at the expansion of the same military industrial capacity which Reagan had praised in his August 1979 article. By the end of the year, there was some talk in both the U.S. and Israel to the effect that the MOU was still in effect. Nothing concrete emerged. Meanwhile, the opinion was growing amongst friend and foe alike that Washington was an unreliable ally at best, and, at worst, a duplicitous one.

Throughout 1981 it was apparent that, while the Reagan Administration was hewing to the rhetoric of its original commitment to confront Soviet designs in the Middle East, it was equally clear that it had settled upon Saudi Arabia, not Israel, as the keystone of its future force projection in the region. Similarly, the Administration has modified its professed priorities to conform more closely with the Saudi position. Moreover, the strategic relationship with Israel never developed: its real advocates were not given key positions in the Administration; its opponents were very well organized, well-connected and unstinting in their hostility; and the strategic relationship became hostage, first to events in the Middle East and later to the pursuit of an "improved" Israeli demeanor and sensitivity to American-Saudi interests. Not surprisingly, those who had been opponents of the strategic relationship all along became the prime movers in this later push for linkage.

While the alignment in the administration for those favoring close cooperation with Israel was thin and scattered, the bureaucratic and petrodollar factions favoring Saudi Arabia's ascension to the primary strategic role for the West in the Middle East became entrenched and energized in the U.S. government. Interestingly, not many Arabists were active constituents of this school, primarily because most of the officials at the State Department understood the parochial priorities and internal limitations of the Saudis, and concluded that the Saudis were both unwilling and incapable of joining in a close, visible strategic partnership with the U.S. Never before, in consequence, has so much been built on so unstable and unreliable a foundation.

The group favoring the Saudi option was based primarily in the Pentagon. It included Major General Richard Secord, head of Middle East Affairs in International Security Affairs. Also included were Lieutenant General Charles L. Donnelly, head of the U.S. training mission to Saudi Arabia; Major General John T. Buck, the Air Force's AWACs program head; the first commandant of the RDF, General P. X. Kelley; the current RDF commander, Lieutenant General Robert Kingston; the former military liaison on the NSC, Major General Robert Schweitzer; the head of the Air Force, General Lew Allen; the Chairman of the Joint Chiefs of Staff, General David Jones; the recent ambassador Saudi Arabia, John

West; and Secretary of Defense Weinberger himself. (Weinberger had come to the Defense portfolio with little foreign policy experience. He had, however, become professionally skilled at cutting deals with the Saudis during his years as a senior official of the Bechtel firm, a company currently holding billions in construction contracts.) These were the major players. Defense sources have identified members of the Joint Chiefs' staff and General Allen's staff as long-time upper-level proponents of U.S.-Saudi military cooperation. Assistant Secretary of Defense Francis West played a key role as conduit and catalyst. He was also a primary point of access for corporate figures involved in promoting a wide range of U.S.-Saudi ventures.

It is important to realize that discussions about U.S.-Saudi military cooperation had begun well before the Reagan Administration came to power. Its bureaucratic sponsors had advantages and momentum that supporters of U.S.-Israeli cooperation lacked. Furthermore, although the Saudis had been vague about their willingness to commit themselves to any strategic cooperation, their style appealed to the experts on logistics and weapon acquisition in the higher echelons of the Pentagon. This fact explained the rationale for the AWACs sales (initially, General Buck's desire to offset research and development costs and lower unit acquisition costs of advanced models; later, the Joint Chiefs desire to establish a surrogate force in Saudi Arabia). The U.S.-Saudi initiative went forward even though the head of the first AWACs group in Saudi Arabia, Major General John Piotrowski, had written his superiors excoriating Saudi security; even as the Army's Doctrine staff was openly revamping U.S. military procedures along Israeli lines; even as the Saudis made public pronouncements against any Western security presence in the region and did their best to bribe Oman into discontinuing arrangements with the U.S. for the use of the Masirah base and other facilities.[11] Given the list of sales the U.S. had made or was considering, there was unquestionably a strong military and corporate bloc favoring the expansion of the American-Saudi relationship and—equally important—intent upon curtailing any alternative. This was particularly true if the alternative—U.S.-Israel cooperation—elicited hostility from the Saudis even though

it would not replace (indeed, ideally would bolster) the American-
Saudi tie. Not only was Israel's strategic value dismissed, but
Egypt's strategic worth was denigrated as well. Given the quality
of the Israeli Air Force and the strategic position of Egypt, such
bias must stand as an example of pure corporate military thought,
wholly indifferent to the primary role of the military—to win bat-
tles.

The continuing drive for Saudi cooperation was also indicative
of no little wishful thinking. The Saudis asserted repeatedly that
they did not share the vision of strategic consensus against the
Soviets. There were also examples of open American courtship of
the Saudis—in overt contrast to the attitude shown the Israelis.
This is the double standard (or more correctly, the petrodollar
standard). The Saudis have said repeatedly that they do not consider themselves strategic partners with the U.S. and do not agree
with or share U.S. priorities. On January 25, 1981, King Khalid
told the Islamic Conference in Taif that Saudi Arabia and other
Muslim countries should align with neither East nor West. On
March 23, Saudi Arabia rejected peace talks with Israel. The next
day, senior Saudi officials rejected the idea of U.S. bases or facilities
in the Persian Gulf.[12] On March 26, the State Department confirmed that the Saudis were permitting Soviet overflights to and
from Ethiopia and South Yemen. On April 8, Saudi Arabia rejected
joint crewing and control of its AWACs. The same day, the Saudis
told Secretary Haig in Riyadh that they did not accept his strategic
consensus or his assertion that the Soviet Union was a greater
threat than Israel.[13] On July 16, Saudi Arabia offered to fund a
replacement reactor for Iraq—this three weeks after Saddam Hussein had asserted that the Arabs must acquire nuclear weapons.[14]
In the wake of Israel's attack on P.L.O. headquarters in Beirut
(July 20) Saudi Arabia pledged $20 million to the P.L.O. On August
20, the Saudis denounced the U.S. downing of two Libyan SU-22s
as "medieval piracy," and encouraged members of the Gulf Cooperation Council to join in a denunciation of the United States.[15]
On September 14, after a statement by Haig suggesting that the
Saudis did not object to U.S.-Israel strategic cooperation, the Saudis voiced their "strong objections" to such an arrangement.

Throughout October, the Saudis continued to reject joint control over AWACs.

The day after the AWACs sale was approved, the Saudis committed an act directly counter to the interests of the Western alliance: they raised oil prices and cut production to try to preserve OPEC's eroding market control. At the end of November, a Saudi official reported an attempt to bribe the Omanis into ending the American presence at that country's military facilities. In essence, all these statements and actions took their theme from King Khalid's repeated calls for non-alignment (reiterated by the Saudi Foreign Minister Saud al-Faisal throughout the year) and from the Petroleum Minister, Sheikh Yamani, who, early in 1981, said that Israel, and not the Soviet Union, was the primary threat to the security of the region!

The Administration's intention of moving toward closer military and political coordination with Saudi Arabia had been evident for some time. It was reported in early February 1981 that Weinberger had been lobbied by the Saudis for enhancements for the F-15s when he was still at the Bechtel Corporation. On February 3, Weinberger said that the Administration would want to make the Saudi F-15s "as effective as possible" and that the U.S. would "do everything it could to assist them [the Saudis]." In early February, it was reported that Haig was seeking the use of Saudi bases, as well as exploring arrangements for the pre-positioning of material. Haig announced on February 22 that the U.S. would be selling sophisticated weapons to Saudi Arabia. In fact, a Defense Department study team had recommended selling AWACs the month before and the recommendation had just reached the NSC for evaluation.[16] In late February, it was reported that the Bureau of Near Eastern Affairs in the State Department regarded the sale of F-15 enhancements as a litmus test of America's regard for the Saudis, and was opposing any *quid pro quo*. On March 6, the State Department said that "changed circumstances from 1978" justified the decision to sell the enhancements in violation of the last administration's pledge to the Congress not to do so.[17] Weinberger stated—revealingly—on March 8, that the U.S. would seek facilities in the Middle East "if acceptable to the Saudi Arabians and other host countries."[18] This is perhaps the earliest evidence that the drive to give Saudi Arabia strategic primacy was in full swing. On March 18, 1981, Haig justified the enhancement sale citing support for it from the previous administration. Yet Carter officials indicated on March 27 that they had, in fact, made no binding commitment.

On March 26 and April 8, Haig committed two blunders that effectively destroyed any chance for implementing a new Middle East policy based on strategic cooperation with Israel and on the abandonment of the mirage of a comprehensive settlement of the Arab-Israeli conflict. On March 26, the Secretary told the Senate that it was "too early" to speak of a Saudi role in the peace process.[19] This send a clear signal to the Saudis that deferential treatment would continue, and that the U.S. was not prepared to impose sanctions on those who opposed its policies—at least not in the Middle East. On April 8, in Saudi Arabia, Haig delivered an airport statement in which he abruptly changed his prior approach—that the Soviet threat was of greater importance than the pursuit of an Arab-Israel settlement. Haig, apparently after tense and difficult discussions with a recalcitrant Saudi leadership, talked of the "twin problems" confronting the region. This effectively put the Arab-Israel dispute on the same level with the Soviet threat. It was at odds with what the State Department, only a week before, had told reporters would be Haig's message. By April 19 one State Department source was articulating the new line—that the Soviet threat was no more and no less important than pursuit of an Arab-Israel settlement, and that policies designed to deal with both were mutually reinforcing.[20]

In early May, Defense Department sources acknowledged that they had failed to negotiate proper joint control over the AWACs. Yet the Reagan Administration was not to be deterred from embelishing the fiction of strategic consensus and cooperation with the Saudis. On May 16, Reagan met secretly with the chief of Saudi intelligence, Prince Turki al-Faisal, in order to win Saudi Arabia's involvement in the Lebanon mediation. Habib carried the same message to the Saudis simultaneously. Hereafter, there were repeated references from the Administration to Saudi Arabia's helpful diplomacy. Two days later the State Department said the Saudis were playing a "very constructive role" in the Lebanese crisis and at the same time on May 18, pointedly decried Begin's slaps at Saudi Arabia.

The Saudi plan was soon revealed: it took as its major elements the retention of the Syrian surface-to-air missiles in Lebanon pending some future withdrawal, Saudi refinancing of the Syrian "peacekeeping force," and a limitation of Israeli overflights. Yet this proposal, which became the basis of the *de facto* resolution of the crisis, was hereafter well received by Administration officials, even though it damaged Israel, aided Syria, and did nothing to promote American interests through removal of the causes of conflict in Lebanon. On June 1, the White House cited Saudi concern over the Lebanon issue. Assistant Secretary of State Veliotes said on June 2 that strategic cooperation with the Arabs depended in large part upon progress on Palestinian autonomy.[21] This was further erosion of the primacy once given the Soviet threat. On June 30, State sent congratulations to Saudi Arabia for its mediation of the Syrian siege at Zahle. Weinberger took pains to note the role Saudi Arabia was playing in the mediation of the Lebanese crisis.

With the AWACs vote looming, Reagan wrote members of Congress on August 5 that the sale was essential to the "security and stability of southwest Asia." Philip Geyelin reported in the *Washington Post* the next day that the USAF looked to the AWACs as a potential adjunct to a U.S. military presence. The State Department refused to comment on the blast Fahd leveled at U.S. policy on the same day (August 7) that he revealed his so-called peace plan. On August 23, acknowledging that the U.S. would have no effective control over the Saudi AWACs, an unnamed Administration official noted that the Saudi "dignity" and "sovereignty" had made it impossible for the U.S. to obtain a Saudi pledge not to use the planes against Israel. He did not mention that two months earlier, Saudi Prince Bandar had indicated (in the *Wall Street Journal*) that the primary reason the Saudis wanted AWACs was Israel—not the Soviets.[22] The very next day, Under Secretary of State Buckley asserted that the AWACs, in addition to defending the oilfields, would restore U.S. credibility with Saudi Arabia and provide a military system that would "facilitate deployment of U.S. tactical forces in the region in time of need if requested." Buckley also said the sale underlined both the Administration's commitment to Saudi security and laid the foundation for U.S.-Saudi cooperation. Haig added a new line to this on September 8: the AWACs would serve the interests of the U.S. and Israel by increasing "America's presence" in the region. This approach was in keeping with Haig's assessment in the spring: that the U.S. had to command the shared confidence of its potential allies.

That America policy had come full circle was apparent on September 17, in Haig's testimony to the Senate Foreign Affairs Committee. The same man who in early February was reportedly seeking Saudi bases now said the desire of local nations for independence made it unfeasible for the U.S. to try to secure such bases. Haig said the U.S. had *many* strategic interests in the region. This further blurred the earlier, clear-cut assessment of priorities. Autumn 1981 seemed to be Reagan's season for personally courting the Saudis. On October 1, he said Saudi Arabia would not be allowed to become another Iran. He repeated this on October 17. He welcomed certain aspects of the Fahd plan on October 19. Three days later he said he looked to Saudi Arabia to bring the P.L.O. into the peace process and on November 19 he called Saudi Arabia "the key to peace in the Middle East."[23]

At no time during 1981 did the Administration spend as much energy on any foreign policy issue as it did in the battle over the AWACs. Officials emphasized Saudi Arabia's "moderation," its sharing of American priorities, its lack of interest in fighting Israel, its crucial economic value, its eminent reputation in the Middle East, as evidence to support the sale (despite the fact that there was little empirical evidence from Saudi Arabia to back up any of these claims, only petrodollars and cents). President Reagan even went so far as to call into question the patriotism of his opponents. A note of desperation crept into the Administration's behavior as the crucial vote on the AWACs neared. The White House floated hints that it might use waiver provisions to circumvent any Congressional resolution disapproving the sale of AWACs. It tolerated the anti-Semitic denigration of the American opponents to the AWACs sale in order to win votes through intimidation.*

As if proof were needed that the Administration had institutionalized its special regard for the Saudis, one can cite more than just the Administration's discarding of the 1978 pledges to Congress not to sell F-15 enhancements and AWACs to the Saudis. No less significant is the fact that on the day after the resolution was pushed through the Senate the Administration began suggesting that the pledges on the use of the AWACs, contained in a letter to Congress and submitted the day before, might not be fully binding.[24] This letter had won over a number of Senators, yet, within hours of the vote the pledges were already being discounted by an Administration all too aware of the true intentions and style of the Saudis. In this manner, the Reagan Administration has established Saudi Arabia—a feudal kingdom that the President had discounted only a year earlier—as a linchpin for anti-Soviet policy in the Middle East. The influence of the Saudis on the Reagan Administration exceeds even that exercised during the Carter years. Jimmy Carter did not sell America's most advanced airborne warning and control system to the Saudis, though he might, perhaps, have been planning to do so during a second term.

In the last week of October 1981, it was apparent that every meaningful pledge made by the Administration had gone by the board: the 1978 promises, the promises in the Reagan letter; even the promises not to sell future technology to upgrade the AWACs. The Administration acknowledged that pledges to sell a "strippeddown plane" applied only to this initial transaction, and not to what would finally be delivered. In fact, the National Security Council had discussed in March the schedule for which AWACs upgrades would be sold, and how high technology items could be sold without Congressional review. The Administration thus placed itself in a position of giving Saudi Arabia control of a system essential to NATO's defense.

---

*OPEC's decision to raise oil prices was well programmed to come only *after* the crucial vote was taken in the U.S. Senate. One can only speculate whether the Administration used information on this to reinforce earlier forebodings of an anti-Semitic backlash were the AWACs to be voted down.

Since the middle of 1981, relations between the United States and Israel have been hamstrung by the Administration's linking the prospect of U.S. support for Israel in one area to Israel's behavior in another. What Israel got depended on what Israel did. Other Administrations have at times employed such a policy, but none had ever used it to such an extent. Candidate Reagan decried the Carter Administration's sniping at Israel and sowing seeds of distrust; yet there is ample evidence that even in this simplest area of relations between allies—or even between courteous strangers—the Reagan Administration, while privately acknowledging the validity of Israel's case failed to back it publicly. Instead, it undercut and distanced itself from Israel, vented anger and bitterness at its leadership and made periodic threats.

The pattern emerged almost as soon as the first conflicts over AWACs and Lebanon had occurred. On May 12, White House officials voiced concern over possible Israeli action against the Syrian SAM sites and P.L.O. concentrations in Lebanon. The next day, James Reston of the *New York Times* ran a story in which the White House leaked Reagan's irritation with Begin over AWACs and his verbal assaults on West German Chancellor Schmidt. Such leaks were intended to reinforce the same negative image as the Administration's policies were to project later that year: that Israel was unreliable, not to be fully trusted and ultimately, that *Israel* was responsible for the United States holding it at a distance. On May 24, when Israel reported, on the basis of hard intelligence, that Libyan troops were in Damour, Lebanon, the State Department said it could not confirm it. The next day the State Department dismissed Israeli charges that Soviet advisers were with Syrian forces in Lebanon. It was reported that Soviet experts made periodic inspection tours of Syrian positions. Their duty was to ascertain that the deployments of Soviet equipment were sound, and they made suggestions. Not only did the State Department not confirm this story, but Department sources privately upbraided Israel for making "provocative" statements.[25] Here again, the inevitable effect was to erode the image of the would-be ally, Israel. On June 2, Assistant Secretary Nicholas Veliotes asserted that the U.S. was not giving Israel "the green light" for action in Lebanon.

He stressed that raids were damaging the chances for peace. Again, Washington was distancing itself from Israel and putting it on the defensive.

Israel's adversaries in the Administration were waiting patiently for the first pretext to portray Israel as a black sheep, and an undeserving and ungrateful one at that. That came with the suspension by the United States of arms shipments to Israel in the wake of the Israeli attack on Iraq's nuclear facility at Osirak. After the Osirak raid, the State Department said there was no evidence that Iraq was violating the Non-Proliferation Treaty, an assertion that contradicted intelligence information available to the White House.[26] In his June 10 meeting with the Arab ambassadors, Reagan was at pains to demonstrate that the U.S. had no foreknowledge of the raid. He also said Israel had not exhausted all its diplomatic options beforehand. In mid-June, CIA briefers at closed door sessions on Capitol Hill were providing extensive support for Israel's case. Yet on June 17, then Under Secretary of State Walter Stoessel testified that the U.S. did not share Israel's assessment of the threat posed by the program at Osirak.[27] The pressure from the bureaucracy was evident here—as it angled for a confrontation with Israel. State Department briefers attacked both Israel's estimates and those of the CIA.

In fact, the Foreign Military Sales Act did not require the United States to suspend arms shipments to Israel until a determination had been made that weapons had been used offensively. Early on the Administration knew that Israel had a legitimate fear of Iraq's nuclear program. Moreover, Iraq had been in a continuous state of war with Israel, having signed neither a ceasefire nor an armistice agreement. If a determination were not to be made on the basis of legalistic hair-splitting, then it was apparent that Iraq's own belligerence could provide the U.S. with a justification for standing by Israel—an ally of longstanding—instead of Iraq, a Soviet client. Yet in a memorandum sent to the National Security Council shortly after the Osirak raid, Weinberger reportedly outlined potential U.S. responses[28] as including: cutting off military and economic aid; suspension of all military deliveries; reparations to Iraq; IAEA inspection of Israel's nuclear reactor at Dimona; and UN condemnation. Having cabled the Arab states on June 9 that it was not in collusion with Israel on the raid, the Administration chose on June 10 to hold up the delivery of four F-16s. Such an embargo of weapons already in the pipeline was unprecedented.

Yet another pattern of behavior emerged. Heretofore the U.S. had asked Israel to trust its mediation of the Lebanese crisis (May 4, May 11); now, however, the White House was indicating privately that it might no longer be pushing for a full withdrawal of the Syrian SAMs. A partial withdrawal might come later, at the end of an undefined pacification process—one obviously requiring Israeli restraint. During this time, and in the ensuing months, the State Department chose not to comment on the constant stream of calumnies and insults being spewed forth from Damascus excoriating American imperialism, Washington's connivance with Zionism, and Habib's unfitness as a mediator. The State Department, one may recall, had slapped Begin on May 19 for calling Saudi Arabia medieval and corrupt.

The administration, in fact, indicated concern over Arab reaction, and was trying to demonstrate "even-handedness" to the Arab states. Not only were F-16 deliveries to Israel suspended; not only did the U.S. begin to back away from forcing a Syrian withdrawal, but the talks on military and intelligence cooperation initiated during Israeli Foreign Minister Shamir's February visit were curtailed.

In June, Secretary of State Haig sent a harshly worded aide-memoire to Prime Minister Begin that infringed Israeli sovereignty by demanding prior consultation on the use of American-supplied arms for offensive purposes (this was an NEA product, and Haig probably signed it as much to mollify the Arabists as to obtain some actual accommodations from Begin).[29] On July 9, State Department officials indicated that failure by Israel to comply with this demand would make resumption of F-16 deliveries more difficult. In Israel on July 13, State Department Counsel Robert MacFarlane requested that the Israelis agree to prior consultation. Haig said the next day that MacFarlane's report on the Israeli government's attitude would affect the decision on the F-16s. The Administration, knowing it had made an error with the F-16s, was prepared to lift the embargo on July 17. However, the same day, Begin was so incensed by the fact that P.L.O. shelling was driving Israelis from Kiryat Shemona, that he ordered the bombing of the P.L.O. headquarters in Beirut. The Beirut raid had been in Israel's contingency plans for many years, and had never been used, reportedly out of concern over the likelihood of an adverse world reaction if massive numbers of civilians were killed. Delivery of the F-16s was held up again. Israel's use of American weapons in reprisals against the P.L.O. had long been established as custom and there had never been a State Department legal finding against it. Arab supporters in the Congress used it periodically as a propaganda lever and as a means of unsettling U.S.-Israel relations. Yet, with the hold-up after the Beirut raid, the U.S. was, in effect, applying the provisions of the Foreign Military Sales Act for actions in Lebanon—something it had scrupulously refused to do in the past.

Nonetheless Haig stated on July 19 that there was no link between the Beirut raid and the F-16 hold-up—an obvious diplomatic lie—and he opined that delivery of the planes would be linked to "moderation in the current levels of tension and a reduction of violence." He outlined a "broad" interrelationship between the F-16s and local turmoil.[30] Haig's statement, like his April 8 gaffe in Riyadh, seemed to be at odds with the Haig who remained throughout the year more friendly to Israel than any other Administration official. As in Riyadh, and in the "I am in control" episode after the Reagan assassination attempt, Haig seemed to be reacting too quickly to the pressures of the moment. Clearly, he was under pressure from his Near East Bureau after the Beirut raid, and was aware of the line that Weinberger and the Joint Chiefs had been taking with the White House about the appropriate course of action vis-a-vis Israel.

On July 21, Administration officials described the F-16 imbroglio as a "watershed" in U.S.-Israel relations. A State Department official cited the "tense situation" as justifying the F-16 delay. Weinberger and Clark spoke up the next day. Both statements were important not only because they represented the most open example of high-level criticism of Israel, but also because they reinforced each other (they also demonstrated how the Administration personalized disagreements with Israel and sought to justify its personal animus towards Begin as being deserved and also a central element of American policy). Weinberger's statement established—for the first time—a formal tie between the events of June and those of July.[31] It also expanded the impact area of the Beirut and Osirak raids: Weinberger said their effect had "set the whole course of security and peace back quite a ways." Clark's statement stressed that the U.S. was concerned with regional responsibilities and had sympathy for both sides.[32] In essence, Weinberger implied that Israel—not the P.L.O., not Syria, not Iraq—was responsible for the general state of unrest in the area. This was the classic Arabist line. Clark dismissed Israel's concerns about P.L.O. shellings and Iraqi nuclear weapons as parochial, even distracting. Within a day, White House officials were giving support to these statements. On July 27, Weinberger expanded the implied demands Haig had made on Israel on July 19. He stated that delivery of the F-16s depended upon a combination of circumstances, not just the Lebanese truce.[33] The image of an Israel on probation was focused somewhat more sharply. It complimented neatly the image of a moderate, helpful Saudi Arabia then being promoted by the Administration. The White House emphasized Saudi Arabia's presumed cooperation primarily as a means of justifying the embattled AWACs sale. But the net effect was to create precisely the atmosphere wanted by the Joint Chiefs and other proponents of a Saudi link, one in which Israel's reliability as an ally was devalued and Saudi Arabia's inflated, one in which Israel would be preoccupied with getting itself back into the good graces of the Administration.

When the F-16 holdup was lifted, the White House added a specific note of reproof even though no finding had been made that Israel had used its American weapons illegally: "Any country we sell arms to we expect to abide by U.S. law concerning these sales" (August 16).[34] Secretary of State Haig cited Israel's willingness to accept the Lebanese cease-fire, as one reason for lifting of the embargo. By the time the embargo ended, sixteen planes, including two F-15s, had been delayed. The Israelis were particularly angered at the F-15 holdup, for they inferred from this that an American arms embargo could be unrestricted, and potentially total. Meanwhile, the issue of the Syrian SAMs had been allowed to lie dormant. Here again, the Administration used the pretext of an Israeli action to accede to something damaging to Israel: the Syrian/Saudi plan to preserve the Syrian presence in Lebanon. It is certain that the Administration did not have the conviction to face down Syria's Assad, whose government's statements, while continually castigating the United States, proclaimed an absolute right to maintain the missiles in Lebanon and a refusal to negotiate.

As the AWACs battle neared its end, the process of linkage manifested itself differently. On August 30, the Administration began what would be a series of stories in which Israel was warned that additional aid, and some of the elements of strategic cooperation would be eliminated if the AWACs deal went down to defeat. On September 11, senior Pentagon officials, briefing reporters "off the record," warned that cooperation with Israel would be reassessed if the AWACs resolution was defeated.[35] Haig reportedly told Begin later that week in New York that, despite Begin's statements to the contrary, there was a link between U.S.-Israel strategic cooperation and AWACs. On September 14, Haig acknowledged that U.S. policy toward Israel would be altered by an AWACs defeat. In mid-September, it was reported that Defense was going so far as to recommend holding up strategic cooperation pending not just the AWACs vote but the autonomy talks as well.[36] It was obvious that elements at Defense would seize upon any device that might block genuine movement toward U.S.-Israeli cooperation. This process would continue so long as it pleased the Saudis.

With the defeat of the AWACs proposition a growing possibility, veiled and not so veiled warnings emanated from an increasingly desperate Administration during September and October. Not a few of these came from the National Security Council staff, notably Admiral Nance and Richard Allen, and from Richard Burt, head of the Bureau of Politico-Military Affairs at the State Department, as well as from others. After a September 14 meeting with Senators, the White House leaked criticism of the opponents of AWACs and of supposed heavy Israeli involvement in the American legislative process. The White House legislative liaison sent a package up to the Congress whose centerpiece was an essay from *Time* magazine questioning Begin's fitness to be Prime Minister. Reagan's October 1 statement (a Meese and Allen product) was aimed directly at Israel: "It is not the business of other nations to make American foreign policy."[37] In a seminar sponsored by the Washington-based Center for International Security in early October, General Schweitzer, representing the NSC, justified the AWACs sale by noting that its supporters included Reagan and Sadat, and its opponents "Begin, Brezhnev, and Qaddafi."[38] It should be noted that from August through mid-October, the Israeli embassy was under orders from Jerusalem to do as little as possible on the AWACs issue, precisely in order to avoid the impression of meddling in American politics (Israel, in fact, had requested its American Christian supporters not to go to the mat on this issue for Israel's sake alone). But the White House's hard-ball lobbying—born of desperation—sought to question the motives of AWACs opponents, even though most members of Congress were primarily concerned not with Israel so much as with the dangers to America's own security. The AWACs appeared certain to be insecure in the hands of the Saudis. It is also useful to note that Saudi Prince Bandar was camped out in Washington throughout the year lobbying energetically for the AWACs.[39] On this the Administration was mute. In conversations during and after the AWACs battle, Administration officials denied any antipathy for Israel; in fact they repeatedly, even heatedly, explained their intense and occasionally invidious lobbying techniques as just rough-and-tumble politics. The net result of this, of course, was materially to increase Israel's suspicion and distrust of the Reagan Administration. President Reagan was doing just the opposite of what candidate Reagan had promised.

In the wake of the AWACs vote, Administration officials moved publicly to demonstrate solicitude for Israel. Yet, at the same time, State Department sources denigrated Israel's concerns over the President's newfound regard for the Fahd plan (November 1 and November 12). Reagan's welcoming of elements of the Fahd plan did not occur in a vacuum. There had obviously been some rethinking at the State Department since the plan was first greeted with indifference in August. Several hours before Reagan made his statement, Deputy Assistant Secretary of State Peter Constable said the U.S. "welcomes . . . constructive elements of the Fahd plan." This suggests that Reagan had been given briefing papers calling for a change in American policy. Both the State Department and the White House called the OPEC price rise on October 29 and the Saudi production cutback "moderate," a classically Arabist view. On November 5, a senior State Department official said that King Hussein's visit in September had restored "confidence and trust" to the relations between Jordan and the U.S. That same day, Jordan announced its intention to buy SA-6s from the USSR, to be paid for by Iraq. U.S. officials later said this would complicate relations. At the UN General Assembly in September, Saudi Foreign Minister Saud al Faisal repeatedly referred to the "so-called State of Israel." The State Department made no comment. On November 14, Saudi Arabia disavowed a statement made two days earlier by its acting UN ambassador, which asserted that the Fahd plan meant recognition of Israel. The State Department made no comment, but Administration sources did use the opportunity to say that Israel was probably trying to intimidate Saudi Arabia by overflying Tabuk. At the meeting with Jewish leaders on November 20, Reagan indicated that he preferred Jerusalem to remain united under Israeli sovereignty.[40] State Department and White House officials issued *"clarification"* within hours. After the collapse of the Fez conference, NEA officials opined that the State Department still viewed the Fahd plan as the best means for broadening the Middle East peace talks.[41]

Weinberger followed his own department's advice, and postponed talks with Israel on strategic cooperation until after the AWACs vote. In the aftermath of the AWACs vote, Administration officials indicated that, given budget restraints, the U.S. would aid Israel not so much with increased aid as with strategic cooperation. Thus, when the MOU was cancelled in the wake of the Golan annexation in December, the U.S., though repeatedly promising Israel strategic cooperation, had delivered very little. Worse yet, the Administration was creating an artificial link between two completely different planes—the Golan action and the MOU. The Administration stated that the MOU dealt particularly with the need of allies to consult, and that Israel had failed to do this in taking an action that (in the Administration's charge) circumvented UN Resolutions 242 and 338.[42] The Administration's position however made little sense in the face of Israeli affirmation that nothing in the extension of its law to the inhabitants of the Golan Heights negated peace negotiations for a final recognized border in the Golan. In any case, the U.S. reaction to Israel's Golan action seemed out of proportion to the supposed offense: it threatened the possibility of a suspension of arms shipments and the imposition of sanctions in addition to the demand for the repeal of the Golan decision. This signal of American unreliability was decried by Israeli Defense Minister Sharon on December 19. The same day the State Department took the time to reject Sharon's criticism (this from a department that had failed even to comment on Saudi Arabia's call for a Holy War on Israel or to respond to Assad's ravings); and three days later the Administration repeated that above all, it did not want Israel to feel it had a "blank check" (December 22).[43] Yet in suspending the MOU, the Administration precipitately stopped a wide-ranging existing program to help Israel's defense industries find customers and expand markets and sales. This had been another goal of candidate Reagan, mutually beneficial for the U.S. to take advantage of Israel's technical prowess. The Joint Chiefs of Staff, an adversary of Israel's arms industry long before there was talk of strategic cooperation between the U.S. and Middle Eastern States, could not have been displeased by this reversal. Their defense industry suppliers were surely also content.

In sum, what emerged during 1981 was a pattern in which Israel was not treated as a primary, trusted ally. It was not favored; it was not rewarded. From the Administration's viewpoint, the reasons seemed to rest with Israel. At the end of the year, Administration officials cited "four disappointments" that had soured them on Israel and its leadership: the Osirak raid, the Beirut attack, the opposition to the AWACs deal, and the Golan "annexation." This claim covered up an underlying reality: there is a faction in the U.S. Government that is constantly working against any fundamental reevaluation of the American-Saudi connection, a faction that seeks to tighten that connection at Israel's expense, that appeases Soviet proxies in the region, that has seized upon pretexts, beginning with Osirak, to accelerate the alienation of the Reagan Administration from Israel, that hopes to achieve this aim by pushing for punishment of Israel out of all proportion to any infraction of agreements, that campaigns to undermine the image of Israel as a reliable and militarily valuable ally, that has succeeded in propagating an attitude toward Israel characterized by distrust, impatience, animus, exasperation, and doubt and that aims at a long-term strategic policy more pro-Arab and self-deceptive than any promoted by the traditional Arabist at the State Department. By the year's end, it seemed that those who still considered themselves Israel's genuine friends—Haig, Reagan—could shake their heads and wonder why Israel had gotten both countries into such a tangled misunderstanding. Yet the reality was that those few in the Administration who planned for a new relationship with Israel in the national interest never had a chance.

In the first two weeks of 1982, several events had a direct impact on America's strategic policy in the Middle East. The most important of these was Secretary Weinberger's tour of the Middle East in early February. The itinerary of the trip was significant, for Weinberger specifically refused to visit Israel, even though the trip was billed as one that would assess the military needs of the United States. In excluding Israel, Weinberger and the JCS implicitly emphasized the Pentagon's downgrading of Israel's strategic value. Israel was not included, according to the Pentagon, because it was felt that a visit would be seen as a U.S. imprimatur to the so-called annexation of the Golan Heights.[44] Publicly, Weinberger said he would visit Israel at a later date. The intention to disengage from Israel was apparent. This became increasingly clear when the press reported background remarks by officials on Weinberger's plane. One senior aide, later identified as Assistant Secretary of Defense Francis J. West, Jr., told reporters that in the future the focus of American policy in the region would be "redirected" from Israel toward the Arab states.[45] This caused an outcry in Israel. The Pentagon subsequently issued a clarification (though not for several days) to the effect that the official (then as yet unnamed) had meant that U.S. policy would be redirected away from purely external

threats and toward the problem of dealing with internal subversion.[46] Nevertheless, the original interpretation remained the dominant one in the public mind, especially after *New York Times*
reporter Richard Halloran identified West as the person who had
made the statement.

There was no better epitome of the Reagan Administration's
problems and approaches to the Middle East than Weinberger's
visit to Saudi Arabia. The Saudis were studiously non-committal
toward Weinberger's call for a formal strategic relationship. One
Saudi general told American reporters that in case of an external
threat, Saudi Arabia would look to itself first, to its Arab neighbors
second, "and to you last." Another member of the party of Defense
Minister Sultan told the press that the U.S. and not the Soviet
Union, was the primary threat to Saudi Arabia's oilfields. A third
Saudi official dismissed suggestions that the sale of the AWACs
had obligated the Saudis to be more responsive to America's push
for an expanded peace process. "You are just arms salesmen," he
said, "and we pay cash." Yet another Saudi official, when asked if
he thought anything good had come from the Camp David Accords,
replied "Yes, the death of Sadat."

Weinberger's meetings were similarly unproductive and politically embarrassing. For several days, he tried unsuccessfully to
convince the Saudis to agree to a formal, written military agreement. He also sought their acceptance of the conditions for the
Saudi's use of the AWACs, which President Reagan had certified
to Congress as guidelines. The Saudis adamantly refused to sign
any written agreement on either subject. They accepted certain
conditions on the use of the AWACs, but officials at the NSC later
acknowledged that these terms, as yet unreleased to the public,
did not fully match those which the President had promised the
Congress. When the press reported later in the month that the
Saudis had agreed to limitations on the use of AWACs, the Saudi
Government issued a denial. Most importantly, the Secretary of
Defense failed to win more than *pro forma* Saudi acceptance of
military cooperation. Emerging from a negotiating session which
lasted until 4:30 a.m. (February 9), Weinberger announced that
the two countries had agreed to form a Joint Committee for Military

Projects. In the news conference that followed, however, Prince Sultan stated that the U.S.-Saudi relationship was not based on "cooperation in the field of military endeavor." Weinberger scrambled to clarify, acknowledging that what the Prince had to say was "of course correct."[47] The Saudis thus once again demonstrated not only their refusal to acknowledge publicly the need for military cooperation with the United States, but also their talent for dissimulation.

On the plane to Jordan, Weinberger told reporters that he would look favorably on a Jordanian request for Improved Hawk Mobile Air Defense missiles (SAMs). He also indicated understanding of Jordan's desire for F-16s. In Jordan, King Hussein reiterated his longstanding criticism of American Middle East policy. Members of Weinberger's entourage brushed this off as so much rhetoric, and privately briefed the press to the effect that the Reagan Administration would be willing to ignore assurance given to the Congress in 1976 that any Hawk missile sold to Jordan would have to be installed at fixed sites.[48] Upon his return to the U.S., Weinberger parried queries about the sale by saying that there had as yet been no formal request. When Hussein told interviewers that he would request U.S. mobile SAMs but not cancel an order for Soviet SAMs, Weinberger and the Administration began articulating a new theme: that it is in the interest of peace, of the West, and of Israel that the U.S. and not the Soviet Union would be the military supplier of Jordan. It was argued that with the SAMs from the USSR would come Soviet advisers, and this would exacerbate tensions. Yet Jordan would not cancel its deal with the Soviets. Israel reacted sharply to these reports. Defense Minister Sharon indicated that Israel "would not permit" Jordan to acquire the I-Hawks or F-16s. This drew private rebukes from the White House; all this stood in contrast to the Administration's tolerant silence toward Hussein's verbal assaults on the U.S. and the assertion of his intentions to consummate the sale with the Soviets.

In essence, the Weinberger visit drove the wedge between the U.S. and Israel deeper, and sowed a new crop of distrust. Simultaneously, it advanced what was now more obviously a sterile strategic policy of American-Arab cooperation. Typically, Administration officials were quick to criticize Israel for stating its concerns, but showed little or no response to positions adopted by Saudi Arabia and Jordan. It is significant that in 1981 the Reagan Administration indicated that Jordan's purchase of Soviet SAMs would affect adversely the U.S. military supply relationship with the Hashemite Kingdom. In 1982, the official attitude was that the U.S. would be more forgiving—so as to regain Jordanian favor.

Of all the minor policy signals given by the U.S. in early 1982, none was more disturbing that the decision to lift Iraq's designation as a country supporting terrorism. Simultaneously, the State Department decided to allow Syria and South Yemen to purchase American commercial airplanes if they so desired; the two nations remained on the list of supporters of terrorism. The decision to change Iraq's status reportedly came because Abu Nidal, an adversary of Yasser Arafat, had decided to leave his sanctuary in Iraq. Also, Iraq, preoccupied with its losing war with Iran, had reduced its involvement with the various guerilla groups in Lebanon. Yet Iraq maintained its sponsorship of the Arab Liberation Front; and its secret services continued their relations with Soviet, Cuban and East German counterparts and through them, with the international terrorists they supported in Lebanon, Libya, South Yemen and Western Europe.

This apparent cultivation of Iraq fits into a larger process begun during the Carter Administration. Beginning in 1977, State Department officials had begun suggesting that Iraq was moving out of the Soviet orbit. Iraq was the special project of NSC advisor Zbigniew Brzezinski, who privately said that he could do with that country what Kissinger had done with Egypt. The cultivation of the Ba'athist regime continued after Saddam Hussein removed his predecessor, Hassan al-Bakr and replaced him as president. It continued even as Saddam was purging roughly thirty percent of the Ba'athist leadership and decimating both the Iraqi Communist Party and major elements of the Iraqi officer corps.

The Israeli invasion of Lebanon at the beginning of June 1982 precipitated a series of consequences and opportunities that are apparently even less understood by U.S. policymakers than the implications of an Iranian defeat of Iraq. While the Israeli assault against the P.L.O. in Lebanon was ostensibly for the purpose of clearing a twenty-five mile zone in southern Lebanon of P.L.O. forces, it soon took on a more dramatic aspect. Predictably, the Israelis decided to take full advantage of their dominance of the battlefield and turned to the pursuit of political objectives that involved nothing less than a reconfiguration of the political map of Lebanon and of political reality in the Arab Middle East.

Israel had made an earlier incursion into Lebanon in 1978 in order to create a security zone between the Litani River and the Israeli border. The purpose of the zone was to preclude P.L.O. attacks on northern Israel, attacks which by definition were against the civilian population since the P.L.O. focuses almost exclusively on civilians. At the time, a United Nations controlled buffer zone was established north of the river to preclude infiltration to the south, a task which, as it transpired, the UN forces seemed incapable or undesirous of performing. Control of the border zone had been taken over by indigenous Christian Lebanese forces struggling for survival in the face of attacks by P.L.O.-Syrian and Muslim "leftist" forces.

Sporadic shelling and fighting took place in the region for years. The P.L.O. had been supplied with long range artillery which enabled them once again to reach into Israel from beyond the Litani River. Then, in an effort to deny Israel further effective control of the airspace over southern Lebanon, the Syrians introduced into the Bekaa Valley a number of advanced Soviet-made surface-to-air missile batteries. This step seriously escalated the nature of the emerging crisis. The U.S. by exerting strong political pressure on Israel got it to agree to a cease-fire with the P.L.O. At the same time there was an explicit understanding that the U.S. would exert pressure on the Syrians to remove their SAM batteries from Lebanon. The U.S. viewed its collaboration with the Saudis in achieving the cease-fire as confirmation of the new role that "moderate" Saudi Arabia was to play in regional security. Indeed, even after the true nature of the Saudi-inspired cease-fire became fully evident merely as a means of rescuing the PLO, Administration spokesman, incredibly, continued to invoke it as an example of what could be achieved through a broadening of U.S. relations with the Arab states, and as vindication of its need for a more "even-handed" relationship with Israel and the Arabs.

The eleven months of the cease-fire were indeed notable, but not for the reasons which continued to send Washington policy-makers into a state of euphoria. During this period, as correctly foreseen by the Saudis, the P.L.O. was enabled to reconstitute its badly mauled forces in order to be able to continue the struggle with Israel. Israel's northern towns and villages again became the target for P.L.O. attack. Furthermore, during this same period, with Saudi financing, the P.L.O. was enabled to amass a stock of arms that went beyond the most liberal estimates made by Israel's intelligence services. These arms were predominantly Soviet manufactured, but included American arms transferred by the Saudis in direct violation of the arms Export Control Act. Israel launched a series of massive air attacks designed to destroy the infrastructure of the P.L.O. in Lebanon. The success of these attacks was so great that the P.L.O. appealed to Saudi Arabia to press Washington to force Israel to desist. The U.S. complied but failed singularly to produce results with regard to its commitment to Israel to get the Syrian missiles removed from the Bekaa Valley.

After a series of renewed P.L.O. provocations, Israel struck again. However, it was clear to all who understood what was happening, which excludes the leadership of the U.S. State and Defense Departments—not to mention an unprecedently uninspired National Security Council, that the Israelis had no intention of paying twice for the same objective. They were not simply going to push the P.L.O. back a few miles further and allow themselves to be forced into a new cease-fire by a combined Saudi-American demand which would allow the P.L.O., after licking its wounds, to resume its attacks as though nothing had happened. As Washington was unwilling to listen to anything but praise of Saudi moderation and responsibility, Israel obviously decided to act in a manner and at a speed which would deny the Saudis the opportunity to spur the U.S. to pressure Israel into a cease-fire which would again nullify their initial gains in the field.

In a carefully planned and articulated assault, the Israelis quickly rolled up to the outskirts of Beirut, destroying the P.L.O. forces in southern Lebanon and besieging P.L.O. headquarters in the capital. In the process it fought a mini war on the ground and in the air with Syrian forces and quickly accomplished what U.S. diplomacy had failed to do. In its brief encounter with the Syrians, Israel destroyed thirty-nine batteries of Soviet-supplied surface-to-air missiles (including the most sophisticated, the SA-8) and more than a hundred Soviet-built MIGs without sustaining a single loss, and destroyed or captured well over five hundred Soviet-made tanks.

To the general surprise of all, including the P.L.O. and their supporters among the Palestinians, the Arab world as a whole showed remarkable indifference to their fate. The Israeli onslaught was greeted by a general silence amongst the Arabs. Except for a few pro forma protests, it seemed as though they were delighted that the P.L.O. was being destroyed as a military force. Although it appears not to have done so, this should have constituted an object lesson to the Washington policy-making establishment regarding some of the realities of the politics of the Middle East. One might have concluded from the event that the Saudis are far less interested in a P.L.O.-led victory for Palestinian Arab nationalism than they are in keeping the radicalism that the P.L.O. represents as far as possible from Arabia. If doing so requires the Saudis to finance the P.L.O. for a hopeless struggle against Israel, they consider it a worthwhile investment in Arab security. If the P.L.O. were to face serious damage as a military force, so much the better. What is important from the Saudi point of view is for the continued existence of the P.L.O. as a political force as long as it is directed at an external enemy. A politically articulated Arab irredentism continues to serve as an expression of the Arab world's fundamental rejection of a non-Muslim political entity wielding state power in the Arab Middle East. Thus Saudi diplomacy has emerged once again to preserve the P.L.O. through manipulation of its American ally, although this time it is a political P.L.O. that they are attempting to preserve.

The Soviet Union, as most clear-headed analysts predicted, also did nothing, even though two of their clients, Syria and the P.L.O. were badly beaten. There is an important lesson to be learned from

Soviet behavior in this event. Soviet concerns in the Arab world relate almost exclusively to their broader geopolitical and strategic interests. In this scheme, the Arab states can serve as dispensable means but not as political ends. The states of the Middle East are to a great extent not nation-states in the European sense of the word. In the Arab world in particular, national identity is not a significant force. Consequently, recent history displays an exceptional number of attempts at confederation or federation or even union of Arab states, each of which implicitly calls for the ceding of a distinct nationality and the adoption of a new national identity. All of these numerous schemes have failed for one reason or another, but nationality has not been the significant factor. The reality is that the Arab states emerged more from the accidents of the administrative divisions of the Ottoman Empire and from Anglo-French imperialist rivalries than from any nationalist achievement of statehood within a specific territory, as Israel did. The Arab world is thus plagued by a pan-Arab identity and an overriding pan-Arab orientation. This being the case, by contrast with Iran which has a historic national identity and is emerging into a nation-state, the Arab states are perceived by the Soviets as too fluid in nature to provide the stability one must expect from a true and useful satellite. Accordingly, the Soviets are unlikely to take high risks on behalf of Arab states which are essentially marginal to their interests. Thus, while the Soviets have already replaced the losses incurred by Syria in the mini-war with Israel, they apparently would not intervene on Syria's behalf unless there was a direct threat to the Syrian state itself. With regard to the P.L.O., which is not a state and has little prospect of becoming one, Soviet support is strictly of the mischief-making variety. It is hardly worth getting involved in a volatile situation in Lebanon on the P.L.O.'s behalf which could easily culminate in a counterproductive great power confrontation.

Turning to the American reaction to the events, what emerges most strongly is the sense of an inability to come to grips with a reality that simply does not correspond to the pattern of misconceptions that tend to inform U.S. policy in the Middle East. While there is incontrovertible evidence that the majority of Americans, an overwhelming majority in fact, support Israel's objectives in Lebanon, Administration spokesmen continue to claim that most Americans are opposed to Israel's action and that unless Israel is forthcoming in meeting reasonable (that is, Saudi) conclusions regarding the future of the P.L.O. and the Palestinians, the Administration may be forced by the American public to revise its relationship with Israel. Indeed, a clear redirection in Administration policy can be detected which is beginning to veer it away from the sound strategic perceptions held by the President when he took office; perceptions which are increasingly being displaced by illusions.

The initial effective control of Lebanon by Israel provided the opportunity to restructure the Lebanese state in a manner which would not only restore Lebanese sovereignty but also significantly advance the cause of peace in the Middle East. It was an opportunity to bring about the withdrawal of all alien forces from Lebanon: Israelis, Syrians, and Palestinians. Alexander Haig, in his waning days as Secretary of State, grasped the significance of the moment and advised the President to adopt this objective as the Administration's goal in Lebanon. However, the essential first step in achieving this reconstitution of Lebanon was the removal of remaining P.L.O. forces from any position of influence, political or military, in Lebanon. Yet, it is on this most essential point that the position of the President and the then Secretary of State was deliberately undermined by those members of the Administration whose understanding of the Middle East is fueled by a set of misconceptions congenial to Saudi interests.

Thus Secretary of Defense Weinberger publicly denounced Israel's operation in the Lebanon (and advocated curtailment of military and economic aid to Israel) while the White House and the State Department backed Israel's goal to reconstitute the sovereignty of that state. When Secretary Weinberger and Vice President Bush were in Riyadh for the funeral of King Khalid in late June, they reportedly agreed to support the Saudis in their opposition to Israel's aims to eliminate the P.L.O. as a military force, although Israel was under the impression that President Reagan had decided that the P.L.O. must be defeated because of its terrorism, its implacability towards Israel and its record of domination in the Lebanon. While the President's Special Envoy in the Middle East, Philip Habib, and Secretary of State Haig were reportedly passing one set of information to the P.L.O., based on disarming them during a ceasefire, the Saudis were apparently passing the word to the P.L.O. that Secretary Weinberger and Vice President Bush opposed Israel's entry into Beirut to finish off the P.L.O. as a military force. With Israel restrained, it was reported, the P.L.O. was encouraged to refuse to agree to terms, including the surrender of weapons and the evacuation of its members to a country not bordering on Israel.

It was in this context that the White House, according to insiders, decided to say publicly that Prime Minister Begin had promised President Reagan that the Israelis would not enter Beirut (a statement retracted by the President a week later). This embittered Secretary of State Haig—who reportedly said this was a misrepresentation of Prime Minister Begin's position to President Reagan and was intended to encourage the P.L.O. to hold out in West Beirut. He thereupon resigned, much to the delight of the P.L.O. and Syrian representatives at the U.N., who regarded it as a victory for their cause (Prime Minister Begin, had in fact told President Reagan that he was reluctant to order an assault on the western part of the city because the P.L.O. was in effect holding its inhabitants hostage).

These contradictory signs within the Administration were not inadvertent mix-ups. They were rather deliberate attempts to fashion a solution to the problem along lines satisfactory to the Saudis, even if it meant sacrificing the opportunity to bring about the resuscitation of the Lebanon. The effect of the false White House leak and the statements to the Saudis was to let the P.L.O. know that they did not have to give in since the United States would bring sufficient pressure on the Israelis to prevent an attack. Thus, the United States government was itself responsible for the prolongation of inconclusive negotiations over the fate of the P.L.O. Further, to compound the folly of American diplomacy in the Lebanon, the President dispatched eight hundred U.S. Marines to Beirut to provide a screen, with the assistance of French and Italian troops, behind which the bulk of the P.L.O. could be safely evacuated. The P.L.O. was preserved by those in the Administration who wanted to use it as a potential partner in any negotiations on the future of the West Bank and the Gaza Strip. The Administration had no plans, however, for removing the P.L.O. forces from northern Lebanon and the Syrians from the Bekaa Valley, where the Soviet threat to the peace and security of the region remains ominous. The P.L.O. regrouping in northern Lebanon behind Syrian forces caused Lebanon to return to open civil war, this time along north-south lines, while Syria continued to maintain its claim to sovereignty over Lebanon and, in fact, occupies more than half of that unhappy country.

Regrettably, U.S. policy did not encourage developments towards a peaceful outcome. Secretary of State Shultz sought to reestablish Lebanon as the middleman between the West and the Arab petrodollar regimes. This policy, which required that Lebanon refuse to associate itself closely with its only friendly neighbor, the State of Israel, proved to be disasterous to the security of Lebanon and a threat to peace in the region. Although a minimum Lebanese-Israeli agreement was signed, it was too weak, and the commitment to it by the Gemayel government was too weak for it to accomplish anything positive for Israel or Lebanon. Moreover, in its haste to eject the Israelis from Beirut and to deny a peace between Israel and a second Middle East country, the Administration made a major blunder; it interposed untenable American power between Israel and Lebanese forces. The situation was in no way analogous to the U.S. military presence in the Sinai. There, participation in the multinational force in the Sinai is sharply defined within the context of an existing Egyptian-Israeli peace treaty; in Lebanon the mandate was as vague and undefined as its tenure. Unlike the situation in the Sinai where U.S. forces are deployed in a sparsely populated and tranquil area, the Marines in Lebanon were placed in a volatile zone of high urban and sectarian unrest. Indeed, from the beginning they already stood as impotent witnesses to continued outrages between local Christian, Sunni, Shia and Palestinian groups. With the Israeli withdrawal behind the Awali River, it became abundantly clear that the Maronite controlled (largely Muslim manned) Lebanese Army could not succeed in a peace-keeping role in the area; and the open ended character of the American-French-Italian deployment was repeatedly tested by Soviet proxies. In short, the U.S. pressed removal of the Israeli protective umbrella resulted in raising the level of risk-taking by all the warring factions concerned. In the absence of established local Lebanese government military superiority, the Western force was virtually hostage within a multi-ethnic tinder box. The Administration thus trapped itself into a choice between three seemingly unacceptable options—withdrawal prior to pacification, escalation in U.S. force levels, or the return of the Israelis. While in 1983 the choice seemed to be withdraw the Marines or employ them in a major way to reunify Lebanon, the political logic pointed toward cooperation with Israel as the only power capable of controlling developments on the ground. But, having been burned repeatedly by duplicitous or at best confused U.S. policymakers, it was unlikely (in 1984) that the Israel government would risk the public furor that would follow its acquiescence to any U.S. request that Israel unilaterally pull U.S. chestnuts out of the fire. And the United States itself showed little heart for a showdown fight.

That the Lebanese government made a tragic mistake by relying on the United States and Saudi Arabia instead of Israel became quite clear with the Israeli withdrawal from the Shuf—where they had maintained a degree of quiet between Druze and Christians. The withdrawal was precipitated by a near ceaseless barrage of U.S. complaints against the Israeli presence and by continuous demands that they remove themselves south. Finally, fed up with taking casualties from both sides for their peacemaking efforts, fed up with the endless U.S. backbiting, beset by complaints of Israeli Peace Now know-nothings (very much influenced by the Western media), the Israelis withdrew to the Alawi. And then only after repeated delays due to Washington's sudden realization that it had created a dangerous situation that it (now) was not willing or able to deal with. Without the Israeli presence, order collapsed and by February orders came from President Reagan to start evacuating the Marines to ships offshore.

The *Wall Street Journal* of Feb. 8, 1984, quoted Alfred Mady, a Christian Phalange Party leader, who voiced the opinion (shared by many Lebanese) that the Gemayel government should have depended less on the U.S. and more on Israel: "That was our first mistake, and it was fatal." That there could be no secure independent Lebanon without a legitimate and full alliance with Israel was an obvious reality from the beginning. This was either forgotten or ignored by Amin Gemayel almost as soon as he took office (and was taken to the bosom of the Reagan administration). In a way, his mistake was understandable. Could a few rag-tag militias and a Syria which had been dealt devastating blows by Israel (almost offhand) resist the might of the U.S. superpower which said it was committed to his regime? To Lebanese, hearing the solid commitments of the United States, and viewing the mighty battle fleet off shore, it was inconceivable that the U.S. could be defeated or would quit. But Washington *never* had the will or the understanding necessary for victory. Only days before the decision was announced to evacuate Beirut ("relocate the Marines westward") the President had declared that we would not be driven out: he declared that the withdrawal of the Marines would mean "the end of Lebanon." Robert McFarlane, assistant to the President for national security affairs, wrote in the *Washington Times* of Jan. 26th: "There are other reasons why we must not leave Lebanon now . . . what we do in Lebanon affects our policies in the rest of the Middle East and throughout the world . . . a premature withdrawal could compromise Israeli security, which in turn could lead to another Israeli-Syrian war . . . trigger greater Soviet involvement and the attendant risk of escalation . . . A withdrawal of our forces could also diminish our hope for a negotiated settlement to end the war between Iran and Iraq . . . Our Arab friends in the Gulf . . . would have no choice but to conclude that the U.S. will not stand by its commitments. They may decide it is more dangerous to be a friend of the U.S. than its adversary . . . We are a nation with global responsibilities . . . The prudent course is to sustain our efforts, continue the hard work of diplomacy, and pursue the cause of peace." Twelve days later the withdrawal began. Unfortunately, a real understanding by the Administration and Congress of the basic prerequisites for peace in the Middle East is still lacking.

McFarlane's strong words were made in the absence of equally strong Administration policy. There was an Alice-In-Wonderland quality to January/February statements by the Administration. Seemingly, those U.S. officers in charge of U.S. forces on the ground in Beirut, and, certainly Secretary of Defense Weinberger in Washington, didn't understand the military situation, at all—or were not willing to tell it like it was. Otherwise, experienced spokesmen for the Administration, like Deputy Secretary of State Kenneth Dam, would not have told the Senate Foreign Relations Committee (and the press and public) on Jan. 11, 1984: *"The Lebanese Armed Forces, with training and assistance from the United States and others, have played an increasingly effective role in helping the Lebanese Government expand its authority and restore order. The army contains elements from all the Lebanese communities and is an encouraging example of a truly national Lebanese institution that works."* [My emphasis.]

By February 6 Druze and Moslem militias had taken control of West Beirut. Upon word from Nabih Berri, the Shi'ite militia leader, forty percent of the Lebanese Army deserted or refused to fight. Tons of U.S. supplied arms were immediately turned over to the Moslem and Druze militias.

The collapse of the Lebanese government in early 1984, and with it the collapse of all hope for a viable independent Lebanon on its northern border (for now at least), left Israel with difficult security problems. Organized hostile forces had to be kept out of southern Lebanon, and the organization of local Shi'ites into terror bands prevented. Sa'ad Haddad, who had led the Free Lebanon militia based in Majayoun, and—with considerable Israeli assistance—maintained peace between Moslem and Christian villages throughout southern Lebanon since 1978, was now dead of cancer. No other pro-Israel local personality had as yet sufficient prestige or following to fill the shoes of this Lebanese patriot. And the Shi'ites were being stirred to violence. An example of local slogans, of south Lebanon agitation being conducted by the mullahs, was published in the Kuwaiti newspaper "el Watan" (Jan. 1984): "Khaibar, Khaibar—Jews—Mohammed's army is coming back!" The reference is to the town of Khaibar in the Hajaz, which was populated by an ancient Jewish community, which Mohammed subdued after heavy fighting in the year 628. Actions against Israeli soldiers were now being planned in the mosques, presided over by Moslem functionaries, one of them being the Mufti of Sidon Sheikhs Muhammed Jelal aDin. In the last week of January, a delegation of Shi'ite sheikhs from south Lebanon met with members of the Iranian parliament in Teheran to coordinate terrorist (and suicide) missions against Israel and the United States.

If peace in the Middle East was the paramount objective of the Administration, it would not be currying favour with Saudi Arabia. Instead it would be striving for the unity and independence of a reconstituted Lebanon and pressing Jordan to follow Egypt's example and make its peace with Israel. But the Reagan Administration continues its patronizing and vacillating policy toward Israel, threatening (openly or by inuendo) to rein in Israel by sanctions or hints of deals with the P.L.O. (with no regard for the fact that the P.L.O. is also the enemy of the United States in Central America): it persists in building "strong links" with the "moderate" Arab states with arms and close policy relations—regardless of "ally" Israel's protests. Whatever pretense the Reagan Administration made of using Israel to counter the growth of Soviet power in the region seems, for now at least, at an end. If continued unchecked, this policy will undoubtedly lead to a deterioration in U.S.-Israeli relations, irrespective of events in Lebanon. Israel has no choice but to rely upon its own military deterrent to safeguard its interests in the region. In a sense, this could prove to be therapeutic for Israel. It will clear the air for a more sobering and realistic dialogue between the two countries.

Israel has demonstrated in Lebanon, as it did in the West Bank, in the Golan and in the raid against the Iraqi nuclear reactor, that it is willing and able to defend itself against any threat to its security. Moreover, Israel has indicated that it is prepared to utilize its new found role as a major regional power to pursue an independent policy aimed at forging a new geopolitical balance favorable to peace. The United States can no longer afford to treat Israel as it would a client state. Israel has come a long way since the Yom Kipper War, when it was threatened by a critical shortage of armaments. Israel now has the capacity to be militarily self-sufficient, albeit at great cost to its standard of living. Israel is, indeed the recipient of some $1.2 billion in military assistance from the United States each year. In exchange, however, the United States has received multiples of this amount—in the form of secret Soviet equipment, Israeli technology advances which have improved the effectiveness of American weaponry, the testing of the battleworthiness against Soviet arms of the otherwise unproven equipment upon which the defense of the United States and NATO must depend, and invaluable intelligence information which is essential to the projection of U.S. power in the Middle East.

Any attempt by the United States to impose an arms embargo upon Israel would prove to be counter-productive. It would nullify such influence as the United States can and does exercise; influence which has in fact served to place some constraints on Israel's freedom of action in the past. It would have the concomitant effect of severely reducing American prestige and influence throughout the Middle East—to the benefit of the Soviet Union and its clients. For the current standing of the United States in the region, since the Arab world rejected the Reagan Administration's concept of a "strategic consensus," is more related to its ability to apply pressure on Israel than to its strategic power.

Israel has demonstrated in Lebanon not only the capacity to exploit to its fullest extent the advanced technology of the U.S.-supplied arsenal, but to augment that technology to make it even more effective. What merits fuller appreciation is the fact that the Israeli Air Force has perfected the technique of completely nullifying the effectiveness of the Soviet Union's most sophisticated air defense systems, and has demonstrated the vulnerability of the MIG fighter to cannon and missile attack. Similarly, its ground forces have perfected the technology for destroying with relative ease the best tanks in the Soviet armored arsenal, the T-72. In the process, the Israelis have displayed a superior ability at coordinating air, land and sea operations down to unit level. The current Israeli experience of combat against the technology of the Soviet Union surpasses without question that of the United States and NATO. Israel's armed forces are being given recognition as being amongst the most powerful in the world (it used only ten percent of its strength in Lebanon). Israel's military capability has grown to such an extent that the Arab States are simply incapable of overcoming it. This is so despite the fact that the Arab countries have been provided with arms from the United States, Western Europe and the Soviet Union.

The suspension of the strategic dialogue between Israel and the United States, however, for a time barred the United States from access to Israeli technological secrets. This incredible state of affairs meant that the Pentagon had to seek solutions to problems Israel had already solved. Aside from the billions of dollars in potential savings to the U.S. defense budget, were Israeli technology and tactics to be harnessed to NATO, Soviet superiority on the Central front could, in the near future, be neutralized with conventional power alone. This prospect reduces and possibly eliminates the need for tactical nuclear weapons, including the neutron bomb, needed for offsetting quantitative Soviet superiority on the Central front. Conceivably, this could revolutionize the overall U.S. defense posture and raises exciting prospects for arms control and disarmament negotiations. Access to these Israeli-developed systems ought to be a matter of the highest priority to the U.S. and NATO.

For these (and perhaps domestic political reasons) the administration decided once again to enter into discussions toward "Strategic Cooperation" with Israel. On Nov. 29, 1983, President Reagan and Prime Minister Shamir announced a decision to lay the groundwork for strategic cooperation. It was decided that a meeting would be held in January 1984 between U.S. Rear Admiral Jonathan Howe, Director of Political-Military Affairs at the State Department and Menachem Meron, Israel's Director General of the Ministry of Defense—to "flesh out" a military cooperation arrangement. Again, almost at once, there were those at State and Defense determined to undermine the new, renewed—whatever—agreement.

On Saturday, Oct. 29, President Reagan had given his approval for a National Security Directive calling for U.S.-Israel strategic cooperation. On the following Monday, Under Secretary of State

Larry Eagleburger left for Israel with a White House delegation to coordinate strategy against Syria in Lebanon and to plan for wider defense cooredination. On Wednesday Eagleburger told Prime Minister Shamir that Washington had decided to permit Israel to spend Foreign Military Sales credits on American R&D for the new Lavi fighter. Yet, on the same day, Defense Secretary Weinberger struck out against the decision. And, while "strategic-cooperation" discussions were taking place in Israel, in fact on Sunday, *after* Eagleburger and Shamir had reached an agreement that the two democracies would cooperate "to counter Syria's increasing military influence in the Middle East," General Vessey, Chairman of the Joint Chiefs of Staff, told the country via NBC's *Meet The Press*: "In Lebanon, we do not side with either the Israelis or the Syrians." *Surprise!* Although true strategic cooperation with Israel is in the vital interest of the United States, it is difficult to believe it will take place with the sincerity necessary to succeed. There are too many powerful figures in (and outside) the Reagan administration set to sabotage it. Perhaps the disaster caused by U.S. vacillation in Lebanon finally will force the utilization of a worthwhile alliance. Israelis, however, might seriously question the value of any one sided U.S.-Israel Security Agreement based upon you [Israel] help us against the Soviet Union and its clients, but we [the U.S.] won't help you (openly anyway) in your conflicts with the Arabs. That the "agreement" did not imply a true friendship or an honest alliance was made clear by the late 1983 revelation that the Reagan administration, for months, had secretly been working with King Hussein of Jordan on plans to form, train and equip a Jordanian Rapid Deployment Force of two commando brigades complete with C-130 transport aircraft, tank transporters, rivercrossing equipment, etc. In appropriating money for the Jordanian strike force, the administration bypassed the Senate Foreign Relations Committee and the House Foreign Affairs Committee. Funds were hidden in the Defense appropriations bill. It was a dirty way to deal with Congress and a reprehensible way to treat our Israeli ally. While the Reagan Administration stuttered about its plans not being a threat to Israel, about the Jordanian force as necessary to aid the U.S. in defense of the Gulf, the Jordanians clarified. Speaking on Amman radio (Oct. 31, 1983) Jordanian Foreign Minister Marwan al Qasim declared that any new Jordanian force would *not* serve U.S. regional interests but would be used "to protect itself and the Arab nation." He was very clear about what he meant by this: "The Jordanian Armed Forces have participated in every place and on all the occasions which necessitated its participation. These forces battled to realize the Arab rights in Palestine in 1948 and 1967; they offered to assist Egypt in 1956 . . . and contributed in 1973." Three months later, while the Reagan Administration was heating up its effort for Congressional approval of 220 million dollars worth of sophisticated equipment for the Jordanian military, King Hussein told a gathering of foreign correspondents that he wouldn't hesitate to use this or any other American supplied weaponry in future wars with Israel. He, like Foreign Minister Marwan al Qasim, stated clearly that he would not use their weapons at the behest of the United States, but only at the request of Arab allies of Jordan, or in self-defense.

The Administration should carefully rethink regional history before creating a Jordanian Rapid Deployment Force. There is a precedent, now conveniently forgotten: in 1941 during the pro-Axis Rashid Ali Revolt in Iraq, the British wanted to use against him "their" Arab forces in the region—the Arab Legion and the Transjordan Frontier Force. These forces refused to fight. Local assistance did not come from supposed official allies. However, in 1948, these forces were used heavily against the infant State of Israel.

It would be futile to go into all the complexities of the Lebanese situation since the Israeli "victory" in 1982: modulated, truncated and aborted partly by the tenacity of Syria, backed by its Soviet sponsor, in refusing to withdraw from Lebanon, and partly by the short-sighted and sentimental hopes of the State Department for a "political compromise" that would entail just such a withdrawal, the purely military success of the Israelis has landed them in a hornets' nest, as indeed many Israeli critics of the Begin government had predicted.

What remains, however, is a cluster of facts:

- Israel, the most powerful military factor in the region, cannot, by itself, impose peace on the area;
- The Kremlin, through its closely-knit institutional interaction with Syria, Iraq, and—to an unknown extent—elements of the Iranian regime, looms with potency over all regional politics.

For this very reason a close relationship between the United States and Israel is vital: the vacillations of the Reagan Administration—which for a time last summer was vacillating in a manner slightly more favorable to Israel—must be replaced by a firm, conscious, and responsible appreciation of the fundamental rationale for the alliance with Israel.

The basis of U.S.-Israeli relations for the future must be a fully reciprocal strategic and political alliance. This offers the United States significant and increasing geo-strategic and military benefits in its fight against the expansion of Soviet influence in the region. Reciprocity demands that the U.S. support Israel's insistence on bilateral peace treaties with its neighboring sovereign Arab States. This precludes the achievement of the Palestinian Arab "self-determination" on the West Bank in any sense other than local autonomy. (Indeed, if the United States continues to pursue the chimera of "self-determination," it is certain to have the unintended consequence of seriously undermining the Hashemite monarchy in Jordan, which already has a Palestinian majority in a land which is itself part of Palestine.)

Any U.S.-Israel strategic-political alliance will have to bridge the enormous credibility gap created by the Administration's pursuit of the misnamed Reagan Peace Plan. First proposed by the President on September 1, 1982, this abomination has since been buried and resurrected repeatedly. As long as the Administration supports proposals such as this its every intention will be suspect; for the plan, if adopted, would end the Jewish State.

In essence, the proposal is for Israel's return to pre-1967 borders. The "West Bank" and Gaza would become an Arab entity (state, statelet, what-have-you) associated with Jordan: the exact association is really irrelevant. In exchange for "peace," Israel would reduce its area so drastically that it could not even deploy its armored forces within its own borders. Such a state, would be of no earthly use as an ally. Under the Reagan Peace Plan, the Israeli border would run through its capital, alongside its principal airport; the entire country—now a mere fifty miles wide on average from the Jordan to the sea—would be reduced to nine or ten miles wide at the waist with most of its population squeezed into this coastal plain at the foot of ridges that make up the spine of the land of Israel. Of course, as the plan is idiotic in this day and age, the ridge would be held by the new Arab entity.

For Washington to press such a plan is a hostile act; for Jerusalem to accept such a plan would be suicide. No Israeli political party would acquiesce to this. An Israel configured without Judea and Samaria (without highland, heartland or security belt) is not politically, socially, economically or militarily viable.

In the end, every country has to determine its essential territory. Some, in fact most of those nations demanding Israel's return to 1967's indefensible borders, accept as legitimate the Soviet Union's stated territorial requirements for security in Poland, Latvia, Lithuania, Estonia, East Germany and Afghanistan. Others accept that U.S. security needs involve Guantanamo (in Cuba) and the holding of territory many thousands of miles from its borders. Only Israel is considered paranoid for wanting to control the area adjoining its population centers, to maintain a buffer on its vulnerable eastern front against the 7,000 tanks that can be fielded by Syria, Jordan, Iraq and Saudi Arabia (not to speak of their allies, or the long term threat from Iran). Having given up the security depth of Sinai for a shaky peace with Egypt, Israel no longer has an inch of territory to spare. Any Israeli official who would bind his country to the Reagan Peace Plan could reasonably be charged with treason. This is not a plan that can bring peace. The only lasting peace that can exist between Israel and the Arabs, for the foreseeable future, must be based on a convincing Israeli strength in arms, populace *and* territory: above all, the state must be geographically defensible.

It should be stressed that the Reagan Plan is not only harmful to Israel; it is very damaging from an American point of view. The whole point of having Israel for an ally is its credibility and utility as a pro-Western mini-power. If Israel is emasculated, if its armored divisions and air force are for most practical purposes eliminated as significant pro-Western factors in the regional military balance, if it is spiritually and economically laid waste, what is the point of strategic cooperation agreements? It is all rendered nonsense. The Reagan Peace Plan would change Israel from an asset to a burden. This is the purpose of the Arabists in the State Department who propose it. For Arab-Islam itself this is a necessary preliminary to the destruction of Israel: its permanent goal.

If the United States continues to pursue a policy in the Middle East inimical to Israel's security then it may force Israel into a position where it feels it has no choice but to establish itself as an unaligned third power in the region, using its capacity to project military and political power as a means of playing off the United States against the Soviet Union in pursuit of its own national interests. Such a development would prove to be disastrous from an American point of view. The Israelis could conceivably remove the Hashemite crown in Jordan which the United States is interested in preserving, and install Arafat and the Palestinians in Amman. It could establish a Druse state in Syria and a Kurdish state in Iraq. And, perhaps, most galling of all to the exponents of petrodollar diplomacy, it could remove the ruling dynasty in Saudi Arabia without even invading that state. The dismal spectacle of a division of the Middle East into spheres of influence, with Israeli hegemony in the Levant and Russian dominance of the Persian Gulf, would represent a tragic failure of statesmanship on the part of President Reagan. An Israeli-Soviet condominium in the Middle East might be expedient for Israel, but in the long-term, it would be inimical to the security interests of both the United States and Israel. Control of the Persian Gulf would enable the Soviet Union to neutralize Western Europe and Japan, encircle China and eventually isolate the United States.

The challenges before the United States in the Middle East are thus several and complex. It had the opportunity to be instrumental in restoring sovereignty to Lebanon and ensuring its neutrality in the future: at this writing, this seems lost. A free and independent Lebanon would have found it in its immediate as well as long-term interest to emulate Egypt and enter into a peace treaty with Israel, as would Saudi Arabia and Jordan. The United States missed its opportunity to exploit the exceptional defeat of Arab-wielded Soviet arms by the Israeli tactics and a combination of American and Israeli technology in the hands of its only wholly reliable ally in the Middle East. Now Washington must reexamine the nature of its strategic alignments and commitments in the Middle East, including a proper estimation of the real asset represented by Israel beyond the mere implementation of the strategic cooperation agreement entered into so reluctantly by the Secretary of Defense, discarded with alacrity at the first opportunity, and revived yet again in the winter of 1983. Perhaps above all, it is essential for the United States to disabuse itself of the pro-Saudi and pro-Arab cant that has for so long substituted for serious analysis and evaluation of America's goals in the Middle East and the ways and means to achieve them with intelligence and realism. It is only through such an approach that the United States and its allies can hope to meet and overcome the increasing Soviet challenge to Western interests in the region that has become the key to Soviet global ambitions.

While Israel represents the greatest strategic asset that the U.S. has in the area, Turkey and Iran constitute the traditional geographic barriers to Soviet expansion southward. These two countries, bordering the Soviet Union, have historically prevented the Soviets from establishing a dominant position of strength in the area stretching from the eastern Mediterranean to Southwest Asia. Without territorial contiguity or the ability to provide air cover and protect the movements of troops, the Soviet position in the Arab states, however, strong it may appear, would be vulnerable. If Turkey slid into neutrality, gone would be the second largest standing army in NATO, and the line of defense in the southern flank would shift to Italy, thus increasing greatly Soviet pressure on the Western Mediterranean and North Africa. The West would lose the basing and support facilities vital to the conduct of military operations in the Middle East. Moreover, since Egypt's strategic value is in part related to Turkey's role in constraining the USSR, the United States would be unable to exploit Cairo's potential in Africa. The impact of a neutral Iran, would not be as serious except insofar as it might influence American-Turkish relations. If however, Iran moved into the Soviet orbit, then the Soviets would be camped on the shores of the Persian Gulf and the Arabian Sea and the region would be threatened by forward-deploying Soviet airpower.

Soviet policy in the Middle East has been characterized by the pursuit of two objectives simultaneously: to reach an accommodation with the non-Arab countries of Iran, Turkey and Pakistan, and to pursue a revolutionary policy (subject to tactical retreat and later a *rapprochement*) towards the Arab states.

The initial Soviet drive on Iran and Turkey during and immediately after World War II (i.e., demands for bases around the Turkish Straits and the annexation of parts of Eastern Turkey and support for separatist movements in Northwestern Iran) was countered by the Truman Doctrine, the inclusion of Turkey in NATO, the creation of the Baghdad Pact, and the presence of the Sixth Fleet in the Mediterranean. If the USSR had succeeded in subjugating Turkey and Iran, it would have been able to thrust its limited naval and air power into the Mediterranean and Persian Gulf unimpeded as early as the 1950s. The Soviets might then have moved to challenge the West's position on both sides of the Suez Canal.

The Soviet Union's policy of economic cooperation with the non-Arab states, however, eventually resulted in an easing of traditional fears of Soviet encroachment and a reduced commitment to CENTO—an alliance that functioned as the geographic barrier to Soviet expansion southward. When the CENTO countries viewed the Soviets in a less threatening light, traditional quarrels in the area reemerged: Turkey with Greece, Pakistan with India, and Iran with Iraq. Moreover, the domestic political conditions of those countries offered Moscow the opportunity to exacerbate the internal "ideological struggle."

In the Arab sphere, the Soviets enlarged their role in the region by concluding their first arms agreement with Egypt. This was garnered by exploiting Arab-Israeli friction and by maneuvering against Western efforts to draw the Arabs into a regional security arrangement. Soviet Middle East policy came to focus preeminently on relations with the Arab states. In this they were aided not only by exploiting hostility to Israel but also by the lack of any Arab historical experience with Russian imperialism. The Turks and Persians had indeed experienced Russian imperialism first-hand, but Arab experience with imperialism was the saltwater variety—the British and French maritime and commercial presence.

In its relations with the Arab states, Moscow demonstrated that it was willing and able to tamper with the essence of Arab politics by promoting a polarization and later encouraging rapprochement between the revolutionary and conservative forces without losing ideological credibility. Prior to the 1967 Arab-Israeli War, Soviet policy was designed to promote solidarity among the radical states while widening the rift between the "progressive socialists" and the "conservative" monarchies. After the 1967 war, the Soviets sought to promote a "moderate" consensus on inter-Arab issues. They were pleased that the Khartoum Conference in September 1967 convened obstensibly for "erasing the consequences of [Israeli] aggression," resulted in a rapprochement between Egypt and Saudi Arabia. In exchange for a phased Eygptian withdrawal from Yemen, Saudi Arabia agreed to an annual subsidy for Egypt to make up the deficit incurred from losses in Suez Canal revenue. This quid pro quo served not only to detach the conservatives from the West, but also relieved the Soviets from the expensive prospect of underwriting Egypt economically. (It is interesting to note that the Soviet Union has studiously ignored the attempts at political union in the Arab world; it regards Arab nationalism as a national liberation movement of individual Arab countries, struggling against Western imperialism.)

Moscow has a clear-cut, rational objective in the Middle East: to neutralize Turkey and Israel, and to consolidate its position in the "radical" Arab states in addition to building up its network of agents and puppets in the other Arab states, such as Saudi Arabia, Kuwait, Bahrain and the various emirates. The network of puppets and proxies, as well as its comprehensive alliances with Syria and Iraq, provides the groundwork for its major projection since 1975: the encirclement of the Persian Gulf, already a fact, and its consummation—the public *acknowledgement* of that encirclement.

Expressed otherwise, they intend to make a proclamation of power. For that the toppling of the Shah and the installation of a radical regime studded with Soviet agents and allies, some of them secret, were prerequisites.

4

Intervention in Africa

Until recently Africa was an appendage of Europe, neatly compartmentalized and administered by the European powers. Europe's dependence on the region's natural resources has the effect of attracting superpower attention. These resources, and the needs of Africa's developing economies, are the stakes for which both the Soviets and Americans play. Between resources and economic growth stands the imperative of strategic balance, which is shaped by Europe's unfettered access and capacity to transport strategic raw material. It is clear that in the next few years, this capability will in turn determine the ability of the western powers to check the spread of Soviet influence.

The region from Zimbabwe to the Cape is the richest area of mineral reserves in the world. Huge quantities of key minerals are concentrated in southern and central Africa. For the United States, Western Europe and Japan, the focus is on chromium, manganese, cobalt and platinum-group metals. All these metals have vital high technology applications, often as important alloying elements.

South Africa is the main U.S. supplier of chromium and platinum and meets a large portion of manganese and ferro-manganese demands. The main alternative source for chromium and platinum is the Soviet Union. The bulk of America's cobalt comes from Zambia and Zaire.[1] Although substitutes exist for chromium, cobalt and platinum in some of their applications, this is not the case for the major uses of manganese. Again, South Africa and the Soviet Union provide more than sixty percent of the world's supply of this metal, which is essential in steel production. Thus, if the Soviets should gain control—directly or indirectly—of the minerals of South Africa and Zimbabwe, serious disruptions of materials vital in the Western defense effort could be experienced. In *Strategy and Conflict*, the Soviet Union's Major General A. N. Lagovsky refers to America's vulnerability in this regard. Modern armaments, he says, are dependent on certain critical raw materials such as chrome, platinum, nickel, cobalt and titanium. The United States, he points out, has almost no chrome of its own. "This mineral is essential for the production of alloys for jet engines, gas turbines, armor-piercing projectiles and other weapons systems." The lack of chrome was, therefore, the weak link in U.S. defense "and one the Soviets should exploit."

The best illustration of economic employment of resources in the superpower balance is provided by the history of Rhodesian chrome exports in the 1970s. American observance of the UN sanctions produced a situation where Rhodesian chrome could only be purchased through the Soviets. Without altering their production quotas, the Soviets provided the chrome, which they had purchased through an intermediary African state, at a suitably exorbitant profit rate that significantly improved their balance of payments. New technology has now enabled South Africa to make ferrochrome from low-grade chrome ores. But if South Africa and Zimbabwe (Rhodesia) are lost, the West is out of chrome. One has to be alarmed at the notion that South Africa can suffer catastrophic change while its economic infrastructure remains unharmed. South Africa and Zimbabwe are the West's most valuable repositories of vital minerals. Loss of access to this supply would be catastrophic.[2]

There are two fundamental strategies a superpower can adopt

to secure the strategic materials of Africa; the United States pursues one, the Soviet Union the other.

America's strategic approach is to enhance the economic system of key countries. Under this approach, it will prove to be in each recipient country's interest, and in that of its neighbors, to support continued Western investment in exchange for the necessary assistance in transferring resources. The Soviet approach is markedly different; it exploits resentment generated by the memory of slavery and colonialism and encourages African nations to accept military as well as economic aid. Soviet arms, which supposedly bolster the internal defense capability of the state, actually have the effect of stimulating tribal conflict, increasing military dependency and thus allow the Soviets to maintain a degree of military influence that tends to undermine Western influence. Russia's strategy is complicated by its rivalry with China over the terms of military aid to various client regimes.

The aims and influence of external powers are, of course, offset to a substantial extent by African nationalism, whose character is alien to the United States and the USSR. In Africa, nationalism often embraces tribalism, which is tantamount to a battle for paramount position among subnational groups. This was the case in the Nigerian civil war of the mid-1960s; it has resulted in horrifying genocide in Uganda, Central Africa and in Equatorial Guinea, all countries whose leaders made a practice of repressing other tribes as "enemies," including killing them in vast numbers. In Burundi, for example, the ruling ethnic group eliminated two hundred thousand rivals, while neighboring Rwanda, controlled by the ethnic group that was being decimated in Burundi, murdered members of the opposing elite. Tribal loyalties are far more important than national sentiment. Changes in government are frequently carried out by means of a coup, and the record on the continent for free elections is hardly impressive.

Many African states lack the solidarity and stability needed to form lasting alliances and tend to align themselves with others only when there is an incidental congruence of interests, such as repugnance for white minority rule in South Africa. Likewise, political convictions as such are often illusory; the seemingly "idealistic" proclamations of the leaders of Rhodesia's black "liberation" armies, which our State Department concurred in labeling the "Patriotic Front," were a facade behind which Soviet power and tribal interests were expressed. If political affiliations are not tribal in origin, then they are fostered for the purpose of securing aid from one of the superpowers. An African "People's War," then, is frequently an exercise in propaganda, a substitute for a broad political base, a mechanism that tribal minorities use to underscore their legitimacy. Destabilizing Soviet influence inhibits the development of the continent, as tribal tensions are enlarged by the supplying of Soviet military equipment.

Soviet strategy in the Horn of Africa is to control the Red Sea and to use the Horn as a base of operations to destabilize the position of moderate regimes in the Sudan, Egypt and Kenya. While this policy cannot be supported with impunity, it depends on Moscow's strategic requirements vis-a-vis the West. Soviet rhetoric, however, remains consistent. Leonid Brezhnev told the Twenty-fifth Communist Party Congress:

> Some bourgeois figures express surprise about the solidarity of the Soviet Communist Party and the Soviet people . . . with the struggle of other peoples for freedom and progress—this is either naivete or most likely a deliberate attempt to obscure the issue. For it is quite clear that detente and peaceful coexistence are concerned with interstate relations—this means that quarrels and conflicts between countries should not be decided by war, use of force or threat of force. Detente does not in the slightest way abolish and cannot abolish or change the laws of class struggle. . . . Our party is rendering and will continue to render support to peoples who are fighting for their freedom.

It is no longer essential, in Soviet eyes, that client states should, as a precondition for aid, accept Marxism, as long as they "follow an anticapitalist policy that goes beyond the framework of general democratic reform and promotes the growth of socialist elements in the economy and social life" [*International Affairs*, Moscow, no. 3, March 1976]. The Soviets stress the need to alter the "correlation of world forces" mainly through economic alignments, which should precede ideological control. Hence the importance, in Soviet eyes, of mineral-rich Southern Africa. And hence their tolerance of conservative, anticommunist Islamic nationalism, because of the harm done the West by Muslim members of the OPEC cartel.

The Soviets have transformed their once precarious foothold in Africa into a major presence in key geographic areas.

In addition to striking geographic advances, the nature of the Soviet presence within a number of African client states has also changed. In the past, a Soviet military presence was normally undertaken at the request and on the sufferance of the ruling group; currently, the Soviets tend to come and go as they please. This reversal is in part our own fault as a result of our failure, in 1975, to assist pro-Western guerrillas in Angola when they were fighting vestigial groups backed by the Soviets. Angola was the turning point. After that, our minimal concern about Soviet encroachment began to give way to haphazardness and capitulation and even support for the Cuban-backed regime. The current situation in Ethiopia, for example, is in part a result of President Carter's termination of grant military assistance to the Mengistu regime because of human rights violations. This decision effectively eroded chances for human rights progress in Ethiopia by causing Mengistu to turn toward Moscow for aid against Somalia. Whatever "human rights" there were ended with Soviet occupation brought on by U.S. influence.

The collapse of colonial rule has opened unique opportunities for the Soviet Union. France still plays a role in the affairs of her former colonies, but the collapse of Portuguese control in Mozambique and Angola in 1975 changed the political climate of the entire continent, creating targets for Moscow which had not been available previously. When events turned in favor of the Soviets, they moved into Angola and Ethiopia, thus beginning, remarkably, their advance toward encirclement of the Persian Gulf. The intended Soviet strategy is to isolate the United States, using control of mineral wealth to cow our European allies. They want at the same time, of course, to exclude China from having any preeminent role in Africa.

The strategem that has been outlined above is speculative and often tends to elicit a conventional objection—that the Soviets play it by ear in Africa, that their involvement is opportunistic (economic) rather than militaristic (adventurist). Such a view denies the evidence of both a stepped-up military aid program and renewed ideological interest.

A comment on the distinction in the Soviet mind between militarism and opportunism is warranted. Marxist thought, particularly in matters of political planning, stresses the need to base judgments on careful observation and assessment of facts. This approach contrasts sharply with the twin trends that currently dominate U.S. policy, namely, the perception of events according to the hopeful expectations of the observer and the attribution of American values to other parties. There is good reason to assume that Soviet military and political strategists desire to exploit weaknesses in the U.S. security network, especially when perceptions of weakness by third parties affect the strategic balance. A strategy of opportunism thus subsumes a strategy of militarism and, once implemented, automatically anticipates maximum gains.

Lenin's doctrine that the Soviet Union is the natural leader of the Third World, the instrument to overthrow "colonialism," has been fully adopted by its present leadership:

> In the present era, which is characterized by a strengthening of the positions of socialism and by sharp antagonism between the two social systems, a deepening of the *external function* of the Soviet armed forces has logically taken place. It must be seen that Soviet military might objectively assists the successful development of the revolutionary liberation movements and that it hinders the exportation of imperialist counterrevolution. In this lies one of the most important manifestations of the external function of the armed forces of a socialist state. [General Yepishev: *Kommunist*, no. 7, 1972, May.]

The primary aim of the Soviet Union in Africa is not the liberation of subject countries but, rather, the support of revolutionary groups that offer reasonable assurance of Soviet influence on coming to power. Chinese weapons shipments to such groups cause the Soviets great alarm. China's shipments to FRELIMO were crucial to the termination of Portuguese colonial rule in Mozambique; it has also established good relations with Zambia and Tanzania. The signal difference between the Soviet and Chinese methods of disbursing aid is that the Chinese are adept at dealing with clients and that their diplomacy is relatively sophisticated and pressure-free. The fact that the crude, coercive Soviet approach has had the greater success is most likely due to the Soviets' more substantial available supplies, which facilitates the radical revolutionary's suppression of opponents. By the time the revolution is over and economic aid is required to stabilize the territory, a strong and entrenched Soviet presence limits the prospects for economic development as incompetent bureaucrats are unleased on an even more impoverished subject population. The net effect of the military supplies is thus an overall radicalization of the regime and a slackening in economic growth.[3]

The final weapon of Soviet penetration is dogma, which is a corollary to military aid. However, the creative match of ideological conviction to the demands of the moment can sometimes reach a climax, as when the Soviet "revolutionary conscience" dictated abandonment of Somalia in 1977 for the richer pastures (metaphorically) of Ethiopia. A pattern has been established of moderating Marxism-Leninism to make it appear compatible with the several forms of African nationalism: a) tribalism, which cares little for the imperatives of class liberation; b) Islamic nationalism, which is absolutely inconsistent with Soviet precepts but coexists with it by means of a loose construct known as "Islamic Marxism," and c) African nationalism, which is suspicious of the Soviets' intentions but responsive to Soviet anti-colonial rhetoric and their weapons diplomacy.

The Soviets' paranoia about the Chinese threat to their third world leadership leads them to actions that hurt the United States as well as China.

China's probings in Africa, although they sometimes damage

Soviet prestige, are more ideological than strategic. The important Moscow-Peking contests take place on China's northern border and on the border between China and Vietnam. The Soviet Union's diplomatic and propaganda activities in Africa (including the coveted scholarships for emerging leaders to Patrice Lumumba University in Moscow, where they are subjected to endless repetition of Soviet dogma and emerge believing, against all logic, that it applies to their countries), serve as a support apparatus for Soviet military programs that damage the interests of both China and the United States. Since Vietnam, we, for our part, cannot see this, because in our view of the world there is a division between conflicts that are local and those that concern the superpowers.

The great strategic advantage that the Soviets have vis-a-vis the United States is that they have a clear inclusive policy, while we have only abstract, high-minded goals. Strategic concerns are nowhere apparent in U.S. policy, which can be characterized as a series of double binds. We said we aspired to a "majority regime" in Zimbabwe-Rhodesia but we encouraged the Marxist forces.

We want to weaken South Africa until it is forced to comply with American demands for more equitable racial policies, which would bring down the infrastructure that supports the existing establishment; we want to assert control over the fate of the continent but do not want to introduce a direct military presence. These dilemmas are the symptoms and the result of two opposing concepts. One is the absence even of a residual strategic concern, after our abdication in Angola (1975). The other, which prevails, is a moral attitude that is professedly idealistic in character: preservation of our economic interests without the necessary geopolitical and military investment. Our economic aid continues to flow to nonsympathetic regimes on the continent (Tanzania, Guinea-Bissau) in a vain attempt to prove our disinterested capacity for love. Little wonder that we are not taken seriously.

A glance at the mechanism of the takeover in Angola should be instructive, especially the role played by the *New York Times*.

In 1975 there was a de facto situation of civil strife in Angola, between the FNLA, the National Front for the Liberation of Angola, headed by Holden Roberto, and the Moscow-trained MPLA

(Popular Movement for the Liberation of Angola), headed by Antonio Neto.

The *New York Times*, through its well-known investigative reporter, Seymour Hersh, reported (on December 19, 1975) that U.S. aid to the forces under Holden Roberto, amounting to $3 million had been transmitted clandestinely. The report suggested that Soviet aid to competing guerrilla movements was being sent in response to American aid.

Yet direct Soviet aid as well as the transfer of Cuban troops was well under way at the time, while the funds allocated to the Holden Roberto group were earmarked for non-military uses.

Competing groups among the anti-colonial guerrillas were able to count on support from various outside sources, including not only the Soviet Union and, to a far lesser degree, the United States, but also Communist China and South Africa. Hersh's dispatch alleged that U.S. funds for the FNLA had been transferred two months before "the first significant Soviet buildup," but ignored the fact that the Soviet-Cuban shipments of men and material, arriving by sea, were clearly in preparation and underway well before the U.S. chose sides.

The U.S. Congress, acting in a post-Vietnam mood of non-intervention, turned decisively against the Administration's plans for more solid support for the non-Communist guerrilla movements. The Hersh report, by its timing, decisively influenced congressional opinion, which recoiled from the image of clandestine U.S. support for political and military forces abroad.

An insider's version of events preceding this congressional decision has been given by Nathaniel Davis, a foreign service officer who participated in the Angolan events. In an article in *Foreign Affairs* (Fall 1978), Davis traced the hesitancy of the United States at a time when the Soviets were introducing more and heavier, and more sophisticated weapons to their MPLA allies. These weapons included tanks, trucks and MIG fighter planes. Angola's position was not only valuable because of its oil and iron ore deposits, but because of the strategic role of the Cape Verde Islands.

Following the death of the longtime ruler of Portugal, Antonio Salazar, a group calling itself the "Movement of the Armed Forces" took control on April 25, 1974. General Antonio de Spaniola became an intermittently controversial figure because his book, *Portugal and the Future*, suggested that Portugal's military control of Angola, Mozambique and Portuguese Guinea (Guinea-Bissau) would prove to be indefensible. The general became Portugal's President on May 15, 1974. Communist leader Alvaro Cunhal returned to Portugal after twelve years abroad.

While leaders and parties in Lisbon were struggling for supremacy in power and policies, Holden Roberto emerged as President of the Supreme Council of Liberation in Angola. By July 27, 1974, de Spaniola announced that his government was ready to declare Angola's independence and to "transfer power immediately." In addition to the FNLA and the MPLA, a third independence movement, UNITA (National Union for the Total Liberation of Angola) emerged under the leadership of Jonas Savimbi.

Radio Moscow set the tone for an international propaganda campaign which advanced slogans that identified the FLNA with the "imperialist" forces of the United States and with Zaire as its ally. At the same time, UNITA was accused of being in alliance with the "racist regime" of South Africa. Meanwhile, the military buildup organized from Moscow climaxed with the presence of 25,000 Cuban soldiers and 5,000 Cuban civilians on Angolan soil. These forces were decisive in securing military superiority for the MPLA. Roberto went into exile.[4]

One incident during the "anti-colonial" campaign that preceded the Soviet-Cuban intervention and was part of a softening-up of "world opinion" deserves special mention. *The (London) Times* (July 9, 1973) carried an article under the byline of one Father Adrian Hastings, which alleged "a genocidal massacre" in Mozambique. The village named in the article was given as "Wiriyamu," and the date on which this massacre by Portuguese troops was supposed to have taken place was given as December 16, 1972. A multiplicity of gory details was provided in the article.

The Hastings article suggested that the alleged massacre was undertaken against villagers who had supported the FRELIMO (Frente de Libertacao de Mocambique) movement. Interviewed by the BBC on July 11, Father Hastings admitted that most of the article had not been documented by him—that details had been provided by "missionaries in the area." Subsequent journalistic investigations could locate no village by the name given in the *Times*; a village with a similar name offered no evidence to support the content of the original report.

The leadership of the MPLA was soon (after Neto's death) taken over by Jose Eduardo do Santos, a member of the movement at the age of 19 and its representative until 1963 in Congo-Brazzaville. He then spent six years in the Soviet Union. Following training as a petroleum engineer, Santos underwent instructions in military communications. Beginning in 1970, he moved within the MPLA hierarchy, to the position of member of the Central Committee (1974) and became Foreign Minister when Angola achieved independence.

In organization and policy, the MPLA is the equivalent of the "Communist and Workers' Party" in Eastern Europe, where they stand under direct control of the Soviet regime and of the Central Committee of the CPSU.

The same movement compounded of local puppets, Cuban troops, and orchestrated propaganda, was taking place around the same time on the other side of the African continent, in an operation reminiscent of the very effective Iranian destabilization.

In Ethiopia, too, Emperor Haile Selassie was the victim of a campaign that entirely reversed the tidal wave of sympathy he had been given the generation before when, in 1935, Italian troops invaded Ethiopia. At that time, Ethiopia, free of colonial rule since time immemorial, appealed to the League of Nations in Geneva. The League, as impotent then as the United Nations now, did nothing. Still, it was obvious that world opinion—for whatever it may have been worth—was on the side of Ethiopia and its Emperor.

In 1973 a train of events was initiated that led to the ousting of the Emperor and his subsequent death. It was accompanied by a propaganda campaign contrasting sharply with the earlier sympathies for Haile Selassie. A military junta, eventually headed by Mengistu Haile Mariam—now the Soviet Union's favorite strongman in Africa—took power in Addis Ababa. Early in 1973, French

President George Pompidou visited the Emperor, at a time when the Eritrean Liberation Front was beginning a military uprising against the Addis Ababa government. The military-political constellations at that time included traditional U.S. support for Ethiopia, Soviet support for Somalia to the south, and various Islamic supporters for the Eritrean Liberation Front (including Al Fatah, and subsequently Syria, Libya, Iraq and South Yemen). Soviet policy was designed to destabilize the region and establish military bases on the Horn of Africa. In the process, it backed the Ethiopian military junta and alienated Somalia.

U.S. policy was confused and hesitant. Washington eventually abandoned its support of Ethiopia and backed Somalia, although it sought to discourage Somalia's backing of the West Somalian Liberation Front—which claimed the territory of Ogaden as ethnically Somalian.

In March 1974, Ethiopian students from Patrice Lumumba University and Moscow State University occupied the Ethiopian Embassy in Moscow. They claimed to protest corruption, "feudalism" and lack of help for the "starving peasants" of Ethiopia. The military junta in Addis Ababa, which captured key buildings and communications facilities, ousted Haile Selassie from his palace. His family was arrested. The Emperor was placed in what was described as a "three room mud hut." Italian Premier Aldo Moro, who was later killed by terrorists, offered asylum to the Emperor. The offer was ignored by the junta; Haile Selassie died under questionable circumstances on August 27, 1975, at the age of 83.

The United States communication center of Kagnew, near Asmara in Eritrea, was the target of a series of attacks. Various international personalities, including UN Secretary Kurt Waldheim, visited Ethiopia in order to arrange for famine relief. Starvation had become widespread, partly because of a drought, partly because of the disruption of supplies caused by the warring factions. The United States economic and military aid continued intermittently during this period, but was finally discontinued during the early months of 1975. Mengistu hailed this development as symbolizing an end to "slavery" imposed by the U.S. on Ethiopia; he made this speech during May Day celebrations (a Communist "holiday"), following a visit by Fidel Castro.

On May 3, Mengistu arrived in Moscow for talks with Gromyko and Podgorny. Cuban troops arrived in Ethiopia. First reports spoke of 50 Cuban military advisors and 400 to 500 troops. This development prompted U.S. delegate to the U.N., Andrew Young, to say that the arrival of the Cubans "might not be a bad thing"; it might help quiet things down in Ethiopia. He eventually also said that Cuba and the Soviet Union might have "bitten off more than they can chew" by involving themselves there (July 7, 1975).

In February 1977, American grant military assitance to Ethiopia was terminated on grounds that the government had been violating "human rights." The consequences of this decision were Ethiopia's overt, rather then veiled, swing into the Soviet/Cuban orbit, which effectively ended any chance for us to influence events in this strategic area. Other reverses in the region, including Bahrain, the Seychelles, South Yemen and, of course, Iran, have further emphasized our lack of a coherent or realistic policy towards the region. This merely has the effect of buttressing Soviet influence, given the entrenched Soviet/Cuban/East German naval infrastructure and military presence in the Red Sea-Indian Ocean area.

The timing of Carter's Ethiopian decision in 1977 was crucial. He could not have chosen a more inopportune moment for his announcement. Had the decision to implement "human rights" policies in the region not been made, the Soviets would have been edged out of Somalia (and effectively out of the Horn of Africa) by events in that country, and U.S. aid to Ethiopia would have prevented them from finding a safe harbor there. It is true that there would have been a contradiction in our providing aid to a radical regime, but our influence could have served as a restraining and moderating factor, as it had been for thirty years. The United States was, instead, in the position of supporting Somali aggression, which placed us at odds with African nationalism. On the other hand, our refusal to assist Somalia left open the possibility of complete Soviet domination of the area and consequent Soviet control of access to the Red Sea and potential domination of the Indian Ocean and Persian Gulf shipping lanes.[5]

Soviet/Cuban involvement in Ethiopia demonstrates that the Soviets and their mercenaries will risk large-scale military commitment to a radical regime, especially when such aid secures communication and trasnport facilities. After initial arms transfers, the Soviets engineered a major airlift in late 1977, the flights originating in South Russia and refueling at Aden. This operation is only now clearly seen as a trial run for the 1980 invasion of Afghanistan. On the basis of the troop transport rate in the Ethiopian operation, it appears that the Soviets could send at least one division to Libya, for instance, in a single day. Among the arms sent to Ethiopia were substantial amounts of artillery and the advanced MIG-23 fighters, flown by Cuban pilots. There was also a parallel transport of equipment by ship through the Suez Canal to Ethiopian-held ports in Eritrea. The Soviets committed senior personnel, including five generals, to this operation. Clearly it was a high level task force.

By February 1978, the number of Soviet-supported troops, mainly Cuban, in Ethiopia was estimated at between 2,000 and 8,000. Analysts suggested that Russian Air Force personnel had been sent to Cuba, thus freeing Cuban pilots and other air force personnel for transfer to Ethiopia.

The estimates of Cuban troops rose to ten and eleven thousand men. Cuban troops were reported in action in Eritrea as well as Somalia. They were instrumental in driving Somalian units out of Ogaden. At the same time, East German security police units arrived in Ethiopia in order to train the Mengistu regime's own secret police in repression techniques and in the use of equipment. East German party chief Erich Honecker visited Addis Ababa early in 1979, while later, in September, Kosygin came to celebrate the fifth anniversary of the revolutionary government.

Soviet leaders, then, do not shrink from commitment to a regime if it is strategically important and their military presence will enhance the security of their own assets. Ethiopia, of course, constitutes the bridge between the African and Middle Eastern theaters, and Soviet control over it enhances its posture in both. Through Ethiopia, the Soviet Union can radically affect both the economic and strategic stability of the West. Soviet attention to Ethiopia demonstrates that the central concern of Moscow is one of territory and geopolitical advantage rather than of social progress.

The emergence of Zimbabwe, formerly Rhodesia, as a new state demonstrates even more strikingly the success of the Soviet regime in manipulating world opinion, all the more so since there it proved unnecessary to involve any Cuban or East German proxies.

Zimbabwe represents a triumph in the pure use of a concept—human rights—that has since become the underpinning, as we shall see, of all the orchestration of subversion in Central America.

The campaign that had been launched a few years ago against the government of Ian Smith, reflecting an electorate weighted against the black majority, produced two black rivals seeking power, Robert Mugabe and Joshua Nkomo, both Marxists, and together representing no more than a fraction of black opinion in then Rhodesia. And the size of that fraction was entirely uncheckable; the outside figure featured in the world media for some years was only 15 percent, yet even that figure was based on mere estimates derived, ultimately, from the Marxist opposition itself (the so-called Patriotic Front, a coalition of the rival Mugabe and Nkomo groups ZAPU and ZANU).

Yet because it was considered that the black majority had to be represented in a way considered normal in western democracies, and hence had a more or less "natural" right to determine the composition of the government, the "rights" of the black majority as a whole were somehow transferred to the "right" of the black Marxist minority to take up a position of power *before* negotiations with the Ian Smith government.

The entire strategy of the Marxist rivals, who for this purpose had formed the coalition, was to ensure a foothold for themselves in a new order that did *not* depend on democratic elections.

Both the British Labor Government and the Carter Administration, amazingly enough, backed this view of the situation in Rhodesia. The mechanisms applied deserve some attention, since it is precisely this same technique—"political compromise"—that is the mainspring of Soviet-Cuban strategy in Central America.

It might have been thought that, since Rhodesia-Zimbabwe was a manifest target of Soviet expansion, the U.S. government might well have opposed radical, Soviet-backed terrorist factions. Yet from the very outset American policy in this crucial African area became the exclusive province of ideologically committed "liberals."

Carter himself regarded Rhodesia as a sort of cause celebre, to demonstrate his high principles and his contempt for mere material concerns. He asserted the primacy of "human rights," despite the evidence that the Patriotic Front represented a tiny fraction of the *black* electorate.

When Andrew Young was made Ambassador to the United Nations, U.S. policy was focused on this "issue" with intense energy. Rhodesia, through the deliberate, well-nigh hysterical effusions of Young, became a domestic American, black political issue. This entirely parochial misunderstanding became, accordingly, a mainspring of international politics.

Carter rejected Ian Smith's 1978–79 internal settlement plan, thereby accepting the Patriotic Front line that the settlement effectively perpetuated white control. So, we continued our sanctions against Rhodesia, at the same time that we aided and recognized a number of African states which were actively supporting Soviet-backed terrorist groups, although many such states were typically repressive one-party regimes.

Our pursuit of a role in Rhodesia because of concern with the Soviets in Africa thus degenerated into the destabilizing and hypocritical policy of encouraging ZAPU and ZANU, the rival guerrilla groups that made up the Patriotic Front. President Carter protested human rights violations in selected parts of Africa under white control, yet promoted regimes with worse track records; deplored Soviet/Cuban intervention in Angola and exacerbated conditions that made Rhodesia equally susceptible; and tried to force the Rhodesian government into disbanding its security forces and making "the liberation army" the basis of the new Rhodesian military.

One of the reasons we were not content with Smith's plan for the transfer of power (implemented by elections held in 1979) was that it protected the white minority. Although Rhodesia's transitional constitution was identical to that of Kenya, Tanzania and Zambia, in conceding seats to the whites to encourage their remaining in the country, Andrew Young said that civilization has advanced since then and that the settlement should therefore have been more equitable. In fact, though, every plan for the solution of the Rhodesian problem had foundered on the constitutionality of the transfer of power. This was primarily because the Popular Front was disinclined to accept free elections, where it would be at a disadvantage, and because of Patriotic Front leader Robert Mugabe's well-known opposition to the electoral process.

The 1976 Kissinger plan had called for a two-tier structure of government with a black majority. The Anglo-American plan of 1978, by contrast, would have given control to a Commissioner during the period of transition. Ian Smith's internal settlement plan, however, produced a standard American complaint, summarized by Senator George McGovern:

> It offers a formula for at least ten years of qualified multi-racial rule in which there would exist a black majority in Parliament, but a central white power block with the ability to prevent fundamental change altering the political and economic structure of Rhodesian society.

McGovern's objection to this settlement was essentially that it gave the white minority (five percent of the population) too much power, twenty-eight out of one hundred seats in Parliament, not that it prevented majority rule (it did not).

The problem was the constitutional safeguards for the white minority. These would, it was argued, impede rule by the majority, not because the new government would not reflect the majority but because the residual white presence would stand in the way of far-reaching constitutional change. What such change might entail is not known. In response to McGovern, it can be said that the protection of the minority was in keeping with the British requirement for recognition of minority rights and would have been revocable after ten years; it also followed an established pattern in British African decolonization and our own human rights ideal. The purpose of the safeguards was not to prolong minority control but to protect the modern sector of the Rhodesian economy. The whites comprised a skilled managerial class whose expertise would be needed in the transition period. The most significant difference between the Anglo-American plan and Smith's, however (Smith's critics say), was his clear intention to prevent the Patriotic Front from playing a role in the new government. Andrew Young wanted to dismantle Rhodesia's armed forces and create a new defense establishment made up, preponderantly, of the Patriotic Front—hardly a prescription for stability, considering the Patriotic Front's preference for armed insurrection, Joshua Nkomo's tilt toward Moscow and its formulation of a "death list" of "black collaborators with imperialists." In short, its demonstrated lack of respect for democratic processes was clearly identifiable.

Carter agreed with Young that any solution without the full participation of the Patriotic Front was doomed to failure, since the Patriotic Front would not support any transition plan in which it was excluded and, hence, would continue to prosecute the war. In addition, the State Department evidently felt that support for Smith's settlement plan would have caused the Patriotic Front to lose all sense of moderation, and would have driven it more completely towards the Soviets. According to State Department Africanists, this would have increased the likelihood of direct Soviet intervention. An equally important consideration was that no African government had yet proclaimed support for the internal settlement. From this the State Department concluded that our endorsement would antagonize most African states. The Africanists ignored the depth of our influence on the continent; if we recognized the settlement, then other states would not have had to worry that their doing so would be repudiated.

Carter's own plan, or more accurately, position (since he made no effort to persuade others to adopt it), included several refinements of the 1978 Anglo-American initiative, all designed, like the maintenance of sanctions, to indicate displeasure with the white Rhodesians rather than to encourage them to compromise. The weakness inherent in his stubborn stand was that it gave America no role in the negotiating process, while not even inflicting discomfiture on white Rhodesia, which had lengthy experience with isolation. When escalating guerrilla raids caused the postponement of elections from November 1978 to April 1979, the United States and Britain used the postponement as an excuse to stop promoting a meeting of all parties. Patriotic Front leader Nkomo said, subsequently, that it was "for the generals" to bring about a settlement; in the face of this threat, Smith repeated his intention to hold elections in April 1979, and announced:

> We stress again that everybody who is prepared to participate in peace will be welcome to take part in free and fair elections—we are excluding nobody. Furthermore, we will welcome international observers to satisfy themselves that elections are free and fair to all.

The Patriotic Front refused, in spite of this statement, to participate in the elections, preferring the tactic of intimidating voters; and the United States refused to send official observers, having already decided, as Secretary Vance stated in March only a month before the voting, that the election offered no hope for settling the conflict. U.S. policy, obviously, was not to encourage the birth of a legally constituted democracy but to include the Patriotic Front in a peace negotiation in the hope that such a strategem might keep out the Soviets. Young made his usual contribution to the debate by saying that the only people who supported the Smith settlement were "neo-fascists."

Beneath Carter's so-called neutrality in Zimbabwe-Rhodesia lies the problem of his implicit support for terrorism. Since the Patriotic Front was armed by the Soviet Union, Carter's attempt to bring them into the government was not only inadvisable but also had the effect of discouraging moderate black African leaders from looking to the United States for support. It diminished prospects that transition to independence could be achieved by negotiation rather than by force. The lesson of the Patriotic Front, which existed as a military organization for some time, is that terrorism in Zimbabwe-Rhodesia was more legitimate than compromise.

Carter also, in his effort to widen sanctions, provided aid to Front Line States that sheltered the Patriotic Front troops, thus almost directly assisting terrorism against both the old and the Abel Muzorewa governments during the difficult initial period of transition. Terrorism, and its encouragement by the West, of course, hurt Rhodesia more than the sanctions; it also diminished our capacity to affect Africa. Instead of encouraging the Patriotic Front, we should have felt compelled to tell Mugabe and Nkomo that we would not recognize them until they ceased their anti-democratic actions, for the principle that is proven true again and again in third world politics, as elsewhere, is that human rights cannot flourish in a one-party state.

U.S. policy toward Rhodesia during its crisis demonstrates our inability to cope with either local or regional issues in Africa and a tendency to conduct diplomacy by endorsing coercion without sensitivity to nuance. There is a failure to separate the black/white struggle from the struggle among black leaders for political supremacy; a failure to distinguish between the worthy aim of majority rule and the existence of civil war. These are complex problems of political power that make a quest for "moral" solutions merely absurd.

The Kremlin, whose role as sponsor of the Marxist Mugabe faction was scarcely ever mentioned in the media, achieved a striking success in the victory of Mugabe in the elections of February 1980.[6] Mugabe's hold on the Zimbabwe government has survived with ease, as it seems, despite some attempts by former associate/rival, Joshua Nkomo, to unseat him and/or establish an independent position.

The confusion, weakness, and venality rampant in all the newly emerged African "states" has enabled Colonel Muammar Qaddafi of Libya to play a spectacular role, sending bribes, arms, and terrorists throughout Africa in an effort to destabilize governments.

Qaddafi, dictator of a large country with a tiny population—some million and a half—has acquired disproportionate importance partly through his possession of substantial oil reserves and partly through his willingness to act as a cat's paw for the Kremlin in various ventures.

Morocco, for instance, had been under constant pressure from Libya, together with Algeria, since 1979, when Morocco annexed the entire territory of the Spanish Sahara—103,000 square miles—on the basis of claims going back to the sixteenth century.

Libya and "radical" Algeria initially created an entity to challenge

Morocco, the "Sahrawi Arab Democratic Republic," sponsor of the "Polisario" guerrilla movement, which has since then been engaged in a military struggle with the Kingdom of Morocco. The Polisario movement was supported by both Libya and Algeria until the former altered its stance in early 1984. It is still equipped with Soviet arms and uses bases inside Algeria.

In early August 1983 the Kremlin, through Qaddafi, put Captain Thomas Sankara in power in Upper Volta. Sankara had been Prime Minister for Jean-Baptiste Ouedraogo, an army major who had been President. As Prime Minister, Sankara had visited Libya and North Korea officially, and had been dismissed in May because of his pro-Soviet activities. By August he had overthrown the Oued-raogo cabinet with Qaddafi's support, proclaiming the "progressive" aims characteristic of such regimes. Qaddafi sent in several planeloads of military and civilian supplies to the capital of Upper Volta.

In August of the same year, Qaddafi actually dispatched a military expedition into his southern neighbor, Chad, a vast and under-populated area that nevertheless has strategic value for military and political activities east, west and south. The Reagan Administration's response to the continuing Libyan aggression in Chad was to declare Chad to be a French responsibility. Paris, in turn, which has interests of its own in Libya, has played an equivocal role in responding to the assault on Chad.

It is plain that the Kremlin has been ramifying its connections with countless African states, especially since the successful coup of its Cuban proxies in Angola in 1975. Its strong-points stretch from Madagascar, South Yemen, Ethiopia, Iran, Afghanistan and Mozambique, in the east, to Libya in the north, and Angola and Namibia in the west.

The Soviets are now a power in African politics not merely through their military positions, but because they can, through their puppets, enter into the normal byplay of politics anywhere. The Soviet involvement has, in short, a popular, "organic" base. Even African leaders who are apprehensive about Soviet expansionism are prepared to use it, for instance, in order to get rid of minority white rule in South Africa.

It is South Africa, after all, that is the prime target of the Kremlin and its many African dependents. And it is imperative to perceive that the destruction of the South African state, even with its distasteful apartheid policy, would be a catastrophe for the West.

5

The Subversion
of Central America

Yet it is in the Western hemisphere, even further from Russia than West Africa, that the Kremlin has worked out its techniques of subversion and infiltration with the most dramatic—and dangerous—consequences.

It is also the area in which the classic, as it were ideological, method utilized by the Soviets has had the most sweeping effect on public opinion in the United States itself.

Latin America has provided the Kremlin with a made-to-order society—complete with feudal conditions, an impoverished peasantry, a handful of rich magnates and a fragmentary middle class, educated beyond practical application of its training and hence the matrix of an alienated intelligentsia that has always been a prime seedbed for Marxist recruits.

This has made "human rights," the paramount slogan of the Kremlin, its spokesmen and its dupes in the United States, a natural, indeed appealing formulation for the public at large and even for the Christian church.

Who can deny the poverty in Latin America, especially Central America? Who can fail to sympathize with people suffering from malnutrition, landlessness, hopelessness? And how easy it is for half-baked intellectuals to be seduced by the panaceas of social reform proclaimed by communists, socialists and other utopians! The church itself—both Protestant and Catholic—has been overwhelmed by utopian extremism, rampant throughout the feudal societies of Latin America, especially Central America, and expressed by the tiny educated minority. How easy it is for the Communist Parties to heighten disaffection and focus agitation!

The United States has traditionally influenced Latin America through active diplomacy, massive economic inter-relationships and support of friendly governments. Yet in recent years the United States has increasingly tolerated or even tacitly encouraged revolutionary movements while straining relations with her traditional allies. Thus, Moscow's progress in the region is retarded not by American counter-measures but by the independence of traditional revolutionary thought among the Hispanic intellectuals and some effective anti-communist regimes. The existing active opposition to American influence derives largely from Cuba, with persistent Soviet direction.

It is obvious that the current global thrust of the Soviet state—based on economic pressure, military coercion, and manipulation of strategic puppets—has been extended to Central and South America. As in Africa and other parts of the Third World, the Soviet campaign manufactures and exploits the idea that the United States is imperialist, that we support dictatorships and that "Yankee meddling" is a variant of colonialism. As in Africa, the Soviets' principal methods of destabilization involve support for radical factions and shipment of arms, which have increased substantially since the United States decided to restrict its own arms sales. Even if the policies of the Soviets are less easy to implement in Central and South America than on the tribal battlefields of Africa, they are still demonstrably feasible, especially because of our policy of benign acquiescence to revolution that has replaced the Monroe Doctrine and, of course, because of Casto's Cuba. U.S. policy with regard to Soviet initiatives has been virtually congruent with Soviet intentions: it has been embarrassed and inconsistent, and hence, has been interpreted as unreliable and weak.

The policy of the Carter Administration, honeycombed with utopian sentimentality buttressed by a fear of excercising power, was shillyshallying and feeble. But the policy of the Reagan Administration, too, has been hamstrung by a refusal to face up to the fact, admitted and indeed made much of in rhetoric, that the Kremlin has total control of key regimes in the Western Hemisphere, of which Cuba is clearly the most important.

Thus, reactions to American diplomacy have been conditioned by the following factors: U.S. nonproliferation policy, as it applies to Argentina and Brazil in particular; the Panama Canal decision, with its immense symbolic importance; the gradual withdrawal of support for Nicaragua's Somoza and other authoritarian governments; and the inability or refusal of U.S. Administrations to confront either Cuba's growing aggression or the rising military presence of the Soviet Union within Cuba itself. Finally, U.S. arms sales and human rights policies seem contemptible in the eyes of most of our allies and make us look like a major power fighting valiantly for an ill-defined principle only in countries we can browbeat into compliance.

The responsibility of successive U.S. Administrations for the loss of Cuba is still not realized. The "missile crisis" of 1962 has been systematically presented as an American triumph, in which President Kennedy, glaring at Khrushchev "eyeball to eyeball," faced him down and forced the Russians to leave Cuba.

Yet the Russians never left; instead, they built up their forces on the island to the point where under the last two administrations they have become unchallengeable. The denunciation of Cuba as the source of agitation that characterizes President Reagan's speeches rings strangely hollow.

What is perhaps most ironic about the present situation is that Cuba fell into the lap of the Kremlin long before its current plans for world hegemony matured. In 1962 Cuba was, indeed, a "target of opportunity!"

The utter simplicity of the maneuver that planted the Soviets squarely in the Western Hemisphere merits attention. In effect, it *bought* Cuba. By assisting a rebel movement at a crucial moment, by subsidizing the economy of a small island, it acquired not only the manpower for the conquest of Africa and the Middle East but an indispensable instrument for the subversion of Latin America.

No wonder the state documents dealing with the "Cuban missile crisis" of 1962 are still secret!

Seldom can there have been a greater stroke of luck for the Kremlin than the confluence of the partisan requirements of an American president and the climate of opinion in the mass media. Together they made it possible to pass off a stunning Soviet triumph of penetration as a rebuff to Soviet aggression. By establishing a bridgehead in Cuba, and then seeming to withdraw some missiles for a short time, the Soviets, with the active connivance of media and the passivity of successive U.S. Administrations, not only retained its Cuban bridgehead but turned it, when the time ripened, into a powerful adaptable mechanism for the subversion of a vital geographical area.

The role of media in the establishment of the Soviet Castro regime is instructive. Just as media contributed to the destruction of the traditional authorities in Ethiopia and Iran, so in the case of Cuba the emergence of Castro was facilitated by the manipulation of public opinion. For decades, the government of Castro's predecessor, Fulgencio Batista, had what can only be called a "good press." Cuba, to the average American newspaper reader, was a colorful island whose population produced sugar as well as exotic music, provided a desirable contrast to the relative drabness of the U.S. mainland, produced excellent cigars, and featured entertainment in its capital city, Havana, that had some of the exotic vibrancy associated in the public mind with Paris or Las Vegas.

The classic use of an American reporter by a Marxist revolutionary was well illustrated in the case of Herbert Matthews, the *New York Times* correspondent who accompanied Castro into Havana. Matthews represented Castro as a liberalizing force in Latin American affairs. Later, in his autobiography, *A World in Revolution* (1971), Matthews recalled that, when he first interviewed

Castro in the Sierra Maestra on February 17, 1957, "he believed that he could work within a democratic system," but by mid-1960 he had "converted himself to a belief in Socialism." His attitude toward the Russians changed from admiration and gratitude to "anger and distrust" and later "to friendly cooperation." Castro has since acted as a direct agent of Soviet power.

The Matthews-type attitude has been duplicated, before and after Castro's takeover, in various politico-military situations, ranging from the Mao takeover in China—where the Communists were originally represented to the West as "agrarian reformers," Afghanistan, Angola and Central America.

The Carter Administration naturally bears a great deal of the responsibility for continuing the duplicity of the Kennedy Administration. In 1979, for instance, when a Soviet combat brigade was uncovered in Cuba, Carter initially took a "strong" line, calling the continued presence of the brigade "unacceptable," but backed down at once.

In a major address (October 1, 1979) Carter was satisfied by "assurances . . . from the highest level of Soviet Government" that "the Soviet personnel in Cuba are not and will not be a threat to the United States or to any other nation." Instead of demanding the withdrawal of the brigade, United States policy would simply be to "monitor the status of the Soviet forces by increased surveillance of Cuba." This striking reversal of policy on an issue of seemingly vital security interest to the United States itself inevitably caused substantial damage to the credibility of the United States' resolve in resisting Soviet/Cuban supported expansion anywhere in the hemisphere.

It is no doubt charitable to pass over in silence the high comedy implied by Carter's acceptance of the "assurances" of the "highest level of Soviet Government." His naivete was at least consistent; President Reagan, entirely aware—in theory—of Soviet-Cuban initiatives, *in fact* does nothing whatever about the Soviet presence in Cuba and the pliability of the Castro regime in carrying out Soviet projects.

This must be even more baffling to friends and foes alike. There was a hopeful element, after all, in the foolishness of the Carter

Administration. It might well have been thought to be unaware of what was going on, hence a subsequent government, once made aware of the true state of affairs, would do something about it. Thus, the Reagan Administration, by showing its awareness and by restricting its reaction to rhetoric, must be even more deeply discouraging to friends of the United States than was Carter.

The inconsistent, half-hearted, contradictory and hypocritical reactions of successive U.S. Administrations have damaged the position of the United States more than even the breast-beating that followed the overthrow of the Allende regime in Chile. American goals present an opaque, confusing picture. No country can be receptive to a diplomacy that is unclear about what it wants and whose logical ends are incompatible with its stated goals.

Both the Carter and the Reagan administrations have behaved, speaking generally, with a maximum of ineptitude with respect to Latin America as a whole. This is due not only to a systematic underassessment of the role of Marxism throughout the hemisphere, but to a profound ignorance of Latin American society.

Many countries, such as Mexico, Venezuela and Argentina, have cultural traditions considerably older and more sophisticated than those of the United States and are, consequently, reluctant to be treated as third world countries inhabited by tribes who happen to control valuable resources. Such states have large middle classes besieged by social unrest and economic problems, which they accept as the source of radical agitation and upheaval.

An examination of the threat to stability that would be created by Soviet-backed insurrection is a natural preliminary to discussion of the most tangible instance of State Department and White House crisis management—namely, reaction to the revolution in Nicaragua. This was a good example of delayed response by the White House planners, who on such evidence need long leadtimes to formulate policies.

President Carter thought that an agreement to return the Panama Canal to local control would be a gesture of our commitment to peace and to self-determination in the region. However, the decision to return the Canal, together with the human rights and arms policies, appears to have been instrumental in persuading

Soviet and Cuban analysts that the United States would not defend Somoza in the face of concerted "popular" opposition. In addition, we did not object when Panama violated both the Neutrality Treaty by supporting the Sandinistas and Costa Rican nonalignment by using its territory as transit route. These developments created conditions similar to those which are facilitating the Soviet-Cuban venture in Africa; and particularly promised to benefit Cuba for whom the prospect of Marxist alignment with more prosperous neighbors was irrestible, considering the desperate state of the Cuban economy.

We can surely see today, with hindsight, the weightiness of the agreement to transfer the Panama Canal. The fact is staring us in the face—Soviet-backed groups are agitating against their governments throughout Latin America. This trend, though clear, was downplayed by the Carter Administration. General Torrijos, avowedly nationalist, had already displayed a bias favoring Marxists long before Canal treaty negotiations had begun. In fact, after coming to power in a coup in 1968, Torrijos used the Canal issue to gain acceptance among the third world countries of the United Nations. He appointed avowed Marxists to his cabinet in 1971 and made a state visit to Cuba in January 1976.

Soviet weapons shipments to Panama only increased the probability that the United States may in the future face restriction of the Canal facilities. Torrijos was an unreliable cosignatory to a treaty of such critical importance; we depend on the Canal for trade, the restriction of which will harm our interests as well as most Latin American nations and benefit the cause of the Soviet Union and Cuba. Lieutenant General Gordon Sumner (Ret.), a former chairman of the Inter-American Defense Board, told the House Subcommittee on the Panama Canal (June 6, 1979) that Torrijos informed him of his sympathies for the revolutionary cause in Central America as early as November 1977. This classified information was not made public during the Senate debate on the Canal Treaty, despite its crucial relevance to an understanding of Torrijos, who, as a party to the Neutrality Treaty, was supposedly restricted from interfering with the affairs of other nations. Suppression of Sumner's information, which included evidence that Torrijos was actively supporting the Sandinista movement against Somoza in Nicaragua, resulted in a systematic misrepresentation of Torrijos by the Administration.

The implications of this distortion are clear: cession of the Canal was the beginning of the loss of U.S. influence in the region.

American weakness exhibited in the Panama Canal negotiations reverberated throughout the area as Latin nations failed to support the treaty with any enthusiasm. Torrijos invited twenty Latin leaders to come to Bogota, Colombia, in August 1977 to exhibit solidarity for his cause, but only five heads of state appeared (and two of these acquired special privileges in the final treaty).

A much more revealing Latin sentiment towards the treaty had been reflected two months earlier at an O.A.S. meeting in Grenada. At that time the organization cast a unanimous 17–0 vote in favor of Resolution 284 which both reiterated a recommendation "that Panama Canal tolls not be increased" and reaffirmed "the principle that the Panama Canal tolls should exclusively reflect the actual operating costs." Panama vigorously dissented but was joined in abstention by only two other nations. Nonetheless, the United States proceeded to negotiate, and eventually pass, a treaty which would quickly raise tolls by forty percent in order to simply provide the Torrijos regime with upwards of sixty million dollars a year of additional revenues, money that could be used to promote insurrection in neighboring countries.

But, if the United States, which incidentally thereby imposed an enormous energy tax on its own Alaska oil flowing to Gulf port refineries, would not defend her own economic and strategic interests in Panama, then certainly one could not expect Latin nations to criticize prospective control by Torrijos.

Thus, if the United States had attempted to marshall Latin support for continued fairness in the running of the Canal and had accurate presentations been made to the U.S. public in the ensuing debate, then not only might the Canal vote have been different and Torrijos restrained in his revolutionary fervor but the prospects for revolutionary change, as in Nicaragua or El Salvador, would have been significantly reduced.

Repeated instances of State Department equanimity concerning the link between Panama and the Sandinistas came to light in the first part of 1979. Intelligence officers of the Panama National Guard were intercepted on U.S. territory in the act of shipping arms to Nicaragua, and evidence came to light of Panama Air Force planes picking up arms in Cuba and dropping them to the Sandinista groups. The U.S. posture increased the instability of Somoza's position because it revealed the unreliable nature of U.S. support, which was conditioned by Carter's desire to see the Canal legislation pass safely; it would not have passed if it were widely known that a regional conflict was in the making. More serious, however, than any specific case of deception is the fact that the Administration seemed to be susceptible to a portrait of events as it would have liked to see them, which produced, again and again, an irrelevant reaction to changes in the global and regional strategic balance.

The strained quality of Carter's footwork to push the Panama Canal legislation through the House was increased by contradictory announcements. At the same time that he was opening talks with governments suspected of supporting the Sandinistas, he declared that the Canal treaty should not be linked to the difficulties that Somoza was then experiencing because the situation in Nicaragua "stood on its own two feet"—even if that stance was at the moment being undermined by Panama's activities. Further, Somoza was repeatedly attacked for violations of basic human rights, while the same standards were completely ignored in dealing with Panama. This duality was carried to its logical conclusion when the Administration eventually conceded (Subcommittee on the Panama Canal, Hearings, Lt. Gen. McAuliffe's testimony, June 7, 1979) that Panamanian troops were fighting with the rebels in Nicaragua. It was rationalized however that this constituted a local disorder that would not threaten stability in the region, because Panama's motive was hostility to the Somoza government rather than support for the overtly Marxist Sandinista guerrillas. After their success, Sandinista trainees were sent to Panama for instruction in maintaining law and order.

Cuban involvement in the Panama Canal Zone and in the Nicaraguan conflict is testimony to a coherent design for the region, a design which should have been understood since Castro came to power. The strategy is to avoid direct conflict with the United States in third party states and to advance by political subversion. There is thus an implicit dependence on the doctrine of detente, which separates local conflicts from strategic conflict. As long as this condition is observed by Washington, there is a chance for Soviet/Cuban influence in the Western Hemisphere to grow, mainly by means of Cuban intervention, which keeps the Soviet position in the strategic balance at low risk while increasing Cuban hegemony. This strategy must be cautious if it is to challenge seriously U.S. interests in the region.

There is evidence that Castro had something to do with the coup that installed Torrijos, but more significant is the close connection between Cuba and the Sandinistas. Thomas Borge of the militant wing of the Sandinistas lived in Cuba throughout the period of his exile, and the small number of Sandinista cadres that existed prior to the uprising in 1979 were Cuban trained and equipped. Castro's motive for this assistance is personal as well as ideological, since, as he recalls, Somoza's Nicaragua was the stage from which the Carter Administration alternately denied and ignored reports in mid-1979 that Cuban troops had disembarked at Panama and had cut through Costa Rica to join the Sandinista campaign. Eventually Defense Secretary Harold Brown conceded (ABC-TV, June 1979) that there was evidence of "Cuban military support" in Nicaragua. In addition, President Carter, when he returned from Vienna after the SALT II ceremony, referred to Cuban involvement in "the problems of Central America and the Caribbean," thereby acknowledging the fact of low-level Cuban penetration of and interest in the affairs of vulnerable states in the region. By contrast, the Sandinistas adamantly denied any ideological links with or military assistance from Castro, in order to retain the cooperation of non-Marxists who were also opposing Somoza.

Somoza was isolated from the neighboring states. There were well-timed statements of support for the guerrillas by their leaders. "Neutral" Costa Rica was used as a "safeguard area." Late in 1978, Costa Rica terminated diplomatic relations with Somoza after his troops had entered Costa Rica in pursuit of guerrillas, although at that time it was teeming with Sandinistas. By June 1979, even the illusion of neutrality had disappeared. Costa Rica, probably under pressure from the Soviets, recognized the Sandinista leaders as the legitimate government of Nicaragua and thus played a central role in Somoza's overthrow. Later it was revealed that Costa Rica had actively aided the Sandinistas not only with bases and material support but also diplomatically. Given the geography of the region, this aid was of incalculable value; the Sandinistas would not have been able to mount as sophisticated a challenge without a haven in a free zone beyond Somoza's reach. The Soviet embassy in the Costa Rican capital was more a center for operations than a diplomatic post. In early 1980, several Soviet diplomats were quietly expelled from Costa Rica for subversive activities.

The moderate governments of Central America were embarrassed by the contradiction between wanting to preserve their own governments and wanting Somoza to be replaced. Extensive examination of human rights violations under his rule only fed Marxist propaganda, particularly since social conditions in Central America are generally more favorable to violent socialist revolution than to peaceful transfers of power.

Thus Nicaragua acquired disproportionate significance as the first target of the Soviets' current effort to undermine or overthrow Latin American governments by direct military and political support of local Communist parties, which they have decided are easier to control than nationalist leaders. Nicaragua, the largest nation in Central America, was naturally seen as keystone to the region if a powerful anti-communist leader like Somoza could be toppled.

The Cuban and Sandinista forces in Costa Rica, the fall of Nicaragua and the Panama Canal Treaty all changed the regional balance in Central America and gave new impetus to radical forces. If Nicaragua moves in any way against American interest—from nonaligned to pro-Soviet—then Panama, Cuba and Russia would have assurance that there would be no challenge or response to any of their moves; that the United States would be denied, by Costa Rica's neutrality, the option to construct either a second international waterway in a country adjacent to Panama, or a trans-isthmus oil pipeline to transport crude oil from Alaska.

El Salvador now teeters on the brink of a repetition of Nicaragua. Without infrastructure to sustain a "moderate" government, and armed leftists determined to establish a Marxist totalitarian regime, its ability to survive as a non-Communist state without appropriate U.S. assistance is in grave doubt.

A Soviet-Cuban alliance with Nicaragua augmented by neutral or well-disposed neighbor states, would therefore be consistent with the Soviet strategy to control waterways and chokepoints all over the world, in order to restrict U.S. access to vital transport links. If control of the oceans is still the preserve of the U.S. fleet, the Soviet navy, configured for a mission of strategic initiative, antisubmarine warfare (ASW) and interdiction, is ideally suited to deter our force. If a conflict on the seas should break out, their navy is capable of deployment from Cuba to support any moves made by pro-Soviet or nonaligned states to limit our access to the Panama Canal.[1]

As usual, a correlation between Soviet force structure and political diplomacy is apparent. Recognizing the scale of U.S. naval coverage, the Soviets, under Admiral Gorshkov, have concentrated on antiship weapons (trying to negate our carrier task force rather than build their own). This approach has led them to stress sea launched cruise missiles and ASW techniques. In the field of strategy, the Soviet fleet has a role of interdiction wherever it is stationed. The perception of such a capability acts to undermine the value of the more sophisticated U.S. fleet in conditions short of total war. At the same time, it presents a coherent picture of Soviet strategy, which reduces confidence in our capability to maintain the supply routes and the few critical chokepoints on which the West's trade largely depends.[2]

The Soviet's strategy for the region, in combination with theories of "human rights," created the conditions under which Somoza could be replaced in Nicaragua by a Marxist movement with an essentially fictitious populist heritage, despite the existence of a sophisticated, well-organized moderate democratic opposition party—the logical replacement for Somoza. Carter's policy was to isolate Somoza so as to force him to change his government and comply with human rights: to this end, all material and financial aid were terminated, although, concurrently, Carter was making overtures to Castro, the leader of a communist police state. The effect of the U.S. aid cutoff was to weaken Nicaragua's ability and its people's ability both physically and psychologically to resist terrorism and to diminish the chances for an orderly, constitutional transfer of power. Our policy regarding Nicaragua, as it was with others, seems to have led us progressively to destabilize the country and make its situation worse by turning power over to well-organized Marxists who had military power rather than popular democratic support.

One of the more serious ramifications of human rights diplomacy, as Nicaragua demonstrates, is that it can result in a very basic violation of a human being's right to live in an autonomous nation. When Secretary Vance, at the Organization of American States (OAS) conference in Washington in June 1979, called for Somoza's resignation, he was merely following the logical dictates of Carter Policy, without considering that his timing was helping the Communist-backed Sandinistas and that a democratic replacement for Somoza could not be called up in time for the next morning's headlines.

American democracy has experienced only a brief period of economic and military dominion, during which it indulged in intervention and eschewed diplomacy. We now, however, seem incapable of exercising diplomatic initiatives based on self-interest, even in a time when this procedure is appropriate and feasible, and we repeatedly force our allies to take measures foreign to their own interests and plans, although the U.S. umbrella no longer protects them. Often our measures virtually deliver them into the enemy camp, which will radicalize them, change their social structure, slow their economy, and reduce the standard of living of every individual. Latin America has become amenable to a bipolar model of superpower relations, following the commitment of the nonaligned movement to Castro's care; thus a zero-sum game is taking place, and the power vacuum created by U.S. losses will be filled by Soviet gains.

U.S. accommodation to this emerging pattern is evident in our kid-glove treatment of Marxist regimes that violate human rights.

The Carter and Reagan Administrations have refrained from initiating or supporting any investigation of human rights violation in Cuba. The Soviets, who wish to use states of the region against us economically and strategically, must be pleasantly surprised to discover at every turn our active cooperation in their enterprise. The Sandinista campaign was able to use the American press to spread disinformation and to raise the Nicaraguan issue in an international forum. Systematic use of political terror by the Sandinistas continues to be ignored. Reports of military activity generally described Somoza's attacks and popular resistance to them, omitting to mention that the Sandinistas ravaged the country, waged war against its people and made examples of resisting populations, particularly local authorities. Thus a form of popular terror unidentified by the U.S. government, was undermining the elected government, which was hardly in a position to retaliate in kind. The U.S. press consistently failed to comment on Sandinista executions or obvious links between Sandinista efforts and Cuban and Panamanian weapons and aid.

More important than the details of U.S. conduct are their implications for the future. Somoza reminded us of the existence of a mutual defense treaty, but such documents are not currently in fashion. He offered to resign, conditional on American economic assistance to a democratic successor and our promise not to support a Marxist dictatorship. Carter rejected his offer. U.S. allies and pro-Western states in Central America no doubt noticed the conditional character of American treaties and agreements. Recognizing the shift in power in the region toward the Soviets and realizing that the United States acknowledges this change, these countries may no longer have the heart to resist Marxist assaults.

The logical conclusion of the Marxist campaign in the region is to put pressure on Mexico because of its vast oil reserves. The same combination of diplomatic initiatives—support for subversion and simple military bullying—can make that country susceptible to Communism. Even if this strategy is not entirely implemented, it will contribute to a perception of Soviet strength; it will be a bold assault on a U.S. neighbor for the purpose of denying us its economic resources. Once confidence is shattered in our ability to safeguard states in the region from the Soviet reach, the natural casualty will be the fabric of our alliances. It is imperative not to concede strategic defeat by failing to respond adequately to Soviet/Cuban maneuvering.

Nicaragua demonstrates the dangers of designing policy to preserve a status quo rather than to adhere to a wise strategy for a particular region. U.S. policy first encouraged moderates to become open in their opposition to Somoza, then failed to give them the support to remove him. As a result, the moderates were discredited within Nicaragua, became disillusioned with the United States and were persecuted for their pains. It quickly became evident that we had no strategy at all, with no importance attached to our regional prestige.

A failure of analysis, more than four years after the Sandinistas took power, still besets the United States in its interpretation of the new regime. This body is distinguished by strongly socialist policy and extreme hostility to the United States. It actively undermines the elected government of El Salvador by its support of the Marxist rebels who are attempting to overthrow it. This regime is stable not because it is popular or wise or restrained but because the revolution decimated the population, shattered the economy and effectively imprisoned six to seven thousand former supporters of Somoza, particularly national guardsmen. Developments are now following a natural pattern; rebuilding has started and "unconditional" assistance is accepted from all who offer it. What is interesting is that the socio-economic programs to repair the devastation, with the help of a carefully controlled press, are changing the country into a radical socialist state.

The provisional government in Managua was at first made up of several factions, the most moderate of which, the Terceristas, stressed continued need to restore the economy. The two more militant factions were the Proletarian and the Prolonged People's War, both of them Marxist and both of them determined to continue the revolution until the remaining democratic structures are eroded. These groups believed that national revolution will develop into Socialist revolution; they rely upon a private military force and the FSLN to influence the junta's decisions. But it is the Sandinistas, who ousted Somoza, who now control Nicaragua.

The Carter Administration's Nicaraguan policy was remarkable for its ineptitude. Having damaged its interests through excessive zeal for liberal reform, it enabled a government to gain power that could create a totalitarian structure controlled by the radical armed FSLN. As happened many times during the Carter years, "principles" produced their opposite in practice.

The Sandinista regime relies heavily on neighborhood "defense committees" for its continued support. These "committees," modeled after a KGB network developed inside Cuba, function as a mutual spy and denunciation system among Nicaraguan families and neighbors. As is now the norm in new Marxist states, East German specialists in internal security have been brought in to supply training and equipment for use in surveillance, interrogation, and prison administration. Estimates in 1983 placed the Nicaraguan regular army at 22,000 troops, supplemented by 25,000 reservists and some 30,000 militiamen. Nicaraguan pilots are being trained in Bulgaria. The U.S. Senate Foreign Relations Committee heard testimony that more than two thousand Cubans were stationed in Nicaragua, in addition to fifty Soviets and thirty-five East Germans.[3]

There are also some fifty P.L.O. pilots in Nicaragua. MIG fighters are expected in Nicaragua, while the Sandinista regime maintains fifty Soviet-supplied tanks, one thousand East German-made trucks, sixteen aircraft—including four transport planes, several propeller-driven training planes, and four helicopters.[4]

In El Salvador there was a ray of hope; an election was held, and despite the threats and brutality the Marxist-led insurgents held over the heads of anyone who took part in it, an overwhelming majority of the people voted for an unequivocally anti-Marxist government. Countless observers, from America and Europe, including many friendly to the insurgents, were obliged to concede that the election was absolutely fair.

One might have thought that the Reagan Administration, after the actual masses of El Salvador displayed their allegiance to the ideals President Reagan is fond of invoking, would take decisive measures to support them in their rejection of the Marxist insurgents who are entirely dependent on Soviet-Cuban support for arms and "advisers."

Yet the Reagan Administration, while rhetorically —again—commending this display of popular democracy, has been unable to cast off the slogan of all pro-Soviet and pro-Castro forces—"political compromise." And the American press has been full of "news," comment, editorials, and articles somehow conveying the impression that despite the shattering blow dealt the Marxist insurgents by the democratic election the insurgents somehow still represent The People, that the tiny group of rebels supported by arms from outside somehow is the majority and hence deserves the benefits of a "political compromise."

Simply put, this slogan, as in Zimbabwe, means only one thing—that a majority ousted from authority by democratic vote can be let into the elected government by the back door. It is, in short, blackmail, yet spokesmen of the Reagan Administration have repeatedly signaled to anti-American forces in Latin America that even the enemies of American who have been kicked out of the government by democratic action can hope for a "political compromise" that will let them back in. Thus, what cannot be won by the ballot will be achieved by bullets.

We now see the Marxist insurgents in El Salvador, supported by "liberal" opinion in the United States, continue to operate against the democratically elected government. The flow of arms continues to arrive and individual members of the insurgent movement infiltrate neighboring countries with apparent ease.

In Honduras, for instance, the active agent of the Soviet-Cuban-Nicaraguan axis is the "Revolutionary Movement of the People," which in 1982 kidnapped 33-year old Xiomard Suazo, the physician-daughter of President Roberto Suazo Cordova, himself a physician. Dr. Suazo was kidnapped during a visit to Guatemala City, and released after fourteen Latin American newspapers agreed to publish the group's "manifesto" denouncing U.S. intervention in Central America.

Honduras' capital, Tegucigalpa, was blacked out in July 1982 as a result of bombs detonated in electric power sources. That September the "Revolutionary Movement" held hostage an entire chamber of commerce meeting in San Pedro Sula, seeking release of a Salvadoran guerrilla leader. When they were at last convinced that the guerrilla had earlier been turned over to the Salvadoran army, the terrorists demanded and received safe conduct to Cuba.

Honduras is a target in the Moscow-Havana-Managua strategy because it has become a refuge for anti-government Salvadorans who live in camps near the border. Most of them are pro-rebel in sentiment, and representatives of international relief organizations tend to support them in pro-rebel protests and actions. By contrast, the anti-Sandinista Miskitos (Indians) are largely neglected and treated with contempt by some self-appointed relief volunteers, both from the U.S. and Europe.

Two further instances will illustrate the ease with which Cuba can exploit the frictions endemic in the fragmented civil order of semi-feudal Central America.

Grenada, for instance, following its independence from Great Britain, was governed by a self-perpetuating regime under Sir Eric M. Gairy. On March 13, 1979, Gairy's government was overthrown by Maurice Bishop, who governed with direct support from the Soviet Union, East Germany, and Cuba. Bishop's one-party government was based on the New Jewel Movement (JEWEL stands for "Joint Endeavor for Welfare, Education and Liberation").

The party, after the Soviet model, was governed by a Politburo and Central Committee. One member of the Central Committee, Don Rojas, told the East German party paper *Neues Deutschland* (March 13, 1982) that the USSR had supplied tractors, trucks and water pumps. Rojas said, "Our nation has been unified by the revolution"; "mass movements" of women, young people and peasants have been organized.

At the United Nations, Grenada had voted strictly along Communist bloc lines on all issues ranging from Afghanistan to the Falkland Islands dispute. The government crafts shop in St. George, the country's capital, sold posters showing Maurice Bishop standing shoulder-to-shoulder with Fidel Castro and Daniel Ortega Saavedra, the Nicaraguan leader.

Cuban supplies and labor and Libyan money were used in building Grenada's new international airport, both as a showpiece for Bishop's People's Revolutionary Government and as a potential base for military aircraft. While serving as U.S. Secretary of State,

Alexander Haig said that, as an air base, the facility would be capable of accommodating "every aircraft in the Soviet-Cuban inventory."[5] Intelligence gathered in the wake of the U.S. invasion of Grenada in 1983 showed that the Administration had indeed understated the full magnitude of the Soviet-Cuban build-up of the island as a forward base.

The pro-Soviet regime of Suriname, the former Dutch colony that is bordered by Guyana and French Guiana, centers around a former physical education instructor, Desi Bouterse, who overthrew the democratically elected government of Henk Arron in 1980 and initially opposed Cuban influence. Then Bouterse sought to complete his high school education with the help of a female tutor, who became his mistress and introduced him to Marxism-Leninism.

Grenada's late Prime Minister, Maurice Bishop, is said to have encouraged Bouterse to yield to Moscow's and Havana's suggestions. As a result, the Bouterse regime fell in line with Soviet policies and startled the world in December 1982 with a ruthless crackdown on all potential opposition groups. Bouterse had once arrested, as a "Cuban sympathizer," the man who later became his Minister of Mass Mobilization. Both the USSR and Cuba have established large embassies in Paramaribo, Suriname's capital.

Some 180,000 persons have left Suriname and settled in the Netherlands. In Suriname, the inevitable massacre began with the arrest of sixteen prominent citizens—including lawyers, journalists and labor leaders—on December 8. The group had formed the Association for Democracy. Within twenty-four hours, all of them were dead, many evidently tortured.

The key to American futility in Central America is the enigma of Cuba. For two decades now this small island of twelve million people has been an open outpost of Soviet power in the Western Hemisphere. The inability of the Reagan Administration even to suggest some way of solving this primordial problem, while at the same time it is bound to acknowledge the fact itself, indicates the bafflement in the topmost strata of government. The very concept of implementing the Monroe Doctrine—i.e., ousting the Soviet intrusion from the Western Hemisphere—lies dormant.

A major reason for this, to be sure—and a reason that is far more alarming than the indecisiveness or passivity of the Administration itself—is the penetration of the Congress both by idealistic dupes and by unavowed partisans of anti-American interests. If the Congress must be called upon to authorize major military expenditures, if all intelligence activities must be channeled through the vast network of congressional committees (that is, if there is no intelligence) it is evident that an effective policy cannot be pursued by the Administration, even if the President were to have a clear idea of what is going on.

"Moderates" may think it sufficient to project some scheme for "containing" Soviet-Cuban aggression, but today even that must be seen to be utopian. There is no way of "containing" Soviet-Cuban aggression, which is the heart of the entire relationship between Cuba and the Kremlin. Some way must be found of altering the Cuban regime itself.

Cuba has always been an enigma for U.S. planners, since they are incapable of grasping the notion of a radical leadership maintaining control precisely through continued political extremism. Castro remains popular by continuing to promote radical thinking and is a stable leader because of his control of the Cuban armed forces; the soldiers, together with the other skilled classes whose abilities go to Cuba's overseas campaigns, are the elite of Cuban society. Such campaigns act, in fact, as a natural sponge for the executive class, which scarcely fits into the Socialist scheme. Cuba's adventures increase nationalist feeling. The economy is subsidized by the Soviet Union with eight million dollars a day, enabling the Cuban leadership to continue its "independent" support of revolution across the globe, particularly in Latin America. The character of the Cuban expansion is ideological; Castro believes in the Marxist cause, is dedicated to the overthrow of capitalism and parliamentary democracies and appears to be content to be a surrogate of Moscow. The resolve and initiative manifested by the Cuban commanders in Africa show that theirs is no mercenary venture but rather an historical mission.

Cuban policy can be understood by the attitudes of its leaders. There is a stable balance of power in Havana among different factions, each of whose interests is served by the expansion and alliance with the Soviet Union. Ideological imperatives conflict with the country's economic needs only to be a limited extent, and this problem was eased by President Carter. An American attempt to inhibit trade with Cuba, by a blockade or other pressure, would polarize the government there, and support the pragmatist wing's claim that military ventures in Africa would hurt the chances for U.S. recognition. This argument for moderation was largely undermined, however, by Carter's courtship of Castro. With no indications of reciprocal Cuban concessions, the Carter Administration opened diplomatic interests sections in the other country's embassies in Washington and Havana, thus bestowing long-sought legitimacy upon the Castro regime. Beyond that, SR-71 overflight surveillance flights were cancelled and Congressional and other delegations tripped to Cuba to examine and often naively extoll the revolution. Castro responded by expanding his overseas adventures and welcoming a Soviet military presence in Cuba, eventually expanding to the installation of a combat brigade. The practical element in the Cuban leadership was, then, largely silenced by Carter's tolerance of extremism, and Cuban policy reflects the interests of the more radical elements, growing bolder with each American retreat.

Since 1970, there has been a reconcentration of power with Fidel and Raul Castro. The circle of leaders has grown broader, encompassing elements from the new class of technical and managerial experts. But through a recent reorganization, Castro remains the determinant voice, with his own men in key positions. Members of the close-knit Ministry of the Revolutionary Armed Forces have also gained new prominence and now occupy several strategic posts in the government and the party as well as in the military command structure. These individuals are personally dependent on Raul Castro and follow the extremely radical line he espouses. Raul Castro thinks of the armed forces as a resource he can direct easily, without having to convince the military commanders of the merits of the missions abroad.

The pragmatic wing of the Cuban party is then disfavored by the prevailing powers, and any improvement in relations with the

United States would probably not affect Castro's support for revolution in Africa and Latin America. This latter effort is now beginning to come to fruition due to our military and political weakness in the region and Carter's reluctance to commit support to friendly states. Both the ideologues and the military need the overseas expeditions to consolidate their power. Increased Soviet economic and military support since the Angolan offensive has especially enhanced the government's international status, probably to a greater extent than would improved relations with the United States.

These facts make clear that the nature of Castro's government is such that its stability is enhanced by a radical posture in world affairs. This imperative will be played out primarily in Africa, where there is already substantial Cuban involvement supported by entrenched Soviet facilities. Cuba uses some soldiers of African origin, so that they are seen as partners in a struggle rather than as foreign interlopers. The other logical area for Cuban expansion is the Caribbean, where Cuba has painstakingly advanced anti-Americanism, both diplomatically and by providing skilled technical and medical personnel. Cuban relations with Guyana have always been excellent, but improved relations with the territory of Belize give analysts cause for concern. None of the Caribbean islands are of strategic value except in the negative sense of denying us access to the region.

In addition to the Caribbean expansion, the Cuban efforts in Latin America, most of which failed in the 1960s, have been revived to coordinate with Soviet commitment of naval deployments to the region. What was in the 1960s an idealistic attempt to export revolution became, in the 1970s, a Soviet-financed campaign to eliminate U.S. interests and to undermine establishment governments.[6] Carter's tacit acceptance of Cuba's accusation that we are an illegitimate actor in the region has helped this initiative, which relies on local people rejecting the present in favor of an uncertain future. In this context, Carter's policy of not selling arms to human rights violators simplified Castro's strategy. Soviet arms shipments not only went unchallenged but also were met with reduced American military assistance at the time when the governments in power most urgently needed it.

The change is dramatic from the early 1960s when the United States provided over half of all arms sold in Latin America, to the estimated present ten percent of a market that has risen to over two billion dollars. The Assistant Secretary of State of the Carter Administration, Lucy Wilson Benson, flatly acknowledged that "we have exercised restraint over the last ten to fifteen years with the result that the Europeans now have seventy percent of the Latin American arms market." Soviet sales rose from negligible in 1972 to three hundred and eighty million dollars in 1977. Rather than exercising any leverage over military development in Latin America, the United States has encouraged both Soviet entry into the area and the development of a large indigenous arms industry in Brazil. Finally, Secretary of State Vance tried to tie to the ever more minimal arms sales alleged human rights progress, which led seven nations in Latin America to completely repudiate their long standing mutual defense agreements with the United States.

The Carter foreign policy was ill-advised, sacrificed imperative regional security for intangibles that in such countries can never be guaranteed (human rights) and relied on other nations to follow our decision not to sell arms; all so that their hope, "if there are no arms, there could be no war," may be realized.

The U.S. has systematically favored leftist regimes and penalized those of a conservative orientation. We have polarized the hemisphere and aided those regimes most opposed to the United States. In short, Washington has encouraged unaligned states to drift to the left (or to let leftist elements have more power), since it is these states that received our aid and interest. This defeatist policy is not defensible even on economic grounds, since no leftist state in the region has yet been able to prosper on its own. The best example of this is Peru, which suffered severe economic setbacks while flirting with leftist policies. The Carter Administration, opposed to arms sales in principle and unwilling to concede them to conservative states as a means of maintaining leverage, ended up using them, in crude attempts to influence their internal policies, as a weapon against its own allies. Arbitrary limits on arms, for example, significantly damaged Mexico's defense needs, its control of airborne drug trafficking and, more critically, U.S.-Mexican relations, which include our access to Mexican oil. Arms are denied the more democratic states in Latin America, while the radical regimes have no difficulty in obtaining, on generous financial terms, the most modern Soviet equipment, which is sufficiently advanced to disturb the generally bipolar rivalries obtaining locally in Latin America. Finally, certain sales were prevented on specious grounds, such as denying Israel's right to sell Kfir jets to Ecuador with U.S. parts. This contempt for the smaller countries of America, as if their political understanding were commensurate with their economic poverty, has also alienated some of our allies.

Poverty is more the dictator than the military. The military only helps to stabilize the poverty and facilitate production and distribution. Clearly, in recent years, aside from the oil rich nations, those countries with rightist authoritarian governments have realized the greatest economic advancement and general social progress. Because economic problems frequently determine political systems, it is poverty that needs to be remedied if we are to help any society eventually develop into a democracy. The mere replacement of a rightist dictatorship with a leftist dictatorship is of no conceivable benefit to the country and results in every imaginable disadvantage for the United States.

In Latin America, as elsewhere, both the Carter and the Reagan Administrations have failed to make the distinction between authoritarian and totalitarian governments. While dealing with unfriendly repressive states, rationalizing that they belong to completely different traditions of political control, the U.S. stigmatizes authoritarian allies because they should have the same political traditions as ours. The result is often that these countries degenerate from dictatorship to totalitarianism.

The main difference between authoritarian and totalitarian regimes, in foreign affairs, is that totalitarian regimes are ideologically hostile to pluralistic societies and want to dominate even those with whom they cooperate, while authoritarian regimes usually want only to resolve local problems by force. Totalitarian regimes are motivated by an all-embracing ideology, authoritarian regimes by a traditional respect for order and dealing with economic and social problems. Because of our failure to distinguish between these phenomena, we have, among other things, repeatedly insulted the governments of Brazil and Argentina, which, given their historic and economic conditions, are relatively liberal.

It is clear that the Soviet-Cuban strategy is aided by the rift between the United States and its natural allies in the hemisphere. Equally evident is that Cuba has a strategy for armed insurrection in the entire region, originating in Nicaragua and spreading through El Salvador and Honduras, where the local Communist Party trained the FSLN. And now, after the Nicaraguan revolution, troops from both Cuba and Nicaragua are working in other Central American states in an operation, code-named "Black December," which will culminate in an assault against Honduras. Simultaneous guerrilla uprisings in Guatemala and El Salvador may coincide with Honduras; in El Salvador, the liberal putsch is currently being driven to desperation by far left and factional violence as part of the "Black December" plan.

These strategies are hardly uncharacteristic for the Soviets, but they are rendered more plausible in this region by declining U.S. stature and by our Latin American policy. This policy is philosophical rather than strategic in its viewpoint; it proposes that America's difficulties in the Caribbean basin and Latin America are the result of flaws endemic to our approach and flatly rejects the notion that they may be caused by hostile forces. It advocates disengagement from the region, regardless of Soviet penetration; diminished U.S. responsibility; and an accommodation to trends which are not innocent but part of a strategy to deny the U.S. interests vital to its prosperity in order to neutralize it on the global stage. Upon reaching office, Carter promptly sought to normalize relations with Cuba on the supposed grounds that Cuba's material support of subversive movements in other Latin American countries has diminished in recent years; and hopes to lure Havana away from Moscow. A basic change in U.S.-Cuban relations was, therefore, presumably necessary and justified, as was a different attitude toward the region. Military security was no longer to be treated as the first priority; the corollary of this sentiment was that there should be an "equitable new agreement" with Panama regarding the Canal.

The official policy was based on the hypothesis that the area had become the testing ground for ideological pluralism. The real situation, however, is not some mysterious social or popular dynamic but a contest for allies and a strategic position between the United States and the Soviet-Cuban camp. Soviet advances have been actively aided by the Carter policy. For this reason, if for no other, it should be at once reassessed before every state in the region is mouthing the platitudes of "Yankee oppression."

6

The Decline
of NATO

The concept of NATO, as articulated in practical measures, has suffered from the same imbalance as the SALT discussions. American planners, mesmerized by the overarching unthinkability of a nuclear war, have abandoned the necessity of maintaining parity, at least, in conventional weapons. The consequent imbalance in conventional weapons between NATO and the Soviet forces (the Warsaw Pact countries included) is radical.

For various military, political and economic reasons, the West has never attempted to match the Warsaw Pact in quantity of conventional forces. NATO has instead relied on American strategic superiority and on the superior technology of its weapons systems to compensate for the disadvantage in numbers. That edge has been eroded by a vast infusion of new Soviet equipment. Because of this erosion, NATO's conventional forces have again become a crucial element in its defensive strategy, which is called flexible response.

Flexible response consists of two principles: conventional defense and, if that fails, nuclear escalation. These two capabilities support each other and enhance deterrence of aggression. NATO conventional forces, by their presence, are supposed to defeat aggression. If this fails, the enemy attack will be met on a level appropriate to its character. The precise nature of the response is not revealed beforehand because uncertainty is supposed to add to the strength of the deterrent. If a defense cannot be conducted successfully on the chosen level, then a deliberate and controlled escalation procedure will be enacted, the purpose of which will be to convince the adversary that he will not be permitted to reach his goals without having to accept sacrifices that will far exceed his expected gains.

The escalation can be conducted in several ways: by geographical extensions of the theater (i.e., by opening new fronts or attacking targets deeper into the adversary's territory); by attacking new classes of targets, such as populations; or by using increasingly destructive weapons. Europe and America agree on flexible response in theory. The abiding problem between us, however, is that the Europeans prefer deterrence and the Americans prefer defense. There is no permanent solution to this dilemma; it is inherent in our geographical positions and our asymmetries in force structure. America has extended it strategic nuclear deterrent to defend allies against not only attack but also nuclear coercion. But the balance to be struck between conventional warfighting and nuclear deterrence is a matter of continuing negotiations. America wants to lower the risk of nuclear war by fighting with conventional troops on European soil; if war breaks out, Europe wants to equalize the risk of nuclear war to include the United States, in the hope that by demonstrating the United States' willingness to mount the escalation ladder even conventional war will be deterred.

The NATO alliance has long been outclassed quantitatively in almost every conventional category, on the prospective battlefield and in the rear, especially in the north-central sector. An impressive Soviet expansion/modernization program which began in the late 1960s included the addition of 100,000 men to Soviet army forces in Eastern Europe, introduction of large numbers of T-72 main battle tanks, replacement of armored personnel carriers with the BMP 60 mechanized infantry combat vehicle, change from towed to self-propelled artillery, and proliferation of a formidable array of tactical air defense systems which can neutralize the antitank capabilities of NATO's multi-purpose tactical aircraft.

The military imbalance is particularly serious in northern Norway, where a single Norwegian brigade faces strong Soviet forces in the Kola Peninsula—two divisions and a regiment of naval infantry as well as nine divisions in the Leningrad Military District and more to the south in the Baltic states. While many of these formations may have missions other than that of invasion, they can all be brought to bear against Norway and Denmark and could rapidly be reinforced. The wide disparity on land is coupled with the massive Soviet naval strength in the region. The strength of the Soviet forces make Norway's defense, in the event of a surprise attack a considerable problem. Since Norway and Denmark refuse to allow foreign military forces to be stationed on their territories during peacetime, a sudden attack would have to be met initially by air and naval support.

In the southern sector, while there is a rough parity in troop strength, the Warsaw Pact is much stronger than NATO in mechanized forces. NATO forces in the south are also, problematically, deployed in three separate land sectors—Italy, Greece, Turkish Thrace and Asia Minor—with scant possibility of moving units from one contingent to reinforce another. Additionally, the antagonism between Greece and Turkey inhibits NATO's defense in the southeast. U.S. efforts to mitigate the disputes over Cyprus and air space over the Aegean have only added fat to the fire: Greece withdrew its military forces from NATO's integrated military structure in August 1974 and is now engaged in talks with the Soviet Union—talks which have already enabled the Soviets to obtain repair and port facility rights on the Greek island of Siros for their merchant ship and naval auxiliaries. The American arms embargo against Turkey, though it ended in 1978, came at a time when Turkish armed forces were already deteriorating. Turkey has a ground force of 485,000 men—the largest in the alliance. With adequate equipment and training, these troops could tie down Soviet and Warsaw Pact divisions that might otherwise be funneled into a massive attack on the central front. Of more immediate concern is Turkey's strategic importance as a buffer between the USSR and the Middle East, whose oil is crucial to the West. Yet Turkey remains a giant on feet of clay: a recent British report concluded that its army is not even up to the standards of the second world war. Negotiations between Greece and NATO concerning Greece's reintegration have foundered on the question of how much control over Aegean air space to allot to Turkey (and Foreign Minister Rallis warned Secretary of State Vance that if some cooperation between Greece and NATO could not be established, U.S. bases would not be able to continue to operate on Greek territory). Turkey, meanwhile, has extended an existing agreement with the United States which allows us to maintain monitoring bases in that country, contingent upon increased economic and military aid. But Turkey deferred to the Soviet Union on the matter of American U-2 overflights and granted overflight privileges to the Soviet Union, as have the Saudis. These difficulties lead observers to conclude that both Greece and Turkey are abdicating their responsibility to NATO as Soviet power in the region expands.

Another problem with NATO's conventional posture has been the injudicious deployment of the forces which make up the central European command. As a result of World War II logistics arrangements and post-war occupation agreements, the strongest U.S. formations have been stationed in more-defensible southern Germany, although it is the open North German plain that is the most likely to be the target of Pact aggression. The Soviets have deployed fully two-thirds of their East European forces in the North where there are few obstacles to an offensive which could drive to the Rhine in a matter of hours. This situation has, fortunately, been partially corrected; an additional U.S. brigade has been stationed in the north, which makes reinforcement in the event of an emergency much easier. Yet much remains to be done. In NATO's eight corps sectors there are few reserve formations capable of being transferred to reinforce a threatened sector.

A certain East-West maldeployment may be just as critical. The peacetime positioning of major combat units well to the rear of the forward defense line, which the Germans have insisted be at the border between East and West Germany, does little to support NATO's forward defense strategy, the basis of NATO's doctrine. For example, five of the six Dutch brigades committed to the forward defense of the area along the Elbe remain in Holland. The French army in Germany (though not under NATO command), the Canadian battlegroup and substantial Belgian, German and U.S. forces are stationed west of the Rhine or in the distant southwest corner of Germany. In the event of a Pact *blitzkreig*, the ability of these forces to move to their wartime positions would be uncertain, especially because many of the bridges that cross the Rhine would be destroyed.

In combat manpower, the Warsaw Pact has maintained an advantage in the north and central sectors for some years, and its advantage has increased since 1976.

The Eastern alliance likewise has better reinforcement capabilities. While the Soviet Union has decreased its armored and mechanized reinforcement divisions since 1977 (by five and thirty-seven respectively) and NATO numbers have remained static, there has been a general improvement in the firepower and mobility of Pact forces, which could enable them to launch an attack without being reinforced beforehand. No movement of reserves means no warning to NATO. The possibility of a surprise attack by the Warsaw Pact has been widely debated. It is the current consensus among war planners that a Pact surprise attack in Central Europe is the most serious threat currently facing the alliance. The Soviet Union's three tank and two mechanized infantry armies in East Germany constitute a *blitzkreig* force for a sudden, massive invasion of Western Europe; and NATO would be hard-pressed to defend adequately, in view of the deficiencies in its forward defense forces, the problems of reinforcement, Soviet neutralization of NATO's theater nuclear weapons and political difficulties in coordinating mobilization and in releasing nuclear weapons. Defense analyst Colin Gray estimates that attacking with only the forces normally deployed in East Germany, Czechoslovakia and Poland would yield the USSR a theoretical first and second echelon of twenty-seven Soviet divisions. Under the cover of exercises and the annual rotation of troops and tactical aircraft into and out of Central Europe, a surge deployment could be achieved which might not look like mobilization for war. Strategic instability is rooted not in the presence of military forces but rather in the prospect of their sudden and unexpected use.

The Warsaw Pact forces could be reinforced faster than NATO's for obvious geographical reasons. Most of the NATO forces are CONUS (Continental U.S.)-based units whose heavy equipment must be moved by sea, with the inevitable time lag. (Only two American divisions already have their equipment prepositioned in Europe, to which troops could be flown from across the Atlantic.) To function effectively, NATO must be able to continually move men and material from the United States to Europe. Since ballistic missile attacks and naval mine blockades could take out NATO's ports and airfields, ACLANT (Allied Command-Atlantic) must be able to contain Soviet attacks against lines of communication to the Middle East and across the Atlantic if the alliance is to survive. Failure to keep essential avenues open could cause NATO's defense to collapse from logistic starvation even if the land war went favorably. ACLANT's tremendous task is further complicated by NATO's self-imposed southern boundary at the Tropic of Cancer, which leaves sea routes in the South Atlantic outside of NATO jurisdiction. The simulated mobilization exercise, "Nifty Nugget," which tested America's ability to mount and logistically sustain a large military force in Europe long enough to be credible against a conventional Soviet *blitzkreig*, showed that we could not presently do so. Ill-equipped, undermanned U.S. Army reserves were simply decimated by attrition once the frontline troops in Germany were overcome.

The Soviet Union, by contrast, can airlift personnel from European Russia to relieve its five category-one divisions that have been in Czechoslovakia since the 1968 invasion and its two in Poland and four more in Hungary (although no equipment is prepositioned for their use). These forward-deployed forces could be further strengthened on short notice from the thirty-six divisions[1] (three are airborne) in seven armies[2] and 6,800 main battle tanks that now are maintained in the Baltic, Beylorussian and Carpathian military districts.

One of NATO's main problems is lack of equipment standardization. Whereas the Warsaw Pact uses mostly Soviet or Soviet-designed equipment, U.S. experts estimate that about ten billion dollars of the ninety billion dollars that NATO member countries spend each year for defense is wasted because of duplication and inefficiency in weapons systems. For example, NATO forces operate some seven different types of armored personnel carriers and twenty-four different families of military aircraft. The most significant disparity is in tanks: in main battle tanks, in place in Europe, the Pact outnumbers NATO 42,500 to 13,000.[3] Moreover, Russian T-72 tanks are equipped with a new form of armor (called by the Soviets "combined armor") resistant to penetration by allied missiles, particularly from the front.[4] The Pact also has more conventional artillery in north-central Europe: its advantage in field, medium, and heavy artillery tubes; heavy mortars; and rocket launchers is 19,500 to 4,550.[5] In the southern sector, the situation is only slightly better, with NATO artillery and mortars of all kinds totaling 6,200 as against 12,000 for the Warsaw Pact—and about one quarter of the NATO artillery is located in Italy, out of the line of forward defense.[6] Over a ten-year period, then, the Pact's artillery inventory has grown by about fifty percent and has shown marked improvement in quality, particularly in the new self-propelled units, which have replaced obsolescent units that needed to be towed.

Logistics pose serious problems for the alliance. NATO's logistics structure is inflexible, based almost entirely on national supply lines with little central coordination. This is perhaps the inevitable result of assimilating the armies of fifteen nations into a single defense system. The Pact has an advantage in centralization in having Soviet satellite nations, and the Soviets have been improving their capabilities so steadily that NATO's superiority in forward logistics is now gone. Indeed, NATO's command, control and communication capabilities have been deficient for some years because of the scarcity of all-weather reconnaissance aircraft; the absence of easy communication among tactical units of different national armies (six different tactical communications systems are in use, each incapable of communicating with the others); the acute shortage of information processing systems; poor air-to-ground communications; and large, unwieldy staffs at some headquarters. The eviction of NATO from France in 1967 constrained supply lines radiating from Bremerhaven, Rotterdam and Antwerp and made them especially vulnerable. Since they run behind and parallel the prospective front, the first sharp Soviet surge could sever them. Even if France were to receive NATO during an emergency, facilities there would have deteriorated or been dismantled.

NATO is also increasingly deficient in airpower. Neither Britain's aging Vulcans nor the U.S. FB-111s compare with the Soviets' swingwing Backfire, seventy-five of which are believed to be in service in the European theater.[7] While NATO has fewer numbers of aircraft, it does have a higher proportion of multi-purpose aircraft, which are specially useful for ground attack. This power is being increasingly checkmated, however, by Soviet tactical air power, which has been transformed from a short-range, defensive force into an air armada of heavy payload aircraft and strike helicopters (the MIG-21J, K and L; MIG 23/27; SU-17; SU-19; TU-22M Backfire bomber and Mi-24) capable of carrying a war into all of Western Europe. Deep air interdiction could threaten NATO's vulnerable fixed-site targets: supply bases, airfields, air-defense sites and nuclear weapons facilities.

Despite this gloomy assessment, however, the decisive defeat of Soviet arms in Lebanon during the summer of 1982 offers the possibility of a quick-fix solution to the Kremlin's ominous superiority in conventional weaponry. The victory of Israeli-modified American weapons and tactics over those of the Soviet Union presents the free world with a tremendous opportunity to reduce the impact of Russia's extraordinary growth in tactical forces and battlefield technology. It is clear that the Israelis made major breakthroughs in conventional and electronic weaponry designed to overwhelm and destroy Soviet-made weapons systems. Advanced, battle-proven technology and tactics offer a unique opportunity to diminish the present quantitative superiority of Soviet forces in Europe. These advances are in the areas of anti-armor, missile site suppression, and aerial combat, as well as command, control and communications (C3):

- ■ a modified 105 mm shell which pierced the honeycomb armor of the formidable Soviet T-72 main battle tank;
- ■ highly advanced Electronic Counter Measures (ECM) and strike techniques which neutralized and destroyed Syrian SA-6, SA-8 and SA-9 Soviet-made missile arrays without loss;
- ■ enhanced air-to-air missilery and other aerial ECM and tactics which resulted in an unprecedented combat kill ratio of at least 85–0 against Soviet aircraft; and
- ■ a unique C3 ability to coordinate air, land and sea operations down to the unit level.

This combination of combat-proven high technology and tactics, together with new NATO arms technology and targeting systems already under development, could conceivably revolutionize the overall U.S. defense posture and offers exciting prospects for arms control and disarmament negotiations. Furthermore, the adoption of these modern, advanced technologies could make a favorable impact upon future defense costs and the national budgets of the United States and our allies.

An enhanced defense for NATO forces, achieved through the incorporation of the lessons of the war in Lebanon, raises the intriguing possibility of reducing the reliance on escalation to tactical nuclear weapons because of conventional battlefield inferiority.

The entire Soviet "Wave Theory" of advance in the Central Front of NATO is based upon swift movement of mass formations of armor and infantry, closely supported by Warsaw Pact air, all protected by integrated mobile missile air defense systems. If Pact tanks can be knocked out with unique penetrating shells, if SAM sites can be neutralized and destroyed in large numbers, and if their aircraft can be shot down in a virtual "turkey shoot," then established Soviet military doctrine comes into question.

Information gleaned by the West since 1978 indicates that the Soviets are adhering to a master plan for the conquest of continental NATO forces without using nuclear weapons. Our war planners postulate that the Kremlin depends upon sowing dissension among the NATO allies in order to hinder, delay or prevent deployment of new weapon systems in Western Europe, as the Soviets have attempted to do in connection with NATO's deployment of new intermediate-range nuclear missiles. The Soviets' present tactics include encouraging the various European "peace" movements through seeming concessions, and appealing to the fears just below the surface in the peaceniks' arguments by a variety of bullying behavior. Some analysts believe that the shooting down of the Korean airliner in September of 1983 was in consonance with Soviet desires to present an image of unrepentent brutality.

Kremlin strategists are completely aware of the horrifying consequences of a nuclear conflict and their military literature makes it clear that they intend to win such an engagement, if it takes place. However, it is also clear that they define strategic victory as the occupation of Western Europe *without* fighting a nuclear war. For this reason, it is apparent that the Kremlin's pledge of "no first use" can be accepted at face value because it is in the Soviet's interests to prevent an escalation to nuclear weapons. Their current strategy depends upon enveloping Paris within ten to fourteen days and in seriously impeding the West's freedom of action by forestalling various contingency actions. The Kremlin expects that, at a minimum, several days will be required for the U.S. President and the NATO allies to agree upon allowing release of nuclear weapons for us in halting a Soviet *drang nach westen* and that therefore their overrunning of Germany must be substantially accomplished within that time frame in order to present the NATO allies with a *fait accompli*.

Their new doctrine was tested as recently as September 1981. ZAPAD-81 utilized 100,000 men in a war game which postulated a drive to the channel ports of Cherbourg and Brest. A key element in this new Soviet strategy of conquest is the Operational Maneuver Group (OMG). The basic division-sized force would be composed primarily of tanks but also would include integral mechanized infantry and mechanized artillery and would be provided with supporting helicopters. The OMG's function is to begin operating behind NATO's main defensive line within the first two days of the offensive. Ranging as far as 150 miles in advance of the main attacking echelon of Soviet forces, the OMG would assault or seize major targets in NATO's rear areas, including operationally important targets such as divisional and corps headquarters and nuclear weapons storage sites, in so doing seriously disrupting NATO's ability to mount an effective defense of its territory.[8]

Revelation of this new military structure highlights Soviet commitment to non-nuclear warfare, even as they continue to expand their nuclear arsenal and train their forces to fight in a nuclear environment. Introduction of their elite units into an invasion of Western Europe, if opposed by U.S. nuclear weapons, would produce high Soviet losses. Therefore, the Kremlin reiterates that *any* use of nuclear weapons by the United States would bring an all-out intercontinental nuclear exchange. Thus, the Soviets wish to threaten the American President with the possibility of destroying the United States if he attempts to save Europe.

Thus, the deployment of Pershing II and Cruise missiles poses a great problem for Moscow. Now that they are deployed, the Kremlin has no choice but to destroy them. The elimination of the West's battlefield threat could present the United States with the justification for *strategic* nuclear retaliation. As we have seen, however, patent Soviet superiority in that area of weaponry would forestall that option. Thus, the Soviets may plan on intimidating the United States with their awesome nuclear power while conquering NATO Europe with conventional weaponry.

Correlation of Sea Forces

NATO is more dependent on the sea than is the Warsaw Pact; its missions in the Atlantic theater are essentially power projection (amphibious missions and air support from carriers to supplement the new forward bases) and sea control (safe passage of merchant shipping carrying oil and other commodities). In the naval arena, too, Soviet forces, with their increasing sea-denial capabilities, are becoming a real threat to NATO. The erosion of NATO's advantage is due to several factors:

- Technology now favors sea-denial rather than control. Targeting and destruction at long range, for example, is enhanced by satellites for maritime reconnaissance and by stand-off systems such as air-to-surface missiles and SLCMs;

- Soviet-mine-laying equipment and techniques have been improving while NATO's mine-sweeping forces have been declining in both size and capability;
- Coverage of Soviet naval land-based strike aircraft has increased continuously, especially since introduction of the Backfire to the Soviet Naval Air Force;
- The Warsaw Pact can now deny substantial areas of sea to NATO, at least in the early stages of a conflict; the Eastern Mediterranean and the Baltic, Black and Barents Seas would probably be very hostile environments, as would be the Sea of Japan as discussed below.

The Warsaw Pact, however, still has some difficulties:

- It has to get into high seas before hostilities break out in order to avoid passing through "chokepoints" under NATO control (Dardanelles, Straits of Gibraltar, Skagerrak), or those which give them advantage to an intercepting force (Greenland-UK gap);
- Pact navies still lack assured sea-based fighter cover and would be vulnerable to sustained attack by NATO maritime strike aircraft when they are beyond the range of their shore-based fighter aircraft cover;
- Anti-submarine warfare advantages still lie with the West because of technology.

Convoy vulnerability is another concern. The United States is no longer confident that sufficient numbers of NATO's warships will be available quickly enough to escort European-bound convoys in the first days of the conflict and now, consequently emphasizes airlift and prepositioned stocks. This will reduce the danger to convoys in the early days of the war at sea and give a number of ASW units the time to hunt Soviet subs or to protect such high-value units as nuclear ballistic missile subs, carriers and amphibious forces. Obstacles to NATO sealift operations, however, continue to intensify, not least because of Soviet capability to sabotage, bomb or capture European ports on which logistic supply lines depend. This threat is particularly important because all of the major European ports designated to disembark NATO supplies for the central front are situated within the narrow confines of the North Sea.

Theater Nuclear Forces (TNF)

Since the mid-1970s the Soviets have modernized their tactical nuclear forces (TNF) to the point of superiority in the crucial categories of survivability, mobility and range. They have doubled the number of warheads targeted at Europe and introduced two new calibers of nuclear artillery and new nuclear-capable, deep-strike tactical aircraft in addition to the Backfire. They have deployed new missiles, including the mobile SS-20, SS-21, SS-22 and SS-23, all of which replace slow-reacting, inaccurate missiles.

In June of 1982 in Brussels, the defense ministers of thirteen NATO nations resolved to proceed with the deployment of 108 Pershing II and 464 cruise missiles, starting in December of 1983, unless a satisfactory arms control agreement was reached with the Soviets.

As we have seen, Soviet strategic offensive weapons capacities have doubled since the early 1970s. They have embarked on a highly successful program of building and dispatching to the corners of the earth highly sophisticated nuclear attack submarines and a powerful surface fleet. They are now busily reinvigorating their offensive bomber capacities, and have developed an ominous troop-carrying airlift capability.

On the ground the rapid offensive capabilities of Soviet and Warsaw Pact armies have been enhanced by marked increases in air assault units and attack helicopters. There is no doubt that Red Army units are in possession of chemical and biological weapons, the latter constituting an absolute violation of a 1972 convention agreement. Every day, their use of these horrifying weapons in Afghanistan enhances their ability to use them against NATO.

This marked acceleration of Soviet-Warsaw Pact capacities for offensive action can be met by NATO modernization and enhanced cooperation programs.

It must be realized, however, that even with the deployment of the Pershing II and cruise missiles, coupled with an undertaking to negotiate balanced arms reductions, the Soviets will *still* enjoy a pronounced margin of superiority in theater nuclear capacity vis-a-vis NATO. The Pershing II and cruise deployments therefore constitute a most reasonable expression of collective will and basic self interest. In view of the current imbalance of INF capacities in Europe, only those who ignore the basic arithmetic of respective force levels could think of the Pershing II and cruise deployment as Western escalation. And yet, the nuclear freeze advocates use just this argument to justify their position.

Great Britain, too, will maintain an independent nuclear deterrent: five new British Trident submarines are scheduled to replace the four boats which now carry the Polaris missile; but the first of the Tridents will not be in service before the mid-1990s.

7

The MX Muddle

When Casper Weinberger took over the Defense Department, the time was ripe for a serious re-examination of prevailing doctrines and contingency plans. There was strong public support for a major rebuilding of American military forces; more importantly, it was generally recognized that the military and diplomatic principles underlying the Carter Administration's policies had been found wanting. The new Defense Secretary and his immediate subordinates, however, were ill-prepared for the challenge. Having come to the Pentagon, for the most part, as outsiders with little or no defense experience, they felt they had to slow down the process of change in order to give themselves time to become familiar with the intricacies of the Department. As the weeks turned into months, they found themselves being caught up in the process of simply keeping the bureaucracy moving. They were soon captured by the defense bureaucracy as a whole and by their own staffs, many of whom, during the first important months, were Carter holdovers. Hence, many Carter defense policies and decisions were reaffirmed almost *pro forma*, without analysis.

In his first testimony before Congress, Weinberger made it clear that his major initiative was to be increased defense spending. He told the Senate Armed Services Committee: "We will build enough—and I hope in time—to redress the inferior position we now occupy. Our commitment to build is the best way to get the Soviets to stop." The priorities he laid out were the improvement of the combat effectiveness of the forces through better pay and more money for training and maintenance, the upgrading of U.S. strategic forces to redress the imbalance favoring the USSR, and the modernization of the country's conventional forces across the board. These priorities, though worthwhile, avoided the fundamental problem—devising a workable military strategy. Weinberger had been captivated by the same procurement mentality that had bewitched so many previous Secretaries of Defense. Secretaries preoccupied with comparing the relative merits of weapons system "X" or weapons systems "Y" have little time to devote to the larger questions of military strategy and the effective application of force. Thus, choice of weapons is made without reference to military strategy. The two major reviews that have so far been carried out in the Weinberger Department have concerned the Planning, Programming and Budgeting System and the Acquisition System. Reform in the Defense Department has been confined to issues of management.

Perhaps no other issue better illustrates the paucity of thinking on strategic arms in the Weinberger Defense Department than the muddle which has occurred over the MX missile. Although early on Weinberger testified that upgrading the country's strategic nuclear forces was a defense priority of the Reagan Administration, he took over the helm at Defense with few ideas as to just how best to upgrade these forces. Ironically, this subject had been a priority of the Reagan Defense Transition Team, but when William Van Cleave's Transition Team was disbanded, its written recommendations on strategic force enhancements were ignored. Thus, the new Secretary of Defense chose to start from scratch.

The Carter MX plan had envisioned the deployment of some two hundred MX missiles, each seventy-one feet in length and weighing 192,000 pounds, in 4,600 horizontal multiple protective structure (MPS). Each missile was to be shuttled among twenty-three horizontal shelters situated on either side of a road. These shelters, made of cast concrete and hardened to withstand up to 600 pounds per square inch (psi) of blast overpressure, were to be separated from one another by 5000 to 6000 feet to preclude the chance of one Soviet nuclear warhead destroying more than one shelter. The survivability of the MX missiles was to be guaranteed by the preservation of location uncertainty (PLU) and the ability to reshuffle the missiles if it was believed that their locations had been detected by the Soviets. Preservation of location uncertainty was to be implemented by equipping each of the shelters in the complex not occupied by the missile with a mass simulator that duplicated the MX's variety of physical and operational signatures. The total land area envisioned for deployment of this system was thirty square miles, exclusive of land for roads and support facilities.[1] The area most favored for such a deployment at the time President Carter left office was the Great Basin of western Utah and eastern Nevada.

From the beginning, Weinberger's position on MX was felt to be somewhat constrained by President Reagan's pre-election campaigning against the suitability of the Carter plan for multiple shelter basing in particular (though not the MPS concept itself). The expense of the Carter plan was also known to have bothered Weinberger.

In March 1981, the Secretary established the Townes committee, a group of scientists, civilians and retired senior military people, to re-examine the various MX basing options and report back to him on the preferred mode of deployment. The establishment of the panel was a bureaucratic maneuver by the Defense Secretary to allow him to postpone a final decision on the politically-sensitive basing question. The public announcement of the group's formation was greeted with dismay by many analysts in the defense community. It guaranteed another postponement of the MX basing decision and raised the specter of the missile's cancellation. After all, the Air Force had already conducted detailed evaluations of scores of MX basing modes and had finally chosen the Carter proposal as the least objectionable option.

During the following few months, the Townes Committee busied itself, first in bringing itself "up to speed" on the complexities of the deployment question and later in examining specific alternate basing proposals. One of the first proposals that the panel members examined was the ideas of deploying the MX aboard surface ships. This concept (designated *Hydra* after the successful Navy Project of the early 1960s) had an early supporter in the Defense Secretary himself. This plan envisioned canisterized MX missiles, equipped with flotation collars for added buoyancy, being carried aboard disguised merchant vessels. On command, these missiles would be rolled overboard and, at a suitable distance from the ships, remotely launched.[2] Panel briefings in the concept, however, disclosed a number of serious drawbacks to the *Hydra* scheme. Perhaps the most important hindrance was the vulnerability of MX-carrying surface ships to Soviet identification and targeting. Another problem had to do with the degraded missile accuracy provided by the sea-launching method employed.

Another alternative basing mode studied by the Townes group was *SUM* (Submerged Underwater Mobile). This proposal called for the deployment of canisterized MX missiles attached to small, conventionally-powered submarines. These coastal submarines, of some 450 tons displacement (in the original proposal) and carrying a crew of between twelve and fifteen, were to operate in 200-mile bands of ocean off the east and west coasts of the United States. The complement—of two or four missiles—was to be attached outside the subs' pressure hulls. Communication with the National Command Authority was to be maintained through the use of VLF (very low frequency) radio signals, using "awash-buoy" antennas; upon command, the canisterized missiles were to be released to float to the surface for launching. Because missile accuracy would be a problem for missiles launched in such a manner, guidance updates were to be provided to the missiles by a network of ground beacons.[3]

The Townes Panel also identified some major problems with this proposed basing scheme. For one thing, the 450-ton submarines initially proposed for use in *SUM* were found to be too small to handle the additional weight of the encapsulated missiles within safe reserve buoyancy requirements. The actual size of the boats had to be about twice as large, at the very minimum. This change in size requirements was found to necessitate the building of specially-designed submarines for the MX-carrying mission—an event that would have meant costs greater than projected and a far longer time to operational deployment.[4] Also, the proposed operating areas for the *SUM* boats consisted of only some 500,000 square miles of ocean, a region significantly smaller than that available to the Trident submarines (estimated to be about 18,000,000 square miles). The relatively small *SUM* deployment area would have made it easier for the Soviet Union to concentrate its countermeasures to defeat the system and thus increase the chances for their eventually finding a way to destroy the MX before it could be launched. Finally, the dependence of the MX missiles' accuracy on ground-beacons meant that the proper functioning of the system as a whole was entirely subject to the vulnerabilities of the external navigational network. Such beacons (and Global Positioning Satellites, for that matter) could be destroyed prior to the launching of a major Soviet attack on U.S. strategic offensive forces, or their data transmission could be jammed or blacked out by electro-magnetic pulse (EMP) effects from nuclear explosions.[5] This made the *SUM* boats' MX missiles capable of only area-target accuracy.

A third alternate basing mode for MX that received attention from the Panel was an air-basing scheme nicknamed Big Bird. It was a proposal that Weinberger later came to find particularly interesting, since it promised to nullify some of the political problems associated with the land-based deployment proposal. In late July 1981, rumors were rife that Weinberger was in favor of such a basing scheme. These reports came as a devastating blow to the Air Staff in the Pentagon, which was convinced that only a land-based, MPS mode for MX could provide the required safety, timeliness and missile accuracy.

The Big Bird concept postulated the installation of the missiles, one to a plane, aboard large, fuel-efficient, long-endurance aircraft. These aircraft would be based at two airfields—in the United States—and would fly long patrols out into the Atlantic and Pacific Oceans. Half the force would always be airborne.[6] This initial proposal went through a number of briefings, studies and revisions before finally being revised into the scheme advocated by the Defense Secretary. In this final version, a two-stage deployment plan was envisioned. In the first stage, the MX missiles were to be placed aboard newly constructed models of the C-5A transport aircraft, redesigned to handle the missiles and hardened against nuclear EMP effects. Some 100 of these aircraft, each carrying one MX missile on a cradle, would be deployed at fifty airstrips. Once airborne, the planes could jettison their deadly cargoes, the missiles being extracted from the rear of the aircraft by drogue chutes. At the achievement of vertical orientation, the MX's would be ignited and sent on their ballistic trajectories toward their targets in the Soviet Union. The necessary guidance updates were to be supplied by some of a network of 1,200 ground-based transmitters. At the end of the decade, when Stage Two was reached, the C-5A transports would be retired from their missile duties and sent to the Military Airlift Command to augment the country's strategic airlift. Their replacements were to be special, long-endurance aircraft. These planes, constructed of composite materials and with an extremely long wingspan for increased lift, would be capable of remaining aloft for forty-eight hours without refueling and could sustain flight with refueling for up to 5–6 days. Operating normally at 100 knots airspeed, they would increase their airspeed to between 130 and 180 knots and climb to between 10,000 and 20,000 feet of altitude before jettisoning their missiles.[7]

The Townes Panel heard a number of briefings that stressed the potential vulnerabilities of an air-mobile system. Cost was one major factor. The Air Force estimated that the acquisition costs alone for the C-5A high airmobile option (100 aircraft on strip alert) would come to about $54 billion and operating costs over a 12.5 year life cycle would add another $22 billion to that figure.[8] However, the survivability of the air-basing option was an even more serious weakness in the airmobile concept. The survivability of the aircraft was highly dependent upon the early receipt of strategic warning that would enable the planes to take off and fly out of the endangered areas before Soviet warheads struck. Soviet submarines stationed off the coasts of the United States, it was calculated could fire depressed-trajectory missiles that could begin arriving on airbases in the country's north central interior as early as six-and-a-half minutes after breaking water. This short time-span would allow little time even for aircraft on strip alert to clear the immediate impact areas since signals detected by the *PAVE PAWS* warning radars at Beale Air Force Base in California and Otis Air Force Base in Massachusetts must be processed through SAC, NORAD and NMCC. A barrage of Soviet warheads could effectively blanket an extremely large area of sky with nuclear explosions to follow up the destruction wrought by the SLBM attacks. Such nuclear barrages would destroy all aircraft aloft in the affected area, making it necessary for planes to be several hundred miles out from their bases by the time Soviet warheads started arriving—something very difficult for the relatively slow C-5A transports to accomplish.[9] Again, the question of missile accuracy was raised in connection with the airmobile proposal. Missiles launched in mid-air from moving aircraft have an even more formidable task in attempting to achieve high accuracy than do water-launched missiles. The inertial measurement units of the missiles must not only correctly reflect their vehicle's exact location at time of launch, but also their firing azimuths. This information can be supplied only by guidance information external to the missile and, as such, is subject to the same potential blackouts already referred to in connection with the SUM system.

The Townes Panel, having reached its negative conclusions regarding the characteristics of the alternate sea- and air-basing options for MX deployment, reported to the Defense Secretary in September. At that time it was widely believed by defense analysts that Weinberger would be forced to choose a land-based deployment for MX. It was expected that he would decide to go ahead with the horizontal MPS system for MX, albeit a somewhat scaled-down version. Thus it came as a complete surprise when, on October 2, 1981, the Reagan Administration announced that the MX missile was to be initially emplaced in fixed silos.

The MX proposal, announced by the President with some fanfare, as part of a five-point strategic package, envisioned the deployment of up to fifty MX missiles in existing Titan II and

Minuteman missile silos, starting in 1986. These silos were to be upgraded to withstand pressure of approximately 5,000 pounds per square inch to resist blast overpressure effects from near-miss nuclear explosions, and thus increase the chances for MX's survivability over the short term.[10] In the meantime, additional studies were to be conducted to determine the best long-term solution to MX survivability.

Weinberger had evidently made the decision against horizontal MPS basing for the MX missile on purely political grounds. Opposition to basing the missiles in Utah and Nevada had been growing in intensity during the previous few months; several Senators from these states, one of whom—Paul Laxalt—was a close friend of the President, had made known their categorical opposition to the proposed basing scheme. Moreover, the President had campaigned against the Carter-approved basing mode.

Whatever his reasons for urging fixed, vulnerable silo basing for the new missile, Weinberger's choice was immediately opposed *en masse* by defense analysts both inside and outside the Pentagon. This was particularly so since the decision clearly flew in the face of hard information regarding the serious vulnerability of American missile silo to Soviet hard-target warheads. In fact, William Van Cleave, who had just been designated the Administration's chairman of the President's General Advisory Committee on arms control (but whose nomination was subsequently withdrawn by the Administration), told Reuter's Press Wire that the MX decision did not "reflect sufficient concern with the window of vulnerability," that it "ran afoul of crisis stability" and "could tempt the other side to launch first."

Throughout the fall of 1981, Secretary Weinberger vainly attempted to convince members of Congress that his ill-conceived plan for MX was strategically sound. In his testimony before Congress he was forced to stress again and again that the emplacement of forty of the new ICBMs in super-hardened Titan and Minuteman missile silos was only going to be an interim solution to the basing problem. He also kept making the point that since the Titan II missiles were already scheduled for deactivation, it would be better to put newly-produced MX missiles into these empty holes than merely to place them into warehouse storage until the new basing systems were ready. Despite the Defense Secretary's assurances about the workability of this scheme, members of Congress with a serious interest in MX remained unconvinced. For one thing, the cost of rendering the silos ready for MX and of superhardening them to 5,000 psi was calculated to be high—a total of from five to seven billion dollars, of which some three billion dollars would actually be needed for the hardening process itself.[11] Yet even more crucial to Caspar Weinberger's credibility on the issue was the conviction of a number of the Members that Soviet SS-18 ICBMs were accurate enough to destroy even MX missiles in superhardened silos. Thus they regarded as illusory Weinberger's belief that such a basing plan could provide even an interim solution.

As the Air Force began to study the Weinberger MX proposal seriously, its impracticality became even more evident. It was discovered that few of the Titan silos could be hardened to anything close to 5,000 psi because of the geological strata in which the silos had been situated. Also, the Titan sites were located further south than the Minuteman missile fields, and this would necessitate reducing the number of RVs carried by the MX missiles in order to provide full-range coverage of Soviet targets. Moreover, the Titan silos' much larger separation distances (ten to twelve miles apart instead of the three to five miles separation between silos in the Minuteman fields) would increase drastically the difficulty of defending each eighteen missile flight with a standard configuration ballistic missile defense system.[12]

Superhardening the existing Minuteman silos was also found to be highly impractical. Although the diameter and depth of such increased-hardened silos could physically accommodate a missile as large as MX, the incapsulated missiles would fit so tightly into the holes that there would remain insufficient "rattle space" (clearance between the missile and the surrounding walls of the silo, needed to allow for the horizontal motion of the missile during nuclear ground shock waves).[13] Correcting this serious deficiency, however, would necessitate increasing the volume of each silo beyond the thirty percent maximum increase allowed under the SALT I Interim Agreement on Offensive Arms.

Congress settled the matter of superhardening in late 1981 by mandating that only twenty million of the $334 million requested by the Administration could be spent in the fiscal year 1982 Defense budget for superhardening silos in connection with an MX interim basing mode. Having already announced that the use of Titan silos for MX had been dropped, the Weinberger Defense Department finally acknowledged the inevitable when it announced on February 11, 1982, that the first forty MX missiles would be placed in existing Minuteman missile silos which had not been reinforced for added hardness. The Defense Department spokesman making the announcement acknowledged that the Administration had finally agreed with Congress that "hardening on an interim basis wasn't necessarily worth the money." The Administration's indecision spurred Congress into pressing President Reagan to announce a final basing mode for MX by 1 December 1982. In desperation, therefore, the Administration chose a method of deployment, Closely Spaced Basing (known also as Dense Pack), which had serious flaws. Under this basing scheme, one hundred MX missiles would be housed in one hundred superhardened capsules, each eighteen hundred feet apart in a column array some fourteen miles long by one mile wide. The combination of capsule superhardness, close spacing and the column array was supposed to assure the survival of more than fifty percent of the MX missiles in the event of a Soviet first strike.[14]

Apart from the technical objections to the Closely Spaced Basing mode (whether the silos can be superhardened against nuclear weapons effects up to 100,000 PSA, and whether the theory of fratricide will actually work in practice), there is the distinct possibility that by 1989 when all one hundred MX missiles had been deployed at Warren Air Force Base in Wyoming, the Soviet Union would have developed the capability of overwhelming the survivability advantages supposedly being offered by Dense Pack basing. Thus it would be necessary to develop an ABM system and introduce deceptive basing to give some measure of protection to the closely-spaced missiles. There were signs of growing opposition in Congress to the deployment of the MX in what could be perceived as a vulnerable fixed basing mode. Failure to acquire congressional approval for Dense Pack would be tantamount to killing the MX. Casper Weinberger should have realized that by substituting his incompetently-drafted scheme for MX, he was threatening the entire strategic forces modernization effort.

Congressional concern about the efficacy of Dense Pack basing was not long in coming. President Reagan formally presented the plan to Congress on November 22, 1982. In early December the House of Representatives and the Senate passed amendments in the process of voting on the second Continuing Budget Resolution which withheld a large portion of the Fiscal 1983 MX funding. Under this Congressional action, funding for MX missile and basing procurement was reduced by $998 million and obligation on expenditure of another $560 million earmarked for full-scale engineering development of a permanent basing mode was restricted until such time as both Houses had approved of the basing mode.[15] The funding for MX was to be withheld until the President had submitted a report (due by March 1, 1983) to the Appropriations Committees on the permanent basing mode for the missile, and detailing technical assessments of basing modes for alternate missile systems. It looked as if the MX program was in danger of being killed.

Almost as a last resort, President Reagan seized upon the idea of forming a commission composed of prestigious former Defense Department officials and other notable individuals to reexamine the strategic modernization effort. On January 3, 1983, Reagan officially established the President's Commission on Strategic Forces, under the chairmanship of Lieutenant General Brent Scowcroft, (USAF (Ret.), who had served as Assistant to the President for National Security Affairs in the Ford Administration. The other ten members of the Commission included such respected individuals as Richard Helms, former Director of Central Intelligence, and Alexander Haig, the recently-resigned Secretary of State. In addition to its formal membership, four former Secretaries of Defense served as senior counselors to the Commission.

During the next several months the Commission held twenty-eight full meetings and many smaller conferences on strategic force modernization questions. Inevitably they retraced the same MX basing issues which had been investigated by the Air Force and DoD years before. Finally, on April 6, 1983, the Commission submitted its report to the President.

In its report, the President's Commission on Strategic Forces dealt with the MX basing muddle by proposing an interlinked three-part solution: initiating engineering design of a new, small, single-warhead ICBM which would have reduced target value and which would permit greater basing flexibility; seeking new arms control agreements with the Soviet Union in order to enhance strategic stability; and deploying one hundred MX missiles in existing Minuteman silos.[16] It is ironic that after years of effort had been expended in attempting to devise basing modes that would reduce the vulnerability of MX to Soviet missile attack, the Commission found a way of finessing the whole vulnerability question. It did so by asserting that missile vulnerability was no longer a very important issue. As the Commission's report stated: "In the judgment of the Commission, the vulnerability of such silos in the near term, viewed in isolation, is not a sufficiently dominant part of the overall problem of ICBM modernization to warrant other immediate steps being taken [to lessen that vulnerability] such as closely-spacing new silos or ABM defense of those silos. This is because of the mutual survivability shared by the ICBM force and the bomber force in view of the different types of attacks that would be launched at each. . . ."

President Reagan endorsed the recommendations of the Scowcroft Commission on April 19th. To the Administration's good luck, despite the report's apparent inconsistencies in strategic thinking, it found strong supporters on Capitol Hill. Some former anti-MX Congressmen found the report's pro-arms control recommendations influential in changing their views on ICBM modernization, while others were pleased by the report's call for development of a new, small ICBM as a follow-on to the limited deployment of MX.[17]

Against all odds, the Scowcroft Commission had turned an unmitigated Weinberger Defense Department disaster into a constrained but ongoing modernization effort. On May 26, 1983, Congress released the fiscal year (FY) 1983 MX funds which had been withheld under the Continuing Resolution. And in September, Congress passed the FY 1984 DoD Authorization containing funding for MX.

Yet although the MX program was again on track, it was a program even more hostage to political pressures from Congress. The deployment of only one hundred MX missiles and the emplacement of these in vulnerable, fixed site missile silos was a far cry from what had been envisioned for MX several years earlier. In addition, the continued health of MX had clearly become tied to Congressional approval of the Administration's arms control initiatives and its support of the small missile program.

The MX missile would be a major addition to the U.S. strategic offensive forces. Planned to carry ten Mk-12A reentry vehicles with enhanced-yield nuclear warheads, it will have an accuracy enabling it to destroy the hardest Soviet targets with regularity, including targets such as superhardened missile silos and Soviet command bunkers. When it is fully deployed, it will fulfill a need that cannot be met with any confidence by any other portion of our strategic forces. For example, the Minuteman III missiles already in the ICBM force, even those equipped with Mk-12A reentry vehicles and NS-20 guidance sets, will not match the MX's hard-target destructive potential.

The new missile, with its larger, more accurate payload, is needed to cope with a Soviet target set that has been expanded and superhardened (up to 5,000 psi for some silos) over the past decade. Nonetheless, the MX missile itself is of little deterrent value if it is not deployed in a survivable manner. In fact, the vulnerable MX force could tempt the Soviets to strike first in a crisis or confrontation.

The Air Force has studied and restudied basing modes for the MX since 1972 and it concluded that the most effective and timely solution to ICBM vulnerability is a multiple protective shelter system. It was unlikely that more study, as envisioned by Weinberger, would reveal a better way of basing MX. Both deep underground basing and an air-mobile scheme (which apparently still retains Weinberger's interest), will not solve the problem of vulnerability.

The most logical approach would be to go back to multiple vertical shelter deployment for both Minuteman and MX. By adopting the multiple vertical protective shelter system originally recommended by the Air Force, the U.S. can improve the survivability of its ICBM force. A vertical shelter is a more effective design than the horizontal MPS system. Conceptually, a vertical MPS basing mode is similar to the horizontal mode rejected by the Secretary of Defense. The vertical shelters would still be connected by a road network, and the MX missiles shuttled from one to another in a random fashion. Decoys would still be necessary to ensure that the location of the missile remain unknown to the Soviets. But a vertical shelter is structurally harder than a horizontal shelter. Thus survivability is increased.

What the vertical MPS plan would give up in missile reshuffling time (taking an estimated 22.5 minutes for removal or emplacement of the MX missile rather than the estimated five minutes for the horizontal system), it would more than make up in individual shelter hardness.[18] Vertical structures are better able to withstand the effects of nuclear blast, both peak overpressure and dynamic pressure (winds). In addition, the vertical shelters' surface-flush doors would be less exposed than horizontal shelter doors to radiation (including radiation-induced EMP) and thermal effects of nuclear blasts. Furthermore, although it was planned to harden the horizontal shelters to 6000 psi (which would be pushing the engineering state-of-the-art), vertical shelters can be hardened well above 1,000 psi, while using less concrete and steel. Finally, surface-flush vertical doors would provide a far more difficult target aspect to incoming warheads than would horizontal ones, and more such shelters could be packed into a given land area.[19]

Against an attempt by the Soviet Union to defeat MPS by either fractionating ICBM payloads or by expanding the number of ICBMs, MPS basing could be designed to accommodate both an increase in the number of shelters and/or missiles above the number in the Carter baseline system (4600 shelters and 200 missiles). Further, ballistic missile defense of an MPS system would be effective in reducing further the Soviet threat. The Army's Ballistic Missile Defense Systems Command has been developing a system known as LoADS (Low Altitude Defense System). The project's staff was specifically tasked with designing LoADS to function with the multiple protective structure basing mode. Each LoADS defense unit would consist of a small phased-array radar, using high power output and a narrow beamwidth to improve anti-jamming protection, a data processor for handling trajectory information, and several interceptor missiles armed with low-yield nuclear warheads. Designed to be enclosed in a cylinder similar to the one housing the MX missile, it would be fitted into place in one of the available horizontal shelters.[20] LoADS could be designed for defending a vertical shelter system. Each MPS cluster of twenty-three shelters would be protected by one LoADS unit, which would be programmed to defend the one shelter in the cluster containing the MX missile. Because of its role as a "preferential defender," only defending the hidden missile, not the decoys, LoADS would force the Soviets to target twice as many warheads (46 for a 23-shelter cluster) to guarantee destruction of the hidden missile. Because of the extremely short engagement times (with intercepts to take place below 50,000 feet, leaving ten seconds from lock-on to intercept) and the limited number of interceptor missiles available to each LoADS unit, it would not be fail-safe.

LoADS could be made more effective if it is combined with an exoatmospheric defense capability—the so-called "layered defense." In the Army's Overlay exoatmospheric concept, rocket-launched infrared sensing probes would be lifted into space as soon as satellite warning sensors relayed information on an impending Soviet attack. The rocket-borne sensors would act to furnish data on the projected trajectories of arriving Soviet reentry vehicles (RVs) to ground stations. These ground stations would, in turn, launch interceptors equipped with infrared sensors and carrying a number of non-nuclear kill vehicles into the threat corridors. Each kill vehicle would be deployed against a single target. Using its rocket motor and on-board scanner to home-in on the approaching RV (at closing speeds approaching 25,000 miles per hour) Soviet warheads would be destroyed either by direct collision with, or by dispensing in their path, a barrier of metal fragments that would disable the warhead.[21] Overlay would work in conjunction with LoADS and would reduce the number of penetrating RVs.

Weinberger's decision not to base the MX in multiple shelters greatly complicates BMD and will force a major redesign of LoADS by the Ballistic Missile Defense Systems Command, further postponing the date on which such a system could be operationally deployed. Weinberger's decision on MX basing and his failure to recommend steps to improve Minuteman survivability reflect a lack of understanding of the strategic concepts underpinning a multiple protective shelter system, and the mistaken notion that MPS per se is a Carter program. Further, the tardiness of a decision on ICBM basing reflects Weinberger's attempt to redefine the "window of vulnerability." Instead of the open window of the early 1980s, Weinberger is now contending that the window will open in the late 1980s—when Reagan programs are planned to begin coming on line. In other words, the campaign statements on the "window of vulnerability" early in the decade were simply rhetorical. Will such a rationalization stand the test of analysis? Such a redefinition of the "window of vulnerability" cannot redefine the Soviet threat. That threat is immediate. It can be expected to grow during the 1980s—it cannot be countered by promises to do something in the late 1980s.

In sum, the overall trend in Weinberger's strategic force enhancement program is actually toward a weakening of the land-based missile portion of our strategic triad. In addition, the strategic modernization proposal of October 2, 1981 is deficient—it provides no strategic force enhancement available for the critical 1982–86 period because it is already apparent that none of the major systems—MX, B-1B, Stealth and Trident II—will be operational before 1986 *at the earliest*.

Not only is Dense Pack less likely to garner final Congressional approval, but the current MX basing plan raises the specter of the destabilizing policy of launch on warning or launch under attack. With a vulnerable force, the incentive to launch before Soviet warheads destroy the force will be great indeed. Although the Administration may hope that threatening the USSR's ICMBs with Dense Pack will both show U.S. allies that the United States is not inferior in strategic arms and give the Soviets an incentive to seek equitable arms control agreements, critics point to the destabilizing aspects, since both sides have incentives to "use or lose" the ICBM force. When moreover, this realization is coupled with the knowledge that strategic warning is often ambiguous and that Presidential release procedures will remain extremely time-consuming, the instabilities and questions inherent in this approach becomes clear.

It is apparent that the Weinberger Pentagon does not grasp the urgent need for improving the survivability of America's deterrent. In the past, it was U.S. policy to maintain a strong triad of landbased ICBMs, SLBMs and bombers. Has the U.S. under Reagan opted for a dyad of bombers and submarine-launched missiles? It is clear that Weinberger has not examined the foreign policy implications of a vulnerable deterrent. Unless these issues are addressed, and revisions made in the program, the Administration's strategic package will continue to lack a sound strategic framework. After years of neglect and underfunding against the Soviet threat, America's security problems will not be solved by a purely management approach. While everyone is for "better management," the fundamental issue remains one of strategy backed by substantial increases in defense spending. There is no other way to restore the military balance of power.

Failure to restore this balance would result not merely in the scaling down of U.S. commitments around the world but also in the termination of security guarantees to Western Europe and Japan. The loss of the Middle East and Southern Africa, regions that are indispensable to the economic security of the West, would portend the final surrender of our Allies to Soviet domination. The security of the West depends on denying the Soviets control of the Middle East and the Persian Gulf. Conceding control of this region to the USSR would be nothing less than the final retreat of America. There would be no second chance. A disturbing inclination to accept the idea of living in the shadow of superior Soviet power seems to have come over Western Europe, encouraging increased neutralism politically, and passivism psychologically. To halt such a decline, and thus block the way to Soviet hegemony in Europe, the United States must begin to recover its squandered strategic assets.

As for the Far East, it is surely clear that one area in which a new global balance could be struck is in the Pacific Basin. East Asia comprises one-third of the world's population and in its bounds six of the largest standing armies are concentrated. It is an area of the globe where interests of the U.S., Soviet Union, China and Japan intersect. Yet the Reagan Administration Defense Department, blind to the interplay of the forces whose control is the true target of the Soviet Executive, approaches national security issues, as well as the global factors that are the background for national security, from a managerial, budgetary perspective. The Department, in short, has made itself a dupe of the Kremlin, just as the White House itself, for all its bursts of rhetoric, remains essentially passive.

8

The Overall Imbalance

Meanwhile, as the Kremlin articulates its overall plan for sub-version, encirclement and penetration, it is also attending indus-triously to the macro factors of military power—its nuclear arms program and its manipulation of diplomacy. The Soviet bureauc-racy, incapable of satisfying Soviet citizens' needs as consumers, is quite capable of defending itself militarily.

In the face of Soviet military power, America is, in fact, ham-strung by substantial deficiencies—all of them self-imposed.

Since 1960, U.S. security has been based on disarmament and the blind search for arms control agreements, accompanied by a massive erosion of the U.S. defense-industrial base and an attempt to moderate Soviet behavior with preferential access to American technology, food and financial credits. The U.S. and the West wanted to believe that Moscow had conceded that it could not afford to overload its budget with military expenditures and that it would have to maintain peaceful relations with the capitalist world in order to cope with its growing economic shortcomings. Even when Soviet actions in the Middle East, Africa and Afghanistan belied Khrushchev's honeyed utterances, the compulsive desire of the West to seek security through consumerism instead of defense readiness led to the rationalizing of Soviet moves as "defensive," "preventive," or as exploitation of random opportunities. Angola, Ethiopia, Nicaragua were explained as events that would have unfolded even if Soviet or Cuban resources had not been present. In short, the legacy of the 1960–80 period is not only one of American decline but one of Soviet expansion aided and abetted by the liberal transfer of savings that was effected through underfunded defense budgets to the Soviet Union and that helped underwrite Moscow's drive for supremacy.

The shift in power can be traced to Nikita Khrushchev's speeches in 1959–60, which represent a supreme Soviet disinformation ploy. Seemingly contradicting Lenin, Khrushchev declared, "War is not inevitable." Russia, he said, because of its space achievements, would not need to make lavish expenditures on strategic and conventional weaponry. The wars of the future would be small, localized and inexpensive "wars of national liberation"—which would strengthen the socialist camp. The USSR, he asserted, would turn its attention to consumerism, overtaking the American economy and becoming a vast new commercial frontier.

Above all, Khrushchev offered to usher in an era of peaceful coexistence. The American drive to contain budgetary deficits required such rationalizations for reducing defense spending. The Soviet drive needed access to American (and Western) resources on a privileged basis to compensate for the budgetary restraints that would otherwise have impeded the Russian military buildup.

In this manner, the USSR, with an economy about half the size of America's, has been able to craft a nuclear and conventional arsenal of overpowering proportions. The U.S., on the other hand, is facing severe pressures to cut its projected defense appropriations on the grounds that it cannot afford to match Soviet spending. The immediate time frame is crucial. Whatever may be considered to be the Soviet lead in the "correlation of forces," Moscow is in a position to extend its lead in the immediate future by virtue of the existence in the USSR of the huge industrial base for military production created while the U.S. was dismantling its potential. The U.S. will need billions of dollars in capital expenditures to rebuild capacity before it strengthens its arsenal. The Soviets, meanwhile, need only operate their production lines close to capacity in order to maintain or increase their lead, especially if they can count on continued Western willingness to underwrite the Russian military budget with technology transfers and credits.

U.S. military forces are now virtually incapable of fighting and winning any war with the Soviet Union. Since the Truman years, the formulation of sound military strategy in the United States has been hampered to some extent by the artificial distinction between strategic offensive—that is, nuclear—forces and conventional —general purpose-military forces. This dichotomy arose because American planners deemed strategic nuclear weapons (and to a lesser extent, tactical nuclear weapons) too destructive for their use ever to be seriously contemplated by rational decision-makers. It was assumed that a capacity to retaliate against the civilian population of either side would be sufficient to deter a first strike. Because of this strongly-held belief, almost the entire military emphasis was placed on the deterrent value of such weapons. The primary focus of strategic planning was the devising of theoretical constructs for crisis management and nuclear war avoidance rather than on determining doctrine, strategy and tactics for the use of these weapons in case deterrence failed and nuclear war occurred. American nuclear superiority thus was not maintained and the 1960s and 1970s were characterized by futile efforts to educate the Soviets in the horrors of mutual assured destruction (MAD).

The United States not only repeatedly stressed that it intended to allow Moscow to match its strategic nuclear capability, but it demonstrated the point by unilateral restraint. Expenditures for strategic weapons in the 1960s were reduced to one-third of the constant-dollar average of the previous decade. This lower level was maintained for fifteen years, with concentration on technical improvements alone. Development of counterforce capability was restrained: only small multiple independently-targeted reentry vehicles (MIRVs), restricted to the purpose of penetrating possible Soviet ABM systems, were built. Improvements in yield and accuracy on the new Poseidon and Minuteman III were purposely limited to those appropriate for attacking economic and industrial targets, and were intended to be relatively ineffective against "hard" targets such as Soviet missile silos. The objective of this weapons policy was to promote MAD as a self-denying ordinance against counterforce capability. Such was the doctrine under which the United States negotiated and then signed the SALT I agreements in 1972.

By contrast, the Soviet Union's leadership did not choose to emulate U.S. theories of stability and deterrence. Their setbacks in the Berlin Blockade, the Korean War and the Cuban Missile crisis merely emphasized their traditional Clausewitzian approach to war as the continuation of politics by other means. There was nothing in Soviet writings and behavior to suggest any acceptance of MAD. On the contrary, Soviet defense literature explicitly rejected such a doctrine. While trying to deter the U.S. from using military means to oppose Soviet expansion, Soviet forces are structured to fight, survive and win a nuclear war regardless of the "unthinkability" of such a war in Western minds. Whereas the United States unilaterally limited its nuclear programs in the mid-sixties, the Soviets forged ahead, on the diametrically opposite view that there is indeed a point of absolute nuclear superiority that can overwhelm the opponent's nuclear deterrent—politically and, if necessary, militarily. The net result of these divergent approaches to strategy formulation since the Kennedy Administration has been the steady erosion of the very deterrent upon which we have lavished so much of our attention and political capital.

Today, within thirty minutes of launch order, the Soviet ICBM force could destroy the entire political-military leadership of the United States; its command and control, its land-based strategic forces, and its military-related industry. The United States' ICBM force cannot inflict similar damages on the Soviet Union. Despite a superior technology, the U.S. has not built forces that can threaten the Soviet ICBM force or Soviet command and control. Even after absorbing the full weight of the U.S. ICBM force, the

Soviet ICBM force could strike back with devastating effect against a wide variety of U.S. military and political targets. Our conscious decision not to threaten the Kremlin's strategic missile force allows the Soviets to maintain a strategic advantage. They continue to invest heavily in first-strike war-fighting capabilities rather than in second-strike deterrent forces.

Today, the Soviet Union exceeds the United States in more than 80 percent of all measures of strategic nuclear capability, and it is rapidly closing the remaining gaps. U.S. strategic forces are vulnerable to attack. At present, our total ICBM retaliatory capability is but a fraction of a single element of the Soviet ICBM force—their SS-18 heavy ICBMs. A brief summary comparison of U.S. and Soviet strategic capabilities will exemplify the problem. The U.S. has 550 Minutemen III missiles, 300 of which are being fitted with three Mark 12-A warheads, each yielding 335 kilotons and accurate to .12 nautical mile. The remainder carry three Mark-12 warheads each, with the same accuracy, but half the explosive force. There are also 450 Minuteman II missiles, each of which carries a single one-megaton warhead and is accurate to .2 nautical mile, plus less than 45 Titan II's (now being phased out in accordance with an Administration plan to have the entire force deactivated by 1987), which carry less accurate nine-megaton warheads. In addition, the U.S. has 34 ballistic missile submarines, 19 of which carry Poseidon missiles, each with an average of 10 warheads; 12 submarines carry 16 Trident I missiles. Six older Polaris subs have been converted to attack roles, and three new Ohio-class Trident submarines are in operation. The U.S. has some 300 operational B52Gs and Hs and FB-111 strategic bombers.

Overall, the U.S. now has about 9000 strategic warheads, none of which are designed to destroy Soviet missiles in their silos. They were designed instead to destroy soft targets such as urban-industrial complexes. Our most capable warhead, the Mark 12-A, would stand only about one-in-three chance of destroying a hardened Soviet silo. Our submarine-launched warheads have practically no such chance at all. The reality is that although President Carter's PD-59 directed the Joint Chiefs of Staff to emphasize counter-military targeting, none of our strategic systems was in fact originally designed for this purpose.

The Soviet Union has deployed about 308 SS-18s, containing almost 3000 half-megaton/megaton range warheads, almost as accurate as any in the American arsenal. There are also 360 SS-19s, each armed with six half-megaton accurate warheads, and 150 four-warhead SS-17s. Altogether, these three fourth-generation Soviet ICBMs could furnish almost 6000 warheads, the majority of them having a high probability of destroying American silos. In addition, the Soviets have deployed almost 600 older SS-11 single-warhead missiles. Finally, the Soviets have some 1250 inaccurate, city-killing warheads deployed in sixty-two strategic ballistic missile submarines. In an attack on the U.S., the Soviet's 130-odd long-range bombers can be supplemented by Backfire aircraft, since the U.S. is virtually without effective air defenses. In this category, the disparity is striking. In air defense surveillance radars, the U.S. has fewer than 120 as opposed to Moscow's 7,000; in interceptor aircraft, less than 300 against 2,500[1]; and no surface-to-air missile launchers against 10,000. The Soviets also have an extensive ABM research and development capability and may be developing a rapidly deployable ABM system.

Curiously, the Department of Defense's Annual Posture Statement for 1980 did not mention what could be read in *Aviation Week* about the Soviet ABM-X-3 system, which depends on existing battle management radars, some rapidly-transportable guidance radars and two missiles superior to the Spartan and Sprint, which the U.S. discarded ten years ago. The ABM-X-3 system could be built secretly, stockpiled and quickly deployed. In addition, the Soviets are reported to be orbiting an anti-satellite (ABAT) battle station (Cosmos 1267) capable of destroying U.S. satellites and even the space shuttle. *Aviation Week* reports that Cosmos 1267 is armed with clusters of one-meter-long miniature ASAT interceptors guided by infrared sensors and possibly radar homing devices. The new Soviet system could destroy U.S. military communications satellites, further degrading the capabilities of U.S. intercontinental weapons.

In 1981, the last year an official assessment was made, Soviet military spending rose at a steady rate—4 percent higher than the previous—even though the economy remained stagnant and there was a systematic decline in the standard of living.

In the area of civil defense, the disparity is even more dangerous. While the Soviets have dedicated blast shelters for that 10 percent of their urban population (and up to 25 percent if necessary) deemed critical to continuity of function of the Soviet Union; the U.S. by contrast does not yet have a serious civil defense program (as required under mutual assured destruction doctrine). It is this disparity that lends credence to the belief of the military and political leadership of the Soviet Union that it is possible to fight and win a nuclear war. Twenty years ago, by their criteria of victory and under the best of circumstances, they would have lost. Today even using conservative assumptions, they would win.

While Moscow emphasized the correlation between military power and geopolitics in the extension of Soviet power and influence, Washington emphasized economic assistance as the best way to stabilize the Third World and to counter Soviet expansionism. The West's erroneous views of the sixties became the détente of the seventies—a decade in which American military power declined further. Thus, under cover of "peaceful co-existence" in the 1960–80 period, the USSR built up history's most powerful constellation of military forces and pre-positioned combat-ready personnel to threaten U.S. security interests. America's unilateral restraint gave the Soviets the opportunity to develop the capability to destroy U.S. deterrent forces. At the same time, the notion that major confrontations are inherently cataclysmic because of the risk of escalation of a nuclear war facilitated Soviet efforts to divide the United States from Western Europe, where the risk of such confrontation appears greatest. Moreover, while trying to use the threat of escalation to paralyze American and European will, Moscow was also able to underwrite and accelerate its military buildup with the help of Western resources, credits and technology.

Since the likelihood of Soviet aggression can be expected to increase in proportion to Moscow's perception of the strategic balance as favourable, the United States must embark on its own two-pronged and integrated military buildup: the restoration of its nuclear deterrent and a modernization of its conventional capabilities.

The fundamental problem is created by the urgent need for a clear strategic framework into which the modernization of U.S. defenses must fit within the broader context of foreign policy goals.

Irrational and emotional fears of nuclear weapons serve to undermine the security of the nation. The United States cannot successfully compete with the Soviet Union if its leaders and people hold erroneous perceptions of nuclear weapons and exaggerated fears concerning the likelihood of general war. There is no need to emphasize how destructive nuclear war would be, but the only realistic alternative to nuclear surrender is deterrence. No strategy can completely eliminate risk. But if the U.S. makes rational decisions in structuring its nuclear deterrent forces and nuclear policy, the risk of nuclear war can be kept very low. The world that we live in is not free of risk and never can be made so. To pretend that it can be so fashioned would be utterly irresponsible. A nation that is unwilling to accept the world as it is—to accept risk—cannot preserve its freedom, and a quest for peace through appeasement and unilateralism will eventually lead to the very war it seeks to avoid.

The U.S. cannot accept anything less than nuclear parity with the Soviet Union (with adequate deterrent survivability), and it should strive for nuclear superiority. With adequate funding the vulnerabilities of our deterrent could be erased within a decade. Nuclear superiority is not unattainable. The level of expenditures devoted to nuclear forces by the Soviet Union is clearly not prohibitive. The Soviets do not invest in the most effective possible fashion. Given our technical advantage, we could regain nuclear superiority within fifteen years—regardless of what the Soviets do. Even if we reject superiority and base policy on strategic parity, we must regain a survivable ICBM force capable of threatening Soviet ICBMs and strategic command and control capability—their nuclear war-fighting capacity. We must be able to threaten the Soviet government in a retaliatory attack and to destroy a high percentage of Soviet conventional and theater nuclear military power. We also need some ability to limit damage through active and civil defenses. Our bomber forces must be modernized to assure effective penetration of Soviet defenses.

Candidate Reagan perceived the "widening window of vulnerability" in the strategic arms posture of the United States and committed his administration to redressing the imbalance as a necessary step in assuring the future security of the nation. Today, however, in the fourth year in office of a presumably strong, pro-defense President, the United States lacks even the first signs that a serious, coherent defense policy even exists. Indeed, the actions of the Weinberger Defense Department show that our defense policy is being determined *not* by strategic urgency but by economic and political considerations.

Ronald Reagan's appointments of Caspar Weinberger to be Secretary of Defense and Frank Carlucci as his deputy, came as a shock to serious analysts of national security issues. Neither man could pretend to having had any experience in military or strategic planning (the former had been Secretary for Health, Education and Welfare and Director of the Office of Managment and Budget in the Nixon Administration and the latter was, as Stanfield Turner's deputy at the CIA, a docile servant of President Carter). When the Department of Defense transition team, headed by William Van Cleave, Ronald Reagan's senior defense policy advisor, was disbanded while in the midst of drafting a detailed set of proposals for implementing a new program, the writing was on the wall.

Despite increased spending, the Reagan Administration has put forward no new strategic ideas; it has merely expressed some hope for the improvement of existing programs. The whole Reagan Administration approach, precludes higher outlays in spite of the fact that the Soviets outspend us by 50 to 100 percent. The presumption is that the American economy cannot bear more than 7 percent annual increases, thus freezing defense spending at about 6 percent of the GNP—a figure slightly higher than that set by the previous Administration. In fact, the major Reagan Administration reform is confined to giving greater leeway of initiative to the Service Chiefs, thus supporting their preferences provided the budgetary limits are not breached. Presumably, if increased inter-service cooperation, responsibility, and efficiency does not materialize, the Administration would then choose between raising expenditures or intervening in the management field.

More serious is President Reagan's apparent failure to realize that his leadership is vital if any serious effort is to be made to restore the strategic military balance. Thus, the importance of the

National Security Council, as a body co-ordinating foreign and defense policies in the greater interest of national security, has been downgraded. This had led to disarray in policy-making, with different interests pulling in different directions without central control. Consequently, in the same way that the foreign policy of the United States is being entirely determined by the State Department, the responsibility for the formation of an overall defense strategy has devolved upon the Pentagon. Campaign rhetoric about closing the strategic "window of vulnerability" notwithstanding, priority has been accorded by the Pentagon to the development of conventional—not strategic—forces. Thus, in the absence of an overall framework, the Reagan defense program is fragmented, lacks definition, coherence and purpose.

Compounding the problem, the Administration, under pressure from business interests, continues to allow the export of computers, microcircuitry, sensors, engines, gas and oil technology, and grains which ease the strain on the Soviet economy created by Soviet militarism. A great disparity exists between the pursuit of profit and professed foreign policy values and goals. U.S. corporate interests are strengthening the military capacity of the Soviet Union at the same time as the Administration is calling for increases in defense spending to counter that rapidly growing capacity, demonstrating a mind-boggling ambivalence and incoherence in U.S. policy.

The five-year $1.5 trillion defense buildup is accompanied by domestic spending and tax cuts resulting in high interest rates. Serious questions arise as to whether the eroding industrial base can deliver the new weaponry on time and within the budget. While to some degree our lagging military expansion is due to economic problems, it is the absence of an integrated, comprehensive military strategy that is the main cause of our defense predicament.

Indeed, any summary comparison of American and Soviet military power shows not only American inferiority in just about every category of capability, but also the inexcusable absence of any winning strategy. Statements by former Deputy Secretary of Defense Frank Carlucci that our response to a Soviet strike against our missiles might be to "launch on warning," i.e., launch all our missiles indiscriminately if we ever become convinced that we are being attacked, bespeak a deep-rooted and sustained detachment from reality. "Launch on warning" would do little to limit escalation; it would most likely invite destruction of the United States by Soviet forces. No less irresponsible is Marine General Paul X. Kelley's statement that we might "sacrifice" one or two U.S. divisions to superior Soviet forces in the Middle East to show our resolve. What then? Would the Former Commander of the "Rapid Deployment Force" (now commandant of the Marine Corps) then call for crossing the nuclear line to exchange one 40 *kiloton* warhead for every *megaton*-range warhead the Soviets could rain on the United States? Such arrant nonsense, born out of Washington's gospel of mutual assured destruction and cost-effectiveness, underscores the bankruptcy of U.S. strategy thinking.

Clearly, new programs and new strategies are needed. The issue goes beyond the disparity in weapons, where merely incremental increases in present programs will not do. Rearmament without a military strategy is deceptively dangerous. In certain categories, such as ICBM production, the Soviets are so far ahead that catching up may be impractical.

The Reagan Administration's strategic weapons program will go only part of the way towards closing the window of vulnerability in the next two decades. There will be a gradual improvement in our strategic position but it will not come fast enough and there is no indication that we will ever regain a survivable ICBM force under the Reagan program. The Administration may even lose the MX missile—the result of its own vacillation on how to base it and because of Congressional opposition. Without a strategic rationale for MX, the limited deployment of MX in a vulnerable basing mode makes no strategic sense.

The most dangerous part of the Reagan program was the rejection of strategic "quick fixes" (e.g., vertical MPS basing of Minuteman III ICBMs, the reinitiation of Minuteman production, re-engining of the B-52 program, and the acceleration of the cruise missile program). The United States cannot afford to wait until the late 1980s to begin to get a significant improvement in its strategic force capabilities. Reagan's program over the next five years is clearly inferior to Carter's because it has fewer ICBMs, bombers and cruise missiles.

The arms control legacy of the 1960s and 1970s is the principal problem we face in redressing the strategic military balance and eliminating the dangerous vulnerabilities that now exist in our ICBM force. SALT I and II not only allowed the massive Soviet first-strike disarming threat to materialize, but also made it extremely difficult for the United States to regain a survivable ICBM force. The United States does not now have, nor will it have with current programs, strategic forces that will give the Soviet Union a compelling incentive to agree to the Reagan Administration's goal—equal, stabilizing and balanced arms reductions. In light of the current military balance, agreements are almost by definition those which are highly advantageous to the USSR, and which contribute greatly to Soviet war-fighting capabilities. It is not even certain that the Soviet Union will accept cosmetic arms control —agreements that are seemingly equitable, but advantageous to the USSR in effect, permitting the continued buildup of Soviet military capability. Significant reductions that do nothing more than freeze the current military imbalance and preserve the current Soviet warfighting capability will do nothing to improve our national security.

The Reagan Administration came into office clearly believing that a realistic approach to arms control was essential, but it has been seduced into taking the path of least resistance by the lure of "NATO unity." President Reagan's Strategic Arms Reduction Talks (START) are a panic reaction to the nuclear freeze movement and an attempt to co-opt or pre-empt it. START is fatally flawed; it preserves Soviet first strike capability against the U.S. ICBM force while reducing U.S. capability to strike back: it concedes throw-weight advantage to the Soviets and accepts equality in warheads, thus preserving the status quo in favor of Soviet overall superiority; and verification of Soviet violations are difficult if not impossible, since the Soviets have rejected on-site inspection and have a notorious record of cheating and trying to conceal past violations of SALT I and II. We are effectively allowing leftward and social democratic regimes in Europe to shape some of our most critical national security policies—in exchange, of course, for the task of defending Europe from Soviet domination. If we do not have negotiating leverage in the true sense—military power—we will be further weakened by the attitude of our "allies." Only the nearly total suspension of the development of nuclear and chemical weapons by the United States will satisfy the American and European Left which the Reagan Administration is now under pressure to appease. The Reagan Administration has been convinced that it can play and win at arms control. It apparently believes that it can increase support for the defense programs by making pious pronouncements about arms control and "peace." While there may be some temporary respite from pressures from the left, Soviet propaganda pressure will increase and the long-term effect will be disastrous. There is simply no way that any Administration, much less a Republican Administration, can compete with the radical left or even the liberal left in proposing arms reductions. The left can always come up with a proposal that is more comprehensive and less verifiable than that which can be put forward by any American government.

The Reagan Administration cannot go on claiming indefinitely that it is more competent than its predecessor to conduct arms control negotiations. It will not get results because its defense programs do not give it the leverage to do so. Moreover, even if it had this leverage, the Soviets take a long view of history and would certainly wait until the 1984 Presidential election before making any significant concessions. By getting caught up in the rhetoric of arms control and peace, the Reagan Administration will only succeed in building up pressure on itself to make concessions to the USSR. It will then reach an agreement only if its position is negotiable—and negotiable means highly advantageous to the USSR. The more the Administration talks about arms control as being able to make a positive contribution to our security, the more pressure will develop for it to achieve results and the only way it can make progress is to make unilateral concessions to the USSR. Indeed, there are signs that this is already happening. The Administration has decided not to deploy fifty additional Minuteman III missiles in Minuteman II silos as originally planned because their multiple nuclear warheads might be violating the limits of SALT II. Also, identifying devices are going to be put on B-52 bombers carrying nuclear warhead cruise missiles in compliance with that agreement. In addition, in late October 1982, with almost no publicity, representatives of the United States and the Soviet Union began the required five-year review of the 1972 Anti-Ballistic Missile (ABM) Treaty in Geneva, with General Richard Ellis (former head of the Strategic Air Command) saying that the Reagan Administration was ". . . thus far satisfied with compliance . . ." of the Treaty's provisions. Yet there is no indication that the Soviet Union has made similar concessions. On the contrary, according to Richard N. Perle, Assistant Secretary of Defense for International Security, there ". . . was considerable evidence that could well have indicated a violation or action inconsistent with the prohibitions in SALT II," as a result of the Soviets deploying the relatively small, mobile, missile, the SS-16.[2]

Since arms control compliance gets in the way of negotiations, it usually is the first casualty. Previous administrations simply suppressed evidence of Soviet non-compliance. By its failure to make the Soviet violations of existing agreements the test for arms control, the Reagan Administration encourages the notion that violations are acceptable. Instead, it should announce that it will not conclude any additional agreements until the USSR manifests full compliance with existing treaties and agrees to the required verification procedures. It should tell the world that arms control will not substantially reduce the risk of war and that it is not a substitute for military forces. It should undertake a major education effort on the overall Soviet arms control compliance record. It should aggressively pursue compliance in all available international forums. The American people must be brought to realize the hard truth that arms control, by itself, is not the answer. The greater threat is not the arms race but the Soviet Union's aggressive behavior in the Middle East, in Latin America and in Europe. Linkage to Soviet behavior must be revived and given more than lip service.

The chronic disparity between what President Reagan promised and what he has achieved, is nowhere more obvious than in his

Administration's plans for the defense of Western Europe. For better or worse, NATO has long been the cornerstone of U.S. foreign policy. When United States dealings with NATO allies have been relatively successful, the resulting situation has often made the particular Administration in office look more competent in its handling of foreign policy than might otherwise be the case. On the other hand, when Major policy disagreements between the United States Administration and the Europeans have become public knowledge, they have often lent the foreign policy of that unlucky Administration an air of amateurishness, despite other foreign policy successes.

Naturally, then, one of the biggest foreign policy concerns that faced President Reagan and Secretary of State Haig at the outset of their Administration was reversing the slide in the United States' relationship with its European allies. This slide had become increasingly evident during the Carter years. Western Europe rightly perceived President Carter as an ineffectual world leader, given more to proclaiming moralistic sentiments than to taking constructive action on behalf of the Alliance. In fact, his last two years in office were haunted by his tragically inept handling, in 1978 of the "neutron bomb" issue, in which he unilaterally cancelled the production of new, enhanced radiation warheads for NATO's tactical nuclear forces after having sought and finally obtained European support for their deployment.

Ronald Reagan was determined to project an image of national strength and purpose to convince the Europeans that the United States' flight from its responsibilities to NATO had at least ended. Indeed, in the first months of the new administration, there were signs that the situation had changed for the better. President Reagan pledged to restore America's military strength and to allow it once again to undertake its myriad international responsibilities. Secretary Haig made it clear that the Administration would devote more attention to the allies' political concerns than had been given by the previous Administration. Yet, despite these positive signs of change, the Europeans began to notice some disturbing indications that all was not well with the Reagan Administration's handling of foreign policy. Defense Secretary Weinberger was the first to stir Alliance feelings when, in February 1981, he made a number of off-hand remarks to reporters indicating that the Administration was considering the production and eventual deployment in Europe of enhanced radiation warheads.[3] These remarks were trumpeted by the European press at a time when many European countries were experiencing a serious revival of appeasement and disarmament movements. The NATO member governments, not having been briefed ahead of time on the direction of Reagan Administration thinking on the neutron weapons issue, were caught totally unaware. As the "peace" groups utilized the Weinberger remarks to criticize the European governments for their tacit support for such a step and also to build up popular support for their own disarmament efforts, these governments were forced to react defensively, denying that they knew of any such plans and even questioning the validity of such a deployment decision.

The violence of the European reactions caused a policy flare-up within the Reagan Administration, leading Secretary Haig to disavow Weinberger's comments, setting off an exchange of fire between the Haig State Department and the Weinberger Defense Department. The sniping increased in intensity over a number of other issues for the rest of the year. The disarray in handling foreign policy, disheartened European leaders even more, since it struck at the core of the President's promise to re-focus America's defense efforts. In addition, European leaders have become worried over what they see as the Administration's increasingly belligerent tone in its dealings with the Soviet Union. They refused to join President Reagan in adopting a tough credit policy towards the Soviet Union as a sanction for the imposition of martial law in Poland, and they regarded his attempt to ban the export of American technology manufactured in Western Europe to the Soviet Union, for use in the building of a natural gas pipeline, as an infringement upon their sovereignty. They see no reason why they should restrict their trade with the Eastern bloc at a time when they are in dire economic straits, especially since the United States resumed its grain sales to the Soviet Union (suspended by the Carter Administration in reaction to the Soviets' aggression against Afghanistan). The diplomacy of the Reagan Administration has had the opposite effect to that intended: it has further alienated Western Europe from the United States.

The Reagan Administration has accorded the highest priority to the modernization of NATO's theater nuclear forces. (The pledge of each of the NATO states to increase its defense spending by three percent a year in real terms, and the request that the allies assist the United States in fielding its "quick reaction forces"—the RDF— for use in the Persian Gulf and other areas of the globe, are regarded as being of secondary importance). NATO had begun to have serious doubts about the credibility of its nuclear deterrent in the late 1970s, when the USSR began to deploy large numbers of a new, highly-capable mobile theater-range missile—the SS-20. The new weapon had not only range and mobility advantages over the old SS-4s and SS-5s which it was ostensibly being fielded to replace, but it carried three independently-targetable warheads, each with dramatically increased accuracy over the single warheads on the older missiles.[4] NATO's doubts about its theater nuclear capabilities eventually culminated in its decision in December 1979 to deploy 572 new U.S. Pershing II and ground-launched cruise missiles (GLCMs), starting in 1983, in order to close the gap in ground-launched intermediate-range missiles.

From the beginning, however, the NATO plan for the modernization of its theater nuclear forces (TNF) was the target of a massive Soviet propaganda campaign designed to prevent the eventual deployment of the missiles. To complicate matters further, the political opposition to the plan in certain NATO member countries was such that, at the time of its original acceptance, both the Netherlands and Belgium deferred decision on allowing the stationing of these missiles on their territories. West Germany had agreed to have these missiles deployed within its borders only because other continental European nations—Belgium, Holland and Italy—had eventually agreed to accept them.

By the time President Reagan entered office, European political support for the TNF decision had eroded even further. This situation made it imperative for the new Administration to reaffirm America's intention to go through with the NATO plan in a clear and forceful manner. When the Administration attempted to do this, however, it was foiled by two circumstances partially of its own making. First, it must be remembered that the original NATO TNF modernization decision had been only one part of a "two-track" decision, the other track being an agreement that NATO would seek to negotiate with the Soviet Union on limiting theater nuclear forces. It was widely believed that if the negotiations were successful, NATO would have no need to go ahead with the actual deployment of the Pershing II and ground-launched cruise missiles. Thus, when public pressure against the perceived remilitarization of America's foreign policy and its bellicose attitude toward the Soviet Union began building up within the European countries in late spring of 1981, the Western European governments, in turn, began urging the Reagan Administration to implement the second track of the two-track decision and begin serious negotiations on theater nuclear forces with the USSR. Second, the manner in which the Reagan Administration announced in August its decision to produce and stockpile enhanced radiation warheads without coordinating it with NATO's member governments, drastically strengthened the hand of the European disarmament movement.

The Reagan Administration failed to come to grips with the gravity of the burgeoning unilateral disarmament movement in Western Europe. For years the Soviet Union has had an extremely well-organized and well-financed disarmament propaganda campaign operating in Europe against U.S. and NATO interests. Yet, until recently, the Soviet effort has had relatively small success in influencing European public opinion against American initiatives. Interestingly, this all changed with the "stop the Neutron Bomb" campaign of 1977 and 1978. The major reason for this change was that the Soviets had started working in a major way with European communist front groups and with the "peace" groups of the European left.[5]

The anti-neutron campaign is instructive. It was started in 1977 on the initiative of the Dutch Communist Party. The campaign quickly picked up organizational strength from two "religious" bodies, Christians for Socialism, a known international communist front group, and the Inter-Church Peace Council, an amalgamation of nine Protestant churches which had begun working with Christians for Socialism the year before. With these "non-aligned" groups in the forefront of organizing activity, "Stop the Neutron Bomb" began bringing into its orbit a range of participants, including not only the "regular" pacifist elements but also "concerned" Christians and other Dutch citizens worried about the prospect of neutron weapons in Europe. As it grew in strength, the Dutch anti-neutron campaign's influence spread to neighboring NATO countries, such as Belgium and West Germany. By the time Jimmy Carter made his fateful decision in April 1978 not to produce and deploy enhanced radiation warheads, the anti-neutron furor in Europe had reached major proportions. In Holland, for example, the "Stop the Neutron Bomb" campaign gathered some 1.5 million signatures against the weapon's deployment.

The Soviets, undoubtedly surprised by, but extremely pleased with, the success of the "peace effort," endeavored to make the campagin against NATO's TNF modernization plans even more effective. They went so far as to encourage all propaganda agencies at their command and all communist front allies to unite totally with the European Left peace and disarmament activities, while purposely downplaying those issues on which the two sides were at odds. In November 1980, the West German Communist Party repeated the success of the Dutch Communist Party three years before by instigating the Krefeld Forum (*Krefelder Apell*) through its front group, the German Peace Union. The Forum was signed by, among others, representatives of the Green Party—Germany's leftist environmental party, the German Communist Party, the Evangelical Church, small trade unions and the German Peace Union. By January 1981, the Forum's call for the West German Government's reconsideration of its "fatal and erroneous decision" to allow the deployment of Pershing II and ground-launched cruise missiles on German soil had attracted 20,000 signatures. By the end of 1981, the total support for the Forum's "peace" position was approaching 1.5 million signatures.[6]

Demonstration after demonstration took place from the summer of 1981 onwards, reaching a frenzied climax in the winter of 1983, but the Reagan Administration failed to see how dangerous it was to stand aloof from the fray. President Reagan assumed that the whole disarmament protest was being orchestrated from Moscow and that the European governments would consequently respond to it. The President's assumption was ill-founded. By bringing into the various peace movements large numbers of citizens who had no Communist connections but who did have very real fears about the proposed TNF decisions, the Soviets and their allies had transmitted the standard Soviet-style propaganda effort into what appeared to be in each country, a kind of nationalistic peace group. It was thus extremely difficult for any of the European governments publicly to paint the disarmament campaigns as Soviet-inspired. The results were a major propaganda victory for the Soviet Union and an increased constriction of general Western European support for the TNF decision.

Just as the Reagan Administration found it necessary to continue with policies toward NATO that had been initiated by the previous Administration, so too its fiscal year 1982 defense budget was drawn up with the Carter budget as a basis. The Reagan budget did allocate additional monies for certain weapons and development categories, but it did not strike out in directions different from those of the Carter defense budget. The actual additional sums provided for strengthening American forces in Europe were relatively small. The bulk of the increases in the budget were allocated to Navy shipbuilding—categories that had little impact on the land and air forces needed in the European theater.

Aside from the budgetary allocations, however, the Reagan Administration's approach to NATO's defense was to continue with force deployments that had long been in use. The primary dilemma facing U.S. ground forces in Europe is not its shortage of military equipment such as tanks, artillery and infantry fighting vehicles —although this shortage is serious—but its present deployment patterns and its tactical and operational plans. The vast bulk of the U.S. Army in West Germany is still deployed with CENTAG in the south, quartered in casernes allotted to U.S. forces at the end of the Second World War. However, in the event of a Soviet armored attack into West Germany, the area under the control of NORTHAG—to the north of present U.S. dispositions—would most likely be the target of the major Warsaw Pact invasion. Therefore, one of the first steps of an Administration serious about defense against a conventional Soviet attack would be to open negotiations with the Germans and other NATO governments for moving the bulk of these U.S. forces into casernes and troop dispositions now occupied by the Dutch, the Belgians, the British and the Germans. The Reagan Administration has so far shown little inclination to do this.

As for the U.S. Army's tactical and operational planning in Western Europe, the Army still clings to an outmoded concept of defense categorized as the "active defense."[7] This is little more than an under-strength, extended linear defense—just the sort of defense that large-scale armored attacks on the German-Soviet model would roll up within hours of an invasion. There is a clear need for the Army to reexamine its tactical concepts in Europe. Yet, here again, the Reagan Defense Department has shown little interest in ordering the Army to do this.

Finally, the Administration has been patently derelict in its responsibility on the subject of NATO standardization. The establishment of standardization and interoperability of military equipment used by NATO forces in Europe has long been a concern shared by both the Executive Branch and Congress. Accordingly, Public Law 94-361, passed as the Department of Defense Appropriation Authorization Act of 1977, provided that the Secretary of Defense shall, to the maximum possible extent, carry out procurement procedures to supply U.S. forces stationed in Europe with equipment that is standardized or interoperable with the equipment of other NATO members. In line with this requirement, the Joint Chiefs of Staff established five top priority areas for interoperability and standardization—one of the five being *ammunition*. Subsequently, the United States and the German Federal Republic reached a Memorandum of Understanding[8] concerning the standardization of 20mm through 40mm ammunition. Thus, it came as a distinctly unpleasant shock to the Germans and other European NATO members when, in May 1981, just five months after the Reagan Administration took office, the U.S. Army selected the Ford Aerospace-proposed Bofors 40mm gun system for the DIVAD air defense program. In making this choice, the Army ignored or failed to note that all of the new European NATO air defense gun systems deployed on the Central Front were 35mm systems, ruling out interoperability between U.S. ammunition and that of the Allies. The decision was a severe blow to the whole NATO standardization program, which had been slowly gaining momentum over the past decade. When the matter was raised with the Reagan Defense Department's leadership, the staff personnel involved declined to intercede, noting that the decision had been handed over to the Army staff to make and was therefore entirely an Army responsibility. Yet this was clearly a case whose repercussions would affect U.S.-NATO relations for years to come.

In President Reagan's fourth year in office it is plain that his Administration has failed to embark upon the redemption of its pledge to repair the ravaged state of America's defenses, after twenty years of willful neglect. In the absence of a coherent strategy to counter the mounting threat to the West posed by the burgeoning military might of the Soviet Union, the Reagan Administration has fallen back upon the bankrupt policies pursued by President Carter. Ronald Reagan was not elected by the American people to spend vast sums of money on programs that will not significantly enhance the ability of the United States to close the strategic "window of vulnerability" within the next ten years. Nor was he chosen to follow in Carter's footsteps and continue to alienate the West Europeans—to the point where the future of NATO is being called into question. The President should take immediate steps to remedy the lack of purpose in his administration's foreign and defense policies. Not only must he involve himself directly in constructing a strategy capable of defending the West from the predatory instincts of the Soviet Union, but he must also ensure that it is implemented, by appointing men who have the intellectual courage and the necessary experience to override the palsied instincts of the bureaucracy. The alternative is the Soviet Union's final achievement of total nuclear superiority, and the blackmailing of the West into gradual submission to the dictates of Soviet totalitarianism.

9

Toward a Coherent
Defense Policy

The present dangerous East-West strategic imbalance reflects the correlation between nuclear missiles and geo-politics, military power and diplomacy. It also accounts for Moscow's increased readiness to undertake higher risks in challenging the U.S. in areas traditionally within its own home defense perimeters.

From the end of World War II until roughly 1969, the strategic balance clearly favored the United States and her allies. Our nuclear superiority served as the ultimate constraint on the Soviet regime's drive for global hegemony. The credibility of America's nuclear arsenal provided us with the capacity to forestall unrestrained Soviet adventurism. Russian knowledge of America's willingness to introduce nuclear weapons, if necessary to break the stalemate in Korea, produced an armistice in 1953 and a Soviet backdown in Cuba in 1962. Under the pressure of our decisive strategic superiority, Nikita Khrushchev was compelled to adopt a policy of "peaceful coexistence" predicated on the belief that the Soviets could achieve their global ambitions without direct military action.

This favorable strategic balance was allowed to erode by an ill-conceived and naive national security policy which assumed that nuclear weapons would be neutralized by mutual deterrence if the Soviets were permitted to reach nuclear parity with the West. However, after parity was achieved by the Soviets in 1969, the strategic balance shifted in a manner which supported rather than restrained Soviet adventurism. In the Yom Kippur War of October 1973, it was the Soviet threat to use nuclear weapons in support of its Egyptian client which loomed as an important element in the United States decision to deny Israel a decisive victory.

Having clearly tilted the strategic balance in their favor, the Soviets are now engaging in nuclear intimidation. They threatened to deploy intermediate range SS-20 missiles in Nicaragua if the U.S. and NATO proceeded to counter the SS-20 missiles deployed in Eastern Europe with their own deployment of Pershing and Cruise missiles in Western Europe. At the same time, the increasing tempo of insurgency by surrogates and direct Soviet aggression clearly reflects the reality of the altered strategic nuclear balance.

The ultimate achievement of Soviet aims is contingent upon the ability of Moscow to preserve the strategic imbalance. Its paramount strategic objective is to separate Europe from the United States, thereby bringing about the collapse of NATO through the denial of access to the critical resources necessary to fuel the economies and defense capabilities of the industrialized democracies. This approach was expressed quite explicitly by Leonid Brezhnev: "Our aim is to gain control of the two great treasure houses on which the West depends—the energy treasure house of the Persian Gulf, and the mineral treasure house of Central and Southern Africa." By reaching for a stranglehold on the economic aorta of Western Europe and Japan, the Soviets seek to force their neutralization in the East-West struggle and the isolation of the United States from Europe, Asia and Africa. The line of East-West confrontation has thus been moved from Central Europe to the Middle East.

In pursuing their objective, the Soviets have capitalized on their advantages in the Gulf Area—geographic proximity, conventional military superiority, and an infrastructure of airfields and naval bases in South Yemen, Ethiopia, Afghanistan, Libya, Iraq, and Syria. The United States, by contrast, has yet to secure the geostrategic base sites necessary to provide flexibility for the projection of American power through a rapid deployment force.

At this moment, Soviet domination of the Middle East has been held in check by our only stable, battle tested, and reliable ally in the vast region between Japan and Western Europe—Israel. Sharing a mutual interest with the United States in denying control of the region to the Soviets, either directly or through client states, Israel by default has assumed the lion's share of America's burden in defending Western interests there, both in manpower and resources. Israel's investment in the defense sector is almost sevenfold that of the U.S. as a percentage of GNP, and thirty-five times as much as Japan. Yet, U.S. military aid to Israel of $2.5 billion, half of which must be repaid with interest, is but a fraction of the $120 billion the U.S. expends annually to maintain NATO and U.S. forces in the Pacific.

Should we, as a consequence of our continued naive undervaluation of Israel as a strategic asset, allow her to be neutralized by an expanding Soviet strategic presence in the region, we will be confronted with a choice of unpalatable options. We will either be obliged to concede the entire Middle East to Soviet domination, thereby accepting the consequences on the Western alliance of such surrender, or be required to deploy substantial ground forces throughout the area at a cost unthinkable in the present domestic political climate.

The Soviet Union has now raised the stakes in the contest for the Middle East by its unprecedented deployment of SA-5 missiles in Syria manned by 5,000 Soviet technicians and advisors—all linked by satellite communications to the Soviet military command in Moscow. Never before installed outside the Soviet Union, the SA-5 dominates the airspace over Israel, Iraq, Jordan, Lebanon, eastern Turkey and presents a direct challenge to carrier-based aircraft of the Sixth Fleet east of Cyprus. We have yet to respond to this threat, even though inaction might be construed as acceptance of Moscow's aggressive designs in this pivotal theater.

Without subtracting from the importance of neutralizing the SA-5 threat, it must be recognized that it is but one of an extensive panoply of dangerous challenges now facing the United States and the free world. Currently, these include among others threats or direct combat operations against Afghanistan, Cambodia, El Salvador, Israel, Laos, the Philippines and South Africa. Meeting such threats requires considerably more than resolute support for these beleaguered friendly nations which stand in the path of Soviet global ambitions.

Admittedly, we must reconstitute our nuclear deterrent capability and upgrade our conventional forces to lend credence to national security policy. But, that policy must be a *coherent* part of a geo-political strategy designed to prevent the paralysis of diplomacy which would result in either a *Pax Sovietica* or a nuclear confrontation. Indeed, the one thing worse than failing to restore our defenses is to rearm without such a coherent strategy.

The positions of the United States and USSR have changed. Now it is the Soviets who are prepared to negotiate agreements requiring exchange of information. What good can it do the United States to know the size and location of Soviet ICBMs when it is not American policy even to be capable of a first strike? Moreover, the Soviet silo-housed missiles are very hard targets, indestructible by any but direct strikes by Minuteman and will, at any rate, not be in their silos in the event of an American second strike. Exchange of information is irrelevant to essential equivalence. The one way to restore stability would be to deploy a system which allows missile survivability. Only a surviving second strike capability of truly frightening magnitude can hope to deter a first strike. Such response capability, in effect, must be of such size and nature as to rule out the very utility of a Soviet first strike.

As we have seen, the relation between missiles and geopolitics is fundamental to world politics, yet it is the forgotten dimension in the arms controls debate. Adverse shifts in the nuclear balance have enabled Moscow to coerce us diplomatically by threatening use of its superior conventional forces, with limited risk of escalation. Soviet leaders are thus able to secure political, economic, and even military gains without force. It is precisely in terms of this delicate interplay of the nuclear balance, conventional forces and diplomacy that one must evaluate the arms control process. No U.S. president, as former head of the Arms Control and Disarmament Agency Eugene Rostow put it, should be in the undesirable position of having to choose between the surrender of vital interests and nuclear holocaust.

If the Soviets risked war in the Middle East when the United States still enjoyed preeminence in forward-deployed ground forces and naval capacity, as well as nuclear strength, they are even more likely to risk it now following the 1982 war in Lebanon.

The Soviet-American correlation of forces has always been a critical factor in Middle East crisis. Four of the five serious threats of nuclear war, the ones other than Cuba, originated in the Middle East: the Suez crisis in 1956, the Lebanon intervention in 1958, the Six-Day War of 1967 and the Yom Kippur War in 1973.

The first U.S. dispatch of Marines to Lebanon in 1958 reflected America's capability of intervening unilaterally to safeguard Western influence in the Levant. The Cuban missile confrontation of 1962 confirmed U.S. superiority, and in the Six-Day War of 1967, Israel won behind the shield of America's deterrent power.

However, Moscow achieved strategic parity in 1969 as the United States began to let its position slide. We refused to challenge the Soviet's assumption of Egypt's air defense in the years 1970–72, even though this extension of Soviet power threatened the U.S. Sixth Fleet in the Mediterranean as much as it defended Egypt. Furthermore, the antagonists in the Yom Kippur War fought behind the mutually deterrent power of the United States and the Soviet Union—perhaps the factor that disallowed a decisive Israeli military victory. In that crisis, the Soviet and American airlifts symbolized a new reality: either superpower could intervene to prevent victories, protect proteges or stabilize situations which threatened to escalate into general war. In the period since then, the Soviets have been capitalizing on their vast military buildup in the Middle East and Africa by raising the level of risk-taking in accordance with their perception of the strategic balance. Hence,

Angola, Ethiopia, Zaire, Yemen, Afghanistan, Iran, Botswana, Grenada, Suriname, Nicaragua and now, El Salvador.

The dimension of the Soviet challenge to America's position in global affairs is delineated by the following:

- While the United States has developed only one ICBM system since 1965, the USSR has developed seven.
- Advances in Soviet MIRV technology and missile accuracy are rapidly overcoming whatever lead the United States once had in the quality of its guidance systems and the capability and quantity of its warheads.
- The Soviets have invested heavily in additional submarine-launched ballistic missiles (SLBMs). While the United States only began to modernize its Polaris-Poseidon SLBM force in 1980, the Soviets were several years ahead of us in deploying long-range (4000 miles-plus) SLBMs, have tested both multiple reentry vehicles (MRVs) and MIRVs and have two MIRV-capable SLBMs being deployed.
- The Soviets are continuing to deploy the Backfire, a supersonic swingwing bomber capable of delivering weapons anywhere in the United States without refueling and are flight testing a new strategic bomber, the Blackjack, which is expected to be available in significant numbers by the end of the decade.[1]
- The Soviets are using chemical and biological weapons in Afghanistan and are making them available to their Vietnamese allies for use against Southeast Asians.
- The Soviets have more naval vessels than does the United States in every category except aircraft carriers. They also have more shore-based naval aircraft. They already have many ship-based anti-ship cruise missiles, with both nuclear and conventional warheads, while the United States is just beginning to deploy its first nonnuclear anti-ship missile.
- The Soviets lead in general-purpose forces: a more than two-to-one advantage in armed forces (4.9 million as against our 2.1 million—the proportions are even worse if one compares fighting categories); larger inventories in all but one category of equipment (helicopters); overwhelming superiority in

many categories of equipment; production of equipment at a much greater annual rate than United States; deployment of both the T-72 main battle tank and an armored infantry fighting vehicle (BMP), both unmatched, until recently, by any U.S. vehicle.

■ Where we maintained limits on size and accuracy, the Soviets built huge missiles which gave them a threefold advantage in ICBM megatonnage and throw weight. Where we targeted industries, the Soviets targeted U.S. air and naval bases. Where we minimized warhead radioactivity, they maintained high levels (despite a stated disinterest in "dirty" bombs). Where we dismantled American air defenses, they have deployed 7,000 air-defense radars, 10,000 SAM launchers, 12,000 interceptor missiles and 2,500 interceptor aircraft. Where we have foregone civil defense, theirs is expanding, featuring hard shelters for about one-quarter of the urban population, protection for vital industries and sheltered food supplies.[2]

Failure to take corrective measures to maintain parity, much less restore the equilibrium, was the fatal flaw in SALT II; whereas SALT I gave the Soviets parity and permitted our decline to inferiority, SALT II conceded decisive advantages to the Soviets.

Another contribution to the erosion of the U.S. position is the Soviet "cold launch" capability. With "cold launch," about half the Soviet silos have been or will be fitted to fire missiles with compressed air before the engine ignites. This technique leaves the silo undamaged; in two hours, another ICBM could be launched from the same silo. By contrast, it takes up to several weeks to repair a Minuteman silo to fire another missile.

America needs to stop saying that all nuclear combat is unacceptable and should begin to view a limited strategic engagement as a possibility. This is, we know, the attitude prevalent in the USSR, which has an advanced civil defense program. The irony is that it is nevertheless an unstated U.S. policy, since our conventional military force is so inadequate and unfit to perform as an international peacekeeper. But because the policy remains unstated, we remain unprepared in areas like civil defense.

The reality today is that the USSR would, after an exchange of weapons, be in a more favorable position. This situation will endure for a while, and if no new missiles except the Trident I on submarines are deployed, it will become worse, until the strategic imbalance is so great that it can be used for diplomatic coercion, including coercion of the United States not to change it.

When SALT I was signed, the Anti-Ballistic Missile (ABM) treaty, of permanent duration, was signed as well. What could be a better way of achieving arms control than by developing an ABM? In hindsight, the logic of the U.S. negotiators, who traded superior ABM technology for the chance to promote the cause of misguided arms control looks deranged. They seem to have believed that the theory of MAD would be violated by the deployment of ABMs but forgot that MAD theory applies only if neither side pursues a policy of destroying the opponent on first strike. ABMs would have helped to prevent the situation that now prevails, in which the Soviets have scoffed at MAD theory by targeting the vulnerable U.S. ICBMs. President Reagan's 1983 "Star Wars" speech promises to eliminate the strategic imbalance by neutralizing the Soviet's nuclear superiority. Only time will tell whether or not this new (but realizable!) Ballistic Missile Defense (BMD) technology will be implemented. Meanwhile, it should clearly be understood that only when our nation's policymakers begin to act on the understanding of the inescapable correlation between military power and a realistic foreign policy will there be a genuine chance to attain the stability and peace for which free people everywhere yearn.

It is obvious, after all, that rhetoric by itself is not only dangerous, it is meaningless. To paraphrase inversely Theodore Roosevelt, walking noisily while carrying a small stick is mere clownishness. If countervailing power must be developed in reaction to the current Soviet thrust, it must be strong enough to demonstrate serious intent—both to the Kremlin and to our allies.

Except for specialists, most people are unaware of just how bad the situation of our armed forces is.

Under the All-Volunteer Force (AVF), manpower levels have become severely eroded, particularly in the Selected Reserve and National Guard components of the Services. For example, in the period from 1971 through 1978, total Guard and Reserve personnel fell to 798,000 men—some 143,000 short of U.S. projected wartime needs. Despite some marked improvement in the quality and numbers of new recruits, the combat potential of both active and reserve forces has declined each year. This has resulted from the ever-larger numbers of recruits who must be brought into the Services in order to meet recruiting goals.

There may be no way that this situation can be reversed without resorting to conscription, since the Armed Forces will require even more forces than are now projected. Additional funding for enhanced military salaries and service-related benefits may prove able to stop some of the hemorrhaging that results from the failure of sufficient numbers of trained officers and noncommissioned officers to reenlist, but it will not do anything to rectify the changing composition of our fighting forces.

It is noticeable that as our All-Volunteer Force continues to operate, the public at large exhibits an ever-greater tendency to view military service to its country as an unnecessary and even illegal demand upon its freedom. At a time of increasing Soviet threat, this tendency to regard duty to country as nothing more than enforced serfdom is harmful to the continuation of national well-being. We have seen how activists who fought against participation in the Vietnam conflict ostensibly on moral grounds have reassembled to fight the institution of draft registration in 1980 when no such moral ambiguities are a factor. During the 1950s and 1960s, the peacetime draft served a very useful purpose in bringing into the Services military recruits from a wide variety of personal backgrounds. This leavening of the Armed Forces served to weaken the regional and professional parochialism most often found in a mercenary military force. The peacetime draft also served to keep the Ready Reserves and the National Guard—so vital for strengthening the active forces in time of war—at highly manned levels.

In the situation in which the United States finds itself today, with a militant Soviet Union expanding its military and political control over large areas of the globe, this country requires greater dedication to its national interests. Under-manned and under-trained volunteer troops will not be capable of performing the myriad tasks required of them in the present decade.

It is in this connection that a national effort to educate the American public about the Soviet threat and the United States' need to counter it will be required. Particularly since the days of the Vietnam war and the antiwar movement, the American public has been propagandized by a combination of groups given disproportional attention by the news media. These groups have utilized every opportunity to preach the need for American withdrawal from its international responsibilities, to stir up opposition to lawful military service and to teach general pacifism. Since the only way that a new national strategy can be successfully initiated is through general acceptance by the American people, it will be vital for the government to educate the public about the need for new measures.

It must be made overwhelmingly clear to the public that a *major national effort* is required: an effort made all the more necessary by the erosion of our military and intelligence capabilities over the past decade.

In order to begin to recap the benefits of this strategy by the latter part of the 1980s we must, accordingly, deploy a permanent U.S. combat force in the Middle East, increase the defense portion of GNP and develop a national manpower service. During the period when U.S. forces are being built up, we will need to rely more heavily on the increased capabilities and readiness of our proven allies.

Economic mobilization is also an important initiative that is now required. A coordinated industrial policy, as part of this initiative, is urgently needed. The government will have to tackle such issues as the need for specialized industrial manpower, increased national resource needs as American military power begins to grow, the subsequent upgrading of strategic materials stockpiles and the accumulation of sufficient military equipment inventories.

Over the course of the last decade and a half, this nation's ability to gear up its industry for such a national effort has been seriously eroded. To cite just one example of this erosion, the phasing out of the bulk of the U.S. space program left the country in a situation where, by the mid-1970s, many highly-developed scientific and technical staffs and the specialized industrial companies that supported them were forced by government spending cutbacks to abandon much of the research and development work that had pushed the country into a dominant position in fields such as integrated circuits, microelectronics and computers. Over the same period of time, one after another of this nation's defense production facilities were closed down in the name of economy. In addition, with the overall government cutback in military research and development contracts, many large, diversified corporations with military equipment research divisions have been forced to decrease appreciably the size of these divisions, thus forcing valuable researchers with specialized military knowledge back into the generalized domestic production pool. When this is allowed to happen, it means the loss of a great deal of defense-related expertise, since such industrial divisions are rarely fully reconstituted even with the addition of new government contracting.

One of the United States' greatest advantages over the Soviet Union has long been its innovation in advanced military technologies. Nonetheless, over the past ten years we have seen our lead in many important technologies matched and even overtaken by the Soviet Union. Among the factors underlying this is the rapid decline in U.S. funding for basic scientific and applied research and the transfer to the USSR of American and Western technologies, either intentionally, through expanded trade, or covertly, through Soviet industrial espionage. An effective policy of national mobilization would address this problem as well.

The positive elements in our national production base that were present only twenty years ago have since turned entirely around. While the U.S. real GNP has climbed during this decade, our manpower productivity has been in decline. Overall national and corporate funding for research and development has been dropping. Plant capacity that in 1960 was underutilized and was thus available for rapid production resurgence is now almost nonexistent. Investment in new plant and equipment has fallen off.

Meanwhile, we cannot wait while plans on such a vast scale are being shaped up; a strategy of active defense must be launched at once.

If one cannot match the opponent's strength at each and every point, then it is necessary to employ strength at points where the enemy is weak in order to counteract pressure upon one's own weak points. Essentially, the strategy would focus strength at the Soviet Union's weak points. The objective is to use forces-in-being, through maneuver, in a way that neutralizes much of the Soviet advantage. Should Moscow continue to disregard the United Nations rules governing the international use of force, it must be subjected to military and/or economic sanctions, including action against Cuba, Ethiopia, Libya, South Yemen, Afghanistan and other exposed dependencies. It is precisely such elements of a national initiatives strategy which give us the ability to surprise the Soviets by initiating actions to sap the enemy's will.

In general, this strategy is composed of three aspects: (1) the maintenance of sufficient force at those points of greatest interest to the United States to deter overt Soviet aggression; (2) the rapid movement of small but powerful forces into third world areas of importance to the United States to forestall overt Soviet moves or to prevent internal changes that would directly benefit the Soviet Union; and (3) the conducting of well-coordinated but limited actions in those areas under indirect Soviet control but which are inadequately defended by its power because of Soviet inattention or overextension. The force at American disposal for the second and third aspects of this strategy would be broad in scope. It would range from economic and military assistance to economic boycott and blockade, from propaganda and psychological warfare to covert operations of some size and from the show of military force to active support of indigenous freedom fighters.

Soviet defense spending has been rising steadily at an annual rate of between 4 and 5 percent for twenty years. The level of such spending is now almost half again as much as that in the United States.[3] This massive amount of military spending has enabled the Kremlin to introduce block improvements into both their conventional and strategic forces every few years as well as to expand the size of their force inventories significantly. There is thus no way that America can catch up if it plans defense increases set at or below the current Soviet rate. Turning the military situation around will require raising defense spending to the Korean War level of

13 percent of GNP instead of the present levels of less than 8 percent.

These additional monies will have to be applied to strategic as well as conventional forces, to manpower as well as military equipment and to basic scientific research. It is vitally important that the United States field strategic forces that are capable of at least balancing those on the Soviet side. The United States would be all the more inhibited to initiate conventional military actions if the Soviets' superior strategic forces gave it the capability of escalation dominance. At the present time, the Kremlin's huge ICBM throw-weight advantage, coupled as it is with its increasing missile accuracy and ability to further fractionate its force, threatens the survivability of the U.S. ICBM force. In order to balance this strategic threat, the United States must find a way of assuring its ICBM survivability while at the same time increasing its own counterforce capability. This balancing will require the initiation or continuation of certain strategic programs that cannot begin to offset Soviet superiority for at least two to three years—a situation which makes the earliest possible decision-making vital.

In strategic defense programs, the United States should begin development of the new ballistic missile defense (BMD) technologies and high altitude interceptors. Radar upgrades and improvements in U.S. interceptor forces will also be required so that the country can cope with the increased Soviet bomber threat posed by the Backfire and follow-on Blackjack bombers. The country also needs to begin a serious effort in civil defense planning. The Soviet Union had long had an ambitious civil defense program involving the relocation or duplication of industrial plants, major funding for city blast shelters and evacuation plans. It is meaningless to speak of parity in strategic offensive weapons without acknowledging that some sort of balance in strategic defense programs is also necessary. The first step in an American civil defense effort will have to include the setting up of operational CD teams at each level of government and the establishment of a comprehensive national civil defense plan. Follow-on efforts will have to tackle such matters as deciding on shelter designs, the provision of effective, blast-resistant municipal shelters, the establishment of food and medical stockpiles and the drafting of lists and lines of authority for evacuation of civilians.[4]

The conventional forces will require equally massive expenditures of money in order to perform effectively their expanded role under the national initiatives strategy. Particular priority will have to be given to the increased requirements for amphibiouslift and airlift to move troops speedily to threatened areas. This will include money for the resurrected Fast Deployment Logistics (FDL) ships, the LSD-41s and the CX transport aircraft. However, the time delay that will be experienced before these new craft become available makes it incumbent upon us to utilize expedients in the near-term, including the use of merchant hulls that are equipped to fulfill the military sealift role.

Because naval power-projection forces are a vital part of the new strategy, additional funding will have to be allocated for the surface combat forces in the Navy's five-year ship-building program. Emphasis must be placed more on obtaining higher-cost but more capable naval vessels rather than on the lower-cost, single-purpose vessels given attention in recent Administration budgets. Continued funding priority should be given to the construction of large-hull aircraft carriers (preferably nuclear-powered), AEGIS-equipped cruisers and destroyers and mine warfare ships. Consideration will also have to be given to providing a limited number of naval gunfire support ships, since present U.S. naval vessels are deficient in both mid-range and long-range guns (eight-inch and above). The need for additional aircraft carriers would be pronounced under the new strategy, since the mobile airpower provided by such carriers could well prove the deciding factor in short-term offensive and defensive operations.

Ground-force needs will require increased production of the new M-1 Abrams and production of the Advanced Attack Helicopter. Ease of mobility will also necessitate development of a capable infantry fighting vehicle and a lightweight armored fighting vehicle similar to the Marine Corps' prototype Mobile Protected Weapon System for use as a tank-killer. The need for adequate antitank and antiaircraft protection of U.S. ground combat units, given the increasing sophistication of weaponry around the world, will call for additional funding in these areas.

Intelligence Capabilities

There is no doubt that a strategy of national initiatives will be heavily dependent upon the rapid and accurate assessment of intelligence information from threatened countries, so that the risks and benefits of action can be calculated. At the present time, the intelligence community in general, but particularly the Central Intelligence Agency, is unable to furnish such information on the urgent basis that would be required. The collection, evaluation and clandestine-operation capabilities of the Central Intelligence Agency have fallen to their lowest levels since the Agency was created.[5]

We have seen the fruits of this disastrous situation most recently in assessments concerning changes in the Middle East. The record of CIA estimates in regard to this region is one of chronic understatement and miscalculation about the extent of Soviet capabilities, the degree of their interests in the region, their direct involvement in wars and their obstruction of the diplomatic process. The failure of the Agency to accurately assess the Soviet role in the radical ferment in Iran, Libya, Saudi Arabia, Pakistan, Turkey and Afghanistan is but one of the results of a general failure in estimating Soviet influence.

Hard as it is to believe, given the United States' continuing concern with the Kremlin during the past thirty-five years, CIA analyses of Soviet military activity have revealed many of the same shortcomings. During a period when the Soviet military machine was expanding at a steady rate, CIA assessments of Soviet defense spending consistently underestimated the extent of their effort. In fact, when the CIA finally got around to upgrading its assessment of Soviet defense spending in 1976, it was forced to nearly double its earlier estimate. And it was not until after the Team A-Team B exercise, when outside intelligence experts and Sovietologists were given the chance to evaluate the CIA's prevailing in-house interpretations of Soviet intent, that the Agency accepted the view that the USSR was seeking strategic superiority.

There are a number of reasons why the Central Intelligence Agency has fared so badly in its assessments during the past years. Some of them have to do with the effects of outside political pressure, but all too many are internal. Congressional investigations of CIA behavior were held in the period from 1974 through 1976. During the course of hearings in both the House and Senate, CIA activities, especially with regard to Cuba and Chile, were subjected to investigation and various accusations of Agency illegality were publicly voiced. During the summer of 1975, hearings by the Church Committee into alleged assassination plots directed against foreign leaders were particularly harmful to the CIA's public reputation. The resulting Congressional and public outcries, strengthened by well-timed, selective leaks of committee testimony, eventually culminated in attempts to limit the Agency's freedom of action through Congressional legislation. Congress had already passed the Hughes-Ryan Amendment to the Foreign Assistance Act of 1974, which among other things required the CIA to report to the Congress on all planned covert activities. Although this amendment had only specifically named two committees to which the CIA had to report this information, six other committees of the Congress also requested and received such highly classified information. These eight committees have a combined membership of one-third of the Congress. This situation put individual Congressmen or their aides who may be against a particular covert operation in the position of being able to veto it by leaking the story to the news media (something which happened in regard to the Angola situation in 1975). Congressional efforts to restrict the CIA's operational freedom have only partially been corrected.

However, actions that were taken within the Agency also served to weaken its abilities. In part as a response to the perceived public distrust of CIA activities, several directors instituted major cutbacks in Operations Directorate personnel and reduced the number of clandestine activities being undertaken by the CIA. These rapid personnel cutbacks stripped the Agency of much of its covert operations expertise, since midlevel employees with years of hands-on experience were let go. Counter Intelligence (CI) was similarly hampered when the long-time head of that section was removed and the CI staff's influence was reduced after a series of ongoing disputes with Director William Colby. Ironically, this occurred at a time when KGB penetration of the United States was increasing.

On the analytical side of the Agency, there has long been a

problem because the Directorate for Plans—now Directorate for Operations—has consistently received the lion's share of Agency attention. It is not surprising that all of the CIA's Directors who have been appointed from inside the Agency have come from the clandestine side. Internal perceptions that clandestine work was more prestigious than the evaluation of intelligence did much to assure that intelligence-side staffing was somewhat less than always first-class.

An additional problem that originated in the mid-1960s, during the tenure of Secretary of Defense Robert McNamara, was the potential politicization of the National Intelligence Estimates (NIEs). There is a great danger that CIA assessments will fail to furnish objective estimates because of a need to conform to particular political judgments.

Equipping the intelligence community to function effectively under the new strategy will require a number of complementary actions. First, the Hughes-Ryan Amendment will have to be amended, setting up one Joint Congressional Committee on Intelligence in place of the House and Senate Select Committees presently overseeing Agency activities. Also, the requirement that Congress be notified prior to the initiation of covert operations should be modified so that it is necessary for the CIA to notify Congress in a timely fashion but not prior to the start of such operations.

Other legislation that unduly inhibits the ability of the nation's intelligence agencies to perform their collection, evaluation and other intelligence tasks effectively must be amended or superseded by new legislation.

Finally, the strength of the CIA's Operations Directorate and Counter Intelligence section should be rebuilt to handle the increased responsibilities under a national initiatives strategy.

Because the planned rebuilding of our military, economic and intelligence capabilities will take a considerable amount of time to complete, it is important that the United States work closely with its allies to bolster the West's position against Soviet encroachment. We cannot expect that our allies will act as a single body (i.e., NATO) to support the United States in areas outside of their geo-political responsibility. We can hope for the support of individual allied countries who have a particular interest in various regions. The colonial empires of Britain and France, in particular, once encompassed large parts of the Middle Eastern, African and Asian territory.

During the time of our buildup, the Soviet Union will use its effective propaganda machine, plus diplomatic and economic pressures, in attempting to drive a wedge between the United States and its allies, particularly in regard to the issue of America's expanding strategic role in the Third World. It therefore becomes vital for the United States to demonstrate its continuing support for its allies. Such demonstration would include rapid and continuing consultation with them on the actions that the United States is taking in connection with its new strategy. Even more important to Allied confidence in American support, however, would be concrete measures for the rapid buildup of American military might.

A hard look at Israel, free of emotional distortion, is vital.

Israel's strategic position is impressive. It is ideally suited for rapid American troop movements into the Persian Gulf area. Southeast of its territory lies Saudi Arabia. Israel's port of Eilat sits at the head of the Gulf of Aqaba. In addition to its strategic geographic location, Israel represents the most effective combat power in the entire Middle East. Its air force, equipped with the most modern interceptor and fighter-bomber aircraft—many American-made—constitutes a powerful offensive air striking force. These are all factors that commend the use of Israel as the focal point for America's national initiatives planning in the Middle East.

Accordingly, we ought to pre-position arms, stocks, munitions, equipment, fuels—the whole range of required war materiel—in U.S. depots on Israeli soil for contingency actions in the Gulf region. The availability of such supplies directly in the heart of the Middle East, within easy reach of the Red Sea, Persian Gulf and Indian Ocean, would prove vital. Such strategic U.S. stockpiles should be over and above increased military supplies for Israel's defense forces themselves. The depots would be under direct United States management and control. They would benefit from reliable and effective U.S.-Israeli protection in a time of regional or global crisis. No other country in the region can offer us a better security guarantee. This would prove to be a very useful first step.

Over the long run, something more will be required—the permanent presence of U.S. ground, sea and air combat forces.

The permanent stationing of American ground combat troops would serve two important purposes simultaneously: it would provide the forces for rapid movement into threatened areas of the gulf while at the same time serving as a concrete demonstration of American resolve to support its allies and friends in the region. Two divisions would be about the right-sized force for this permanent presence—one mechanized infantry division and one armored division. These heavy units would provide excellent support for Marine amphibious forces afloat in the Indian Ocean and paratroop units quickly transported from the United States by air. Together with naval and Air Force tactical power and constituent artillery support, this composite force would prove a formidable intervention corps with good staying power. The deployment would of course be backed up by secured access to Israel's own ports, airfields and logistical and technical facilities.[6]

A new alliance structure in the Middle East should be among the first fruits of this new determination to pose effective countervailing power to the Soviet Union. After Iran, Turkey is the last geographic bulwark against Soviet military and political designs in the Middle East. Israel alone is a potential wall against Soviet designs through radical Syria. Jordan is a buffer state between Israel in western Palestine and the Syrian, Iraqi and Arabian deserts. And Egypt, with the greatest concentration of manpower in the Middle East and North Africa, is an important pivot point for influence in and defense of the eastern Arab states from Cuban and radical designs. Furthermore, Egypt's control of the Suez Canal and American-Israeli defense of that control are important geopolitical advantages.

America can promote such an alliance structure by sticking resolutely to the path started with the Egyptian-Israel Peace Treaty. The United States should thus actively promote economic and military conditions for other bilateral peace treaties to be signed with Israel by countries in the region. Any talk of a comprehensive

solution" to Arab-Israeli conflict in today's world will inevitably
shipwreck on the Arabs' lowest common denominator—the determination to liquidate Israel.

The United States should particularly avoid being seduced by
the idea that the "Palestinian question" is the overriding factor in
the Middle East equation. It is not. Our long-term interests will
best be served by the maintenance of a strong, allied Israel on
which we can rely to support our permanent Middle Eastern force
posture. It is in the Middle East that our new initiatives strategy
will either succeed or fail, and we must give it every chance to
work by relying on our strength and the strength of our true and
permanent allies.

The key to the success of this strategy would be the ability of
the United States to be the initiator of action, striking out at times
and places of its own choosing. While still maintaining a defense
of its vital interests, it could unexpectedly seize the initiative to
upset Soviet geo-political planning. It should be remembered that
it is most often the concentration of force at the key point of the
battle rather than the overall preponderance of force that carries
the day. A brigade in control of a vital junction point early in a
battle may be worth more than two divisions deployed late in the
engagement. With American naval forces forward-deployed and
U.S. logistics and air bases situated in friendly countries proximate
to the threatened region, it would be possible to move troops and/or
supplies into an area rapidly enough to forestall overt Soviet military action or the collapse of friendly governments from within.
These forward-deployed forces could be used to threaten pro-Soviet regimes on the periphery of the USSR's expanding empire.

This is not to say that a strategy of national initiatives would be
easy to maintain. It would call for a sustained effort of national will
of major proportions. But then, no coherent strategy for dealing
with the Soviet threat would be easy. And though a continuation
of American strategic vacillation may appear to some decisionmak-
ers to be cheaper than a sustained effort to counteract Soviet domination, in the long run the costs of such a course will be far higher.

Yet at the very moment the whole of the above is being brought
into being—national mobilization, a new industrial policy, the in-

creasing of the defense budget and the establishment of permanent
ground forces in the Middle East—we must remain aware of the
absolute indispensability of a spiritual dimension in all this activity.
We must look to the war of ideas.

Initiatives Against the Soviets

As we curb the new expansionism of the Soviet regime by a
demonstration of our determination and ability to respond with
conventional weapons applied on an adequate tactical and strategic
scale, we must—peacefully but resolutely—undermine its control
over its population by a broad-gauge, ramified, concentrated campaign of information designed to smash totalitarian censorship.

The Soviet system has internal vulnerabilities we must seek to
penetrate. It is, after all, a vast organization with no true roots in
the people; co-opting its members, it evolves its leadership from
within its own ranks. Totalitarian in structure since the Bolshevik
seizure of power in 1917, and totalitarian in substance since the
consolidation of the neo-Bolshevik dictatorship by the Stalin mas-
sacres of the end of the thirties, it is wholly alienated from the
hundreds of millions of people in its grip.

The notion that it is upheld by an "ideology"—that it is sincerely
dedicated to the spread of "Marxism-Leninism"—is an illusion.
When the Bolsheviks succeeded in holding onto power in a back-
ward peasant country, their theory of Marxism twisted out of shape
and turned into a state cult, an institution designed to justify slaughter and repression at home and, later on, expansion abroad. The
Soviet Union as a concept is a cover for imperium on the part of
the Russian nation, less than one-half in the population of the
USSR.

At present the summits of the Kremlin are clinging for dear life
to their state cult and to their capacity for making weapons and
forming strategies. They may be in the grip of a do-or-die
mood—they must strike out, as indicted, before being overwhelmed by Chinese and American superiority *strategically
applied.*

Thus it is vital to make further military adventures impossible while we undermine the passive or grudging support the Soviet regime can squeeze out of its subject populations.

The key to the realization of a genuine environment for a lasting peace, indeed, is a tandem, interlinked effort: military strength for security against overt attack, and ideological—cultural—strength for the building of a brotherhood of shared concerns for peace for the vast diversity of peoples both inside and outside the Soviet orbit.

There is no question here of rolling back the Kremlin's far-flung boundaries. This is in no sense an engagement based on the use of weapons, nuclear or conventional. It is a campaign aimed at the minds of the many millions now deprived of all information by the totalitarian stranglehold on communications.

The priority to be given this campaign is paramount. We are an open society, highly diverse: peoples of all origins and cultures are intertwined. It is time we remembered the sources of this heritage and its results and applied this testimony to the expansion of our own awareness as a free society.

Sixty-six years ago the Bolsheviks wiped out the socialist-liberal government that had eliminated the monarchy, their communist totalitarianism was based on the premise that only the Communist hierarchy (1 to 10 percent of the total population of the Soviet state) had to be aware of the motives behind policy, and even the great majority of this small percentage was itself dominated by a handful of true policymakers at the very summit.

Thus we must proceed on a dual campaign of information—aimed at the Russian population proper, its satellites and its "Third World" (the complex non-Russian peoples now straitjacketed within the Soviet state by the dictatorship) and, most importantly, increasing far more rapidly than the Russian population itself.

We must step up our overt information agencies—Radio Liberty and the Voice of America. They must be taken away from the half-hearted bureaucrats who tell their Russian-language audiences little about the true nature of America and still less about the true evils of the Soviet regime. We must expand in a major way all our informational agencies, and, more particularly, insist on the linkage of information to any economic concessions we make the Soviet Union, such as telling the Soviet population, for instance, just where the wheat they get from us comes from. We must broadcast as widely as possible the essence of what is going on in the Soviet Union itself: a wall of ignorance smothers its people.

A special effort must be paid to the dissemination of information to the non-Russian peoples in the Soviet state, especially the Muslims.

When Russian tanks and helicopters bombarded and poison-gassed the Muslim tribes of Afghanistan in the early months of 1980 the Muslin peoples around the world were outraged. But what would be still more important than *their* knowledge of the Soviet global campaign against the Afghans would be the same knowledge if it were brought to the 50 million Muslims living inside the Central Asian areas of the Soviet Union. These Soviet citizens are most cruelly deprived of all information by the Soviet regime's wall of silence; they remain largely unaware that their own sons are part of the Soviet forces that have been murdering whole villages of Afghan Muslims. The Afghans' fierce resistance is exacting a heavy toll of the invaders; many Muslim soldiers will not be returning to their Soviet homeland, to their Muslim villages; others may one day return bearing the terrible scars of battle inflicted by this attack on their fellow-Muslims.

Even now some Muslim troops in Soviet units are deserting; they have discovered that their initial Moscow briefing, which prepared them to go to Afghanistan to "fight against U.S., Chinese and Pakistani armies" has proved false.

We must begin, together with all the nations of the world that share this concern, a global effort to reach, with specific facts that directly affect them, the various language, ethnic and religious groups behind the Soviet boundaries.

By cooperating with the ensemble of nations all over Asia, the Middle East and Africa, strengthened by a mutual intellectual and cross-cultural reinforcement, sharing money and resources, we can help mobilize language and culture to advance peace as surely as we can deter overt military aggression by the enhancement of our arms.

By radio, visual and printed matter (the Koran sells for hundreds of dollars on the black market caravan trails inside the Soviet state's Muslim region), the word of mouth messages about the events that are super-relevant to these peoples can become part of the increased information flow to the peoples behind the Soviet frontiers of silence.

The public nature of this effort is crucial. We should neither hide nor deny nor fuzz over the fact that we and our global partners and colleagues are making this effort, nor should we feel "uneasy" about such specific tasks as letting Muslim families within the USSR know in great detail what human and cultural cost Soviet military operations in Afghanistan entail for the Muslims on both sides of the boundary.

While the West, slumbering within its conviction of fundamental nuclear superiority, was still hypnotized by "detente," the Soviets made a determined effort to catch up—and succeeded. Now the West, belatedly, is alarmed, and is galvanized into efforts aimed at arms parity or sufficiency—at arms parity and, ultimately, at superiority.

The real problem is that there has been no incentive thus far for the Soviets to cease their preparations for war, to cease nibbling away at exposed political flanks and invading weaker countries outright as in Afghanistan. The balance of power is shifting in their favor or, as they see it, the correlation of forces on a global scale has shifted to their advantage. America's first priority must be to rebuild our military power so that the Soviets see more risks than gains in using their military forces.

We must give top priority to disincentives to use military power. Only then can we create incentives to show the Soviet leadership that each new venture abroad will create more troubles at home as the focus of attention and the spread of information organized by our own effort provides the non-Russian Soviet peoples with a whole new store of data from which to draw entirely self-interested conclusions contrary to Moscow's "Party line."

Nothing is likelier to jolt the Soviet regime and oblige it to diversify its resources and reevaluate its foreign adventures than the penetration of the walls of silence with information.

We have never attempted this openly, timed for a cause-and-effect sequence in a concertedly global procedure of consultation and cooperation, where the traditions and insights of the Third and Fourth World nations most concerned can be brought into contact with kindred peoples within the Soviet Union.

This fusion of Western military superiority (making the option of a Moscow first-strike attack on the West impossible) and a global informational campaign directed at the populations of the Soviet Union and its satellites will force the Soviet leadership to refrain from risky adventures and begin coping in a serious way with internal domestic shortages, consumer production disasters, deplorable housing, brutal repression and the flimsy managerial base for non-military production—what is, at present, the wholly inadequate Soviet springboard for entering the next century on any but domination terms.

Consider the dilemma that will confront the Soviet regime if their future aggressions and subversions in other countries touch off an immediate increase in the flow and impact of global information detailing Soviet activities to the diverse peoples they seek to control. They will find this flow of information from our agencies hampering their ability to raise new brush fires of aggression and subversion at will around the world. Even more sensitive repercussions will be created within groups of their own population and their bordering satellites stretching from the Elbe River to the frontiers of Afghanistan, China and Korea.

The cause-and-effect relationship of this effort may provide the first serious institutional leverage within the Soviet-West relationship to oblige Moscow to take a path of caution and restraint. The Kremlin leaders may arrive at compelling new reasons to regret such attacks as the one on Afghanistan if they realize that it will merely exacerbate the problem of ruling the fifty million Muslims who learn of the genocide being waged against their co-religionists.

If this effort is seriously performed, it will be the moral and philosophical counterpart to the alleged Soviet concern for the "oppressed masses" of the world that are being urged to look to Moscow for salvation. We in the West truly represent a global constituency of immense diversity. It is time for us to join together with our global allies in other countries. Such a joint effort would be an excellent beginning in focusing attention on the Soviet Union's role as prime aggressor and seeking to build a coalition of participation in dealing with the threat by enlisting the involvement of the Soviet non-Russian peoples themselves.

The tactical priority involved is vital. A public effort to reach the concerned peoples within the Soviet Union is the missing element of leverage to balance the purely military aspects of Western capability to deter aggression and prevent a nuclear holocaust.

This is, quite simply, the root of the matter: the Soviet leadership must cease to seek a way out of its domestic dilemmas by foreign adventures that in this age endanger all mankind. They must be obliged to set their own house in order.

Thus, for the first time since its foundation, the Soviets may conceive or envisage *genuine* detente. If it is made to realize that new adventures abroad, doomed to failure, will also lead to immediate troubles at home, it will be shifted, gradually, into a new stance: accepting a leading but not supreme position among the countries of the world.

Its behavior will be transformed.

It is ironic that our use of power—our strength and our concomitant programs for implementing it—has not to date given the Soviets an interest in taking *real* detente seriously. Yet this subject, a vessel for distortions, lies and failed hopes, is not now literally defunct. Out of its ashes will rise a new concept of detente grounded not in illusions but in factual relations and in fruitful initiatives for bringing peoples together. If we adopt an initiative of "open minds" that will parallel our achievement of military superiority, and if both of these efforts, material and spiritual, are combined to deter any possibility of a nuclear strategic Soviet military option on a global scale, then we may surely find ourselves closer to the creation of a real peace than at any time since 1945—a peace on both sides of the line between us.

Even if the Soviets recoil and decide that the only riposte to such efforts of global, concerted persuasion is still more repression of their population, they will at least take a step away from foreign offensives and begin to face in a new way the reality of the unquenchable spirit of freedom and its matchless stamina in the teeth of all totalitarian efforts to extinguish it. If the Soviet leaders could be compelled to act differently, it may internalize that acceptance and turn aside from aggression against the outside world. With the expansion of such a campaign of information generated within the Soviet orbit by our efforts, the Soviet leaders might well become literally the lepers of the global community. In such an environment of internal seige, an embargo on shipments to the Soviet Union from outside could have a real effect.

The final reason for supporting the open-minds effort is that it would ally us with the spirit of our own American Revolution roots, emphasizing our respect for "facts to a candid world," in Jefferson's words, and the inevitability of the yearning of human intellect and character for knowledge, ideas and exchange of information. We dare not proceed to attempt the creation of a new world environment of development growth and progress to meet the challenge of the year 2000 by abandoning the countless millions of proudly diverse peoples in their solitary confinement behind the Soviet walls of silence.

Our approach must be two-pronged: we must add weight to the scale of peace by increasing our military strength while at the same time encouraging dissidents, minorities and other isolated elements in the Soviet Union by giving them information suppressed by the Soviet censorship. In this way we can tilt the balance toward a peaceful resolution of the great conflict of the century.

We owe our children no less than this: an awareness of the necessity for global involvement in an effort to build a shared, informed framework for peace. The world of the year 2000 may feature as many as thirty countries possessing atomic weapons capability. Adding that harvest of the next twenty years to the record of failure in our efforts to resolve the global crisis which has hovered on the brink of nuclear holocaust for more than thirty-five years, we can understand the urgency of incorporating this missing element of open-minds potential into our 1980's efforts for moving toward peace. There is literally a role for all. The advice and counsel of every race, creed and ethnic root is needed to do the job the way it should be done. We will end being more cross-culturally aware than we have ever been—and we have never been anything but a disappointment on this score, given our potential and opportunity to learn, our world responsibilities in a post-World War Two world and our pathetic habit of refusing to consider as serious constraints the specific attributes embodied in each new situation in which we find ourselves taking a global role.

Having an open society, some Americans often find themselves full of unwarranted admiration for the covert, especially in operations involving foreign affairs. We have an indelible image of the spy-warrior which connotes clandestine broadcasts, unattributed leaflets and all manner of skullduggery to evade identification.

The Soviets, having a closed society, appreciate the image value of the purportedly public position claiming legitimacy and support even in matters preposterous beyond belief (i.e., the Soviet claim that their invasion of Afghanistan was really an assistance mission, helping a neighboring country that had requested a Soviet blitzkrieg; or the outrageous Soviet insistence that Korean Arlines flight 007 was shot down while conducting a spy mission). Despite the incredibly flimsy nature of these lies, the Soviets strive mightily for the legitimacy it seeks to create.

There are of course covert means of getting information across totalitarian boundaries. But the spirit and concept of the program itself must be completely, indeed blatantly, public: the fact that such covert means are being used must itself be public without, of course, being identified or described in detail. Public, too, must be the pride we share with other nations in reaching the diverse peoples in the Soviet Union who have a raging need to know.

This open-minds initiative must rely on the spirit of mankind in its goal to convey crucial awareness of events to peoples who have been for so long deprived of information, surmounting the walls of silence and thus obliterating the information monopoly of the Soviet regime.

Thus, an overwhelming unity of purpose may actually eventually transform the interior structure of the Soviet system, inching them toward the need to make genuine spiritual concessions to the human beings whose spirits they have been straitjacketing.

This may be feasible not because the dynamic thrust of the

Kremlin will have lessened but because the open-minds effort will demonstrate indisputably that Soviet brutal methods of the past are bound to produce a harvest of new troubles at home—a fact that the Soviet leaders of the next twenty years will be obliged to acknowledge.

If, at that time, Moscow's military option is foreclosed by the clear military superiority of the West, the Soviets will have to initiate a historic reassessment of the legacy of the Bolsheviks of 1917 or else face the risk of being bypassed, quite literally, by the world at large.

Only this formula stands a chance of bringing about any real progress toward global cooperation and the peaceful resolution of crises that we have had the right to hope for up to now.

It is with hope, not with malice; with dedication, not in a spirit of belligerence; that this initiative is advocated. These have been the elements missing from our inventory of strengths and skills for thirty-five years.

Our existing information efforts do not come remotely near this new effort; they do not come remotely near this focus.

Nonetheless, we no longer dare overlook the necessity for this new enterprise. Muslims, Christians, Jews, Asians, Middle Easterners, Africans, East Europeans, Latin Americans—all deserve no less. History will not forgive a continuation of past failures to understand the need for this perspective and to take the necessary measures in its behalf.

Without the combination of military strength and the new endeavors based on a national initiatives strategy, there may well be, within the next two decades, no longer any history for free peoples to write.

10

What is to Be Done Now

If this gloomy assessment of the global balance is correct, what are we to do?

How can we cope with the current Soviet movement aimed at a strategic position throughout the world that will excel that of its rivals—the United States and China—and thus result in a position of hegemony?

The subjective intentions of the Soviet leadership are wholly irrelevant: what is beyond dispute is that it has a consistent strategy and cluster of policy goals. Since military superiority is the precondition for world hegemony, we must take seriously the problem this presents.

For the Soviet leaders it was routine under detente to sow disruption, subversion and violence throughout the third world countries. Their ability to evolve, together with their desire to form infinitely more fruitful partnerships with the West, was radically inhibited.

In this age of global integration, now overhung by the dreadful jeopardy of nuclear war, the primary problem facing not merely the West but all mankind is the taming of the adventurous spirit now driving the Kremlin.

Shaky in its socioeconomic institutions, unable, in the greatest granary in the world, to feed its own people, unable to satisfy its consumers, the Soviet regime is gambling on worldwide hegemony precisely in order to elude its disabilities at home. The general instability of the regime was given global urgency, as indicated earlier, when the semi-covert campaigns of subversion current under detente were replaced, in the summer of 1975, by the ramified pincer movement targeting the Persian Gulf.

If we are to respond, and respond without resorting to nuclear decision, with their unpredictable consequences, we must develop methods for coping with the Kremlin that will be aimed not at its destruction but at its transformation into a partner in a new harmony of peoples. This will require the United States to embark on a concerted national initiative strategy vis-a-vis the Soviet Union.

But before such a broad view can even be contemplated, we must reassess all our perspectives—we must broaden the context to take in the whole world.

And to do this we must reanalyze the strategic interrelationship of the many factors of strength throughout the world.

A cursory view should make it obvious, that, despite the growth of many power centers in the world, the area of the Middle East remains crucial, both in the absolute sense and in the sense in which its vast oil reserves lend it a power that radiates far beyond its boundaries. Soviet control of the oil resources of the Gulf would entail immediate, inexorable pressure on the industrialized economies of Western Europe and Japan. It would also entail immediate, inexorable pressure on Africa and Asia as a whole.

Thus the control of the Persian Gulf remains crucial, and since this is where the greatest, most urgent Soviet threat is looming, it is plainly imperative for the United States to begin coping with the greatest threat America has faced in its history.

First of all, we must become conceptually aware of the inadequacy of the measures taken during the past few decades by *all* U.S. administrations.

The essence of current Soviet strategy, as indicated, has been its drive for the achievement of nuclear superiority while at the same time carrying on a vast and ramified campaign of conquest in Africa and the Middle East via surrogates using conventional arms. In 1980, it even dispensed with the figleaf of surrogates in Afghanistan.

It is just this two-pronged strategy that has brought about the current paradox in world affairs. It is precisely the expansion of nuclear weapons systems, whose very existence entails a danger too grave to be risked, that enhances the indispensability of conventional military power. Our urgent need for a strategy to replace detente is evident the moment we assess the implications of the Soviet advance, specifically since the penetration of Angola by Cuban surrogates. When we think of the arms buildup in south Yemen, the Soviet manipulation of the Iraqi military, the penetration of Iran, the invasion of Afghanistan, and the backing of Syrian mischief-making in Lebanon, the urgency of our need becomes incontrovertible.

The security policy we have now, structured to fight "one and a half" conventional wars, is grossly inadequate. This was clearly demonstrated in 1978 by "Nifty Nugget," the first simulated government-wide mobilization exercise since World War II. This exercise was designed to test our ability to mount and sustain logistically a conventional military force in Europe long enough to be credible against an attack by Warsaw Pact nations. It was a disaster. The planners found that nothing worked according to mobilization plans: much of the mobilization capability needed to support a large-scale conventional war had been lost, there were critical manpower shortfalls, crucial equipment shortages and none of the airlift and sealift capability necessary to remain credible in *one* major war was available.

Admiral Elmo R. Zumwalt, Jr., former Chief of Naval Operations, estimates that anything less a three-front capability risks the loss of at least one front to save the other one or two. This translates into such questions as: should we lose the Persian Gulf to save Japan and Korea, or vice versa? Lose Western Europe to save the others? Can we afford to save all three? Can we afford *not* to save all three? The choices imposed on us are as chilling as they are few.

A strategy with positive goals utilizes the panoply of state power attributes—military, political, economic and psychological—in order to further national interest. American decision makers, unaccustomed to viewing global events in terms of the calculus of changing but interrelated factors, continually fail to perceive the linkages that frequently lie beneath the surface of genuine "crisis management." On the few occasions when they do discern the linkage, the response is usually piecemeal and inadequate. This is to be expected: without a national strategy, decision makers had nothing more than a reaction position in regional flare-ups. Containment—enunciated in the early stages of the cold war—is neither a strategy nor a policy but an objective. Entirely reactive in character, it imposes objectives too broad to be sustained by a democratic state formally at peace. The objective itself is negative—the maintenance or restoration of the status quo instead of the defeat of the opponent's will. Its practice puts the United States into a position of having to react to each threat in the global balance potentially beneficial to the Soviet Union. Failure to do so engenders a perception that American will and determination have faltered. Success in any particular conflict merely restores a previous situation at high cost. And if the United States acts and fails to maintain or restore the balance, the validity of the objective itself is questioned. At its worst, containment policy promises defeat at the weakest link in the West's defensive chain. At its best, it inexorably saps the will and determination of the American people to sacrifice in defense of its static place on the security treadmill. Hence the Korean conflict in the 1950s was generally perceived as an inconclusive standoff, and the rejected withdrawal from South Korea contemplated by the Carter administration vitiated the rationale behind containment. Manifestly, defensive reaction is bound to prove inadequate to cope with the continuing Soviet offensive.

Over the long term, there is no alternative to a strategy aimed at the opponent's capability to wage war rather than destruction of civilian and industrial centers as under Mutual Assured Destruction. This cannot be done unless the fundamental asymmetries in strategic doctrine that give the Soviets a superior strategy as well as military superiority are eliminated. One cannot speak of nuclear stalemate and Mutual Assured Destruction when the opponent acts for survival and victory in peace or war. In the Soviet view, "rough equivalency" or "parity" is but one step toward superiority. Any diminuation of the U.S. nuclear deterrent permits an increased measure of coercive diplomacy. Therefore, the likelihood of Soviet aggression is certain to increase in proportion to Moscow's perception of the strategic balance. If Soviet power is to be curtailed, if aggression is to be deterred or repulsed, then Soviet military forces must be made hostage to acceptable behavior. Accordingly, the United States must embark on its own military buildup, two-pronged but integrated: the achievement of superiority in nuclear weapons and a narrowing of the gap in conventional formations.

The last two administrations (Carter's and Reagan's) have both been woefully astigmatic, for different reasons, with respect to the aggressive thrust of the Soviet regime. The Reagan Administration, precisely because of the President's penchant for "firm-sounding" statements, has pointed up the real passivity underlying the rhetoric: "firm-sounding" on El Salvador—silence on action against Cuba; "firm-sounding" on the MX—silence on conscription; "firm-sounding" on his outrage about the shooting down of the Korean airliner—silence on expelling Soviet diplomats or cancelling grain sales.

The global thrust of the Kremlin must be countered by a global response—beginning in the Middle East and in Central America.

There is only one way the United States can stabilize the Middle East in time to forestall a major, and perhaps irreversible Soviet action camouflaged by one or more of its many puppets.

The United States must station—at once—a permanent American ground presence in the region.

The Carter Administration, awash in sentimentality, could not grasp this, yet the Reagan Administration, too, has done no more than adjust itself to plodding along in the same rut as before instead of grasping the geo-political realities of the region.

Current plans for a Rapid Deployment Force (RDF) to be used

in the Persian Gulf area are insufficient. It would take a minimum of five years to establish a full military force capable of playing such a role.

The last of the fourteen planned Maritime Pre-positioning Ships will not be completed until 1987, and the CX transport aircraft—the Administration's candidate for this rapid movement of troops and supplies to the area—has again run into budget trouble in the Congress. In the absence of visible countervailing American power in the region during the next five years, the Soviet temptation to support their destabilization campaign in Iran, Saudi Arabia, Kuwait and Oman will prove irresistible. Furthermore, the more that America's position in the area appears vulnerable, the greater will be the willingness of Gulf rulers to accommodate Moscow's drive for geo-political primacy.

The very concept of the RDF in the current situation highlights the fumbling, half-hearted, radically insufficient measures contemplated by both the Carter and Reagan Administrations.

Having seen that some sort of presence in the region was needed, the Administration began conducting negotiations for access to "facilities" on the island of Masira off Oman and the installations at Berbera in Somalia and at Mombasa in Kenya. Meanwhile, it began expanding its base on the island of Diego Garcia in the Indian Ocean.

The piecemeal activity will not be sufficient, however, to alter the Soviet Union's ever-more-dominant position in the region. In seizing Afghanistan, the Soviets have gained land-based air superiority over the Indian Ocean—their Backfire bombers now have the operating range to effectively target our aircraft carriers deployed in that body of water. The Soviet Union's new proximity to the oil fields of the Gulf and its open support for radical regimes in the area—such as South Yeman—serve to intimidate the more traditionalist shiekdoms in the Gulf region that we desire to protect. The problem then lies not in obtaining overflight rights or access to ports and facilities from allied or friendly countries for future contingencies but in the need for sustained action of a sort designed to arrest the drift toward regional anarchy and possible war.

In turning to Oman, Somalia and Kenya, the State Department

showed that it had learned nothing from its experiences in Iraq, Libya, Ethiopia and Iran. A security policy cannot be built on the strength of an autocratic ruler, a royal family, or a military dictator. Over the long term, the viability of a security alliance requires that the allies partake of a certain measure of shared values and interests in addition to the commonly perceived threat. Out of the whole series of multilateral defensive alliances that were set up under the Truman and Eisenhower Administrations, only NATO remains functioning today. It is the common values and political heritage of Western Europe and the United States and the desire that both sides have to maintain it that keeps the Alliance going forward despite times of mutual political stress. Obviously, the large infrastructure of the Alliance—the political and military staffs, the installations and deployed forces—makes the political arrangements harder to dissolve, but without those shared values and purposes, NATO would have crumbled away once the perception of the immediate threat of the 1940s, 1950s and early 1960s faded and the Alliance entered the detente period of the later 1960s and the 1970s.

It is incredible, in fact, that the single preeminent military power we have refused to factor into the security equation in the Middle East is the only society in the region which shares our democratic values and whose affinity with the West is unquestioned—Israel. Despite its proven value as a stabilizing force, as a deterrent to radical hegemony and as a military offset to Soviet power, American policymakers continue to downgrade Israel's importance for defense of resources vital to our security and national well-being.

If we clear away the emotional cobwebs that obscure our vision of the true necessities which must underlie our policy in the Middle East, we will be able to grasp why the presence of permanent American ground forces in that region is essential.

By its appeasement and strategically counterproductive courtship of Arab regimes, the administration has further eroded America's capacity to thwart the Soviet advance into an area so essential to the vital interests of the free world. Further compounding the problem is the failure of the Reagan Administration's highly publicized enhanced defense program to plan and prepare adequately for facing and winning a showdown with Moscow or Soviet-backed military power in the Middle East and adjacent regimes. The Reagan Administration's most significant failure in strategic analysis concerning the Rapid Deployment Force has been its inability to grasp the fact that only the permanent stationing of U.S. ground forces in the Middle East can ensure the timely deterrence of a Soviet thrust into the Persian Gulf or to prevent the rapid downfall of a friendly regime through subversion. Secretary of Defense Weinberger has accepted the Carter Administration's emphasis on naval forces. Naval power, by itself, cannot prevent an internal coup in Saudi Arabia, a Soviet drive into Iran, attack on our ally Morocco by Soviet surrogate forces (such as Libya, Algeria or Cuba), or a move on the headwaters of the Nile in Ethiopia for the Sudan.

Soviet penetration into the Middle East and Southwest Asia was greatly aided by Great Britain's abandonment of its centuries-long commitments ranging from the Persian Gulf to Singapore. This raised critical questions, which still remain unanswered, about the entire Western security system, and it left a geo-political vacuum in the vast region between Suez and the Pacific Ocean. It is generally agreed that until Britain's precipitate withdrawal in 1971, the deterrent effect of its forces preserved a balance of sorts in the Gulf. With the British withdrawal "East of Suez," however, the often conflicting ambitions of Saudi Arabia, Iran, and Iraq have acquired new importance in the light of increased radical pressures and continuing Soviet machinations.

The British retreat from Arabia and the Gulf marked the end of a special relationship with the United States, in which the two allies shared the responsibility for safeguarding Western interests west and east of Suez, and it heralded the beginning of a permanent Soviet naval presence in the eastern Mediterranean and a frequent Soviet presence in the Gulf and Indian Ocean. Politically, the Soviets recognize that the acquisition of a naval power projection capability involves more than the symbolic showing of the flag. With naval power, the Soviets seek to extend their influence in an area which has become a political and military vacuum.

The Soviet naval presence tends to raise the cost and/or inhibit the use of American power, thereby casting doubt on the credibility of U.S. commitments to prospective aid-seekers. Nowhere is this point better illustrated than in contrasting Soviet behavior during the crisis in Lebanon in (1958) and Cuba (1982), and the Arab-Israeli War of 1967 with that during the October War of 1973. Whereas local American naval superiority played a decisive role in each of the previous crises, its inferiority *vis-a-vis* the Soviet Mediterranean "squadron" in 1973 limited in no small way U.S. diplomatic freedom of action.[1] This contributed to the American decision to deny Israel a decisive military victory. Moscow had clearly learned the importance of seapower as an instrument of foreign policy.

Although the emergence of a Soviet naval presence in the eastern Mediterranean marked the end of exclusive domination of those waters by a single power and constituted the most conspicuous change in the region's strategic environment, Western policymakers, slow to grasp its significance, tended to downgrade the strategic importance of the Middle East. Between 1967–73, it was argued that the Suez Canal was no longer vital since the world's oil tankers could go around Southern Africa, that the Middle East's oil supply was not threatened since the Soviets could not provide a substitute market, and that the development of nuclear technology and long-range missiles had supposedly removed the need for bases to contain Soviet power. These illusions obscured the reality that, after 1967, Israelis at the Suez Canal denied the Russians access to the short Black Sea-Red Sea water route—a condition that imposed some delay on Soviet military support for North Vietnam. At the same time, complacency over British withdrawal from Aden (1968) and from the Gulf (1971) brought about a drastic revision of the military balance "East of Suez." In yet another exercise in American self-deception, Iran, under the Shah, was supposed to fill the power vacuum by developing a major regional military capability. This was based on the assumption that neither the Soviet Union nor the U.S. would seek to replace Britain's naval monopoly in the Gulf and that the region's security would be protected by local powers.

There are severe restrictions on the deployment of a substantial naval presence in the Persian Gulf, despite Secretary of the Navy

Lehman's assertion that the United States could operate a carrier force there, if necessary, and survive. Major naval vessels have a difficult time maintaining maneuvering room in the Gulf and its contiguous waters. Even aircraft carriers in the Arabian Sea must allow themselves sufficient stand-off distance as protection against attack from land- or sea-launched surface-to-surface missiles. The shallow waters of the Gulf make navigation hazardous for large vessels, while facilitating the rapid passage of fast patrol boats and unconventional vessels common to small-scale navies. Also, the short distances between the two opposing land masses and the jutting coastline on the Iranian side of the Gulf greatly facilitate the achievement of tactical surprise, particularly during hours of darkness. The Gulf offers excellent possibilities for both the offensive and defensive use of mines, whether moored or bottom-emplaced (U.S. capabilities to sweep mines are woefully deficient). Furthermore, carrier-based aircraft would prove to be an inadequate counter to Soviet-backed aggression in the region. Air power when used by itself has been found to be ineffective in stopping ground forces intent on seizing territory. In both the Korean and Vietnamese conflicts, U.S. commanders attempted early-on to use airpower to slow down and stop enemy offensives, in both cases to little avail. Certainly the results achieved fell far short of those expected. Also small unit landings of amphibious-based infantry forces, while able to achieve short-term successes against larger ground forces—because of the inability to achieve tactical and even operational surprise—cannot cope with sustained, high-intensity combat, particularly if it involves combat with enemy armored and mechanized forces. Units the size of Marine Amphibious Units (reinforced battalion landing teams) lack the heavy equipment, including armor and supporting artillery, to fight effectively for more than short periods against heavier and more mobile combat forces. Many countries in the Middle East and Persian Gulf areas can today field sizeable numbers of Soviet-, British-, and American-made tanks, armored fighting vehicles and artillery pieces, while surface-to-air missile and multiple-gun air defense systems threaten U.S. tactical air power.

If a primarily naval strategy is unsuitable for the Rapid Deployment Force, a strategy dependent upon the timely movement of a sizeable number of troops from the continental United States is even more unrealistic. Closure times for delivery of a complete airborne division (combat, service, and support) and a mechanized division have been estimated at twenty-one and fifty days, respectively.[2] The entire strategic airlift fleet available for delivery of troops and equipment consists of some seventy C-5A and 252 C-141B aircraft.[3] Only the C-5As are capable of carrying outsize equipment such as the M-60 A3 and the M-1 main battle tanks (at a rate of one per aircraft). With the strategic airlift capabilities presently available, the United States simply could not deploy a large CONUS-based combat force in the early days of a conflict in the Persian Gulf.

RDF planning assumes desert operations against a numerically superior enemy. Yet U.S. tactical doctrine, which is preoccupied with firepower attrition, is ill-suited for the force that will be deployed in any emergency in the Middle East, since masses of main battle tanks and heavy armored fighting vehicles cannot be moved quickly to the battle area.[4] American ground combat troops must be taught to fight a battle of maneuver, using units lightened of their logistical tails and equipped with lightly-armored fighting vehicles whose cannons pack a considerable anti-armor punch. The Army is still very far away from this new doctrine of maneuver. Its forces continue to be hidebound by outmoded concepts and burdened with ever-heavier equipment.

The Marine Corps, in recent years, has shown a more purposeful interest in new doctrinal concepts, perhaps because of its need to look for missions beyond the landing of amphibious forces on heavily-defended shores. Its fight for aircraft capable of performing the close support role for its ground combat forces and for armored vehicles capable of being ferried around by heavy-lift helicopters is additional proof of its interest in recent tactical thinking. Clearly then, one of the most important responsibilities of the Rapid Deployment Force is to develop its tactical procedures in such a way that the integration of Army and Marine Corps combat units will not only be successful, but will furnish the combined arms concept that will enable the force to stand, fight outnumbered against superior numbers—and win.

In this context it is hard to understand why the United States has not made better use of the incomparable experience of Israel in desert warfare. Israel's skills in maneuvering and battlefield tactics in the face of a rapidly shifting front are directly applicable to tactical situations likely to confront forces of the Western alliance. Similarly, Israel's skills in wartime maintenance of equipment, including the restoration of damaged armor to battle in a short period of times, would be crucial to NATO's theater operations in the region especially given better than three to one disadvantages in armor relative to the Warsaw Pact. RDF forces could certainly benefit from an institutionalized maintenance arrangement with Israel, covering especially armor and aircraft. NATO could also benefit—at a minimum, in acquisition of skills necessary to provide the winning edge on a European battlefield.

Israel is a natural partner for the West in upgrading the defense of Europe. Yet the Reagan Administration has done little to expand its ties with Israel in this direction. Instead, the U.S. has chosen to rely upon Egypt and not Israel as its primary instructor in desert warfare. "Bright Star 82" exercises demonstrated that while the U.S. has made strides in learning how to deal with the problems of water supply and some aspects of desert maintenance, its level of proficiency in the skills required for desert combat remains markedly inferior to that of Israel, and probably other Middle Eastern states as well. Although Egypt has a role to play in U.S. strategy, Israel clearly is more capable of training American troops in the real conditions of desert warfare. The U.S. is cutting its combat capability by refusing to expand its training relations with Israel and by refusing to conduct joint ground exercises with Israeli forces.

The Reagan Administration seeks greater emphasis on combat readiness, yet it has failed to take advantage of the skills Israel offers in this field. Pursuing the chimera on in-country storage and servicing in Saudi Arabia, the U.S. has not accepted Israel's invitation to store material and use Israel's bases. This could be a significant mistake because of reduced American readiness and also the low odds for American success in any military operations. Of states in the region, only Israel offers an infrastructure and personnel which meet or exceed American standards. The assumption that the U.S. will be able to use Saudi facilities is not only naive, but is based on the misconception that what assets are available to the U.S. there will be useful or in good repair.

As currently constituted, the RDF is not a credible combat force. Its deterrent value is questionable and its combat effectiveness is highly suspect. It apparently serves only to placate the "beyond the horizon" political requirements for Saudi Arabia's strategy in the Persian Gulf area. The only solution to these thorny problems is to devise a strategy based on a permanent deployment of ground forces, landbased airpower, and air defense in areas contiguous to the Gulf along with increased stationing of Marine amphibious forces afloat in the Indian Ocean and Arabian Sea. The Arab states in the Persian Gulf region have made it clear that they have no desire to see American ground troops stationed in their territories. Thus, the only countries near enough to the Gulf and at least potentially disposed toward a permanent American military presence are Egypt and Israel.

There are a number of likely sites for the stationing of U.S. combat troops in Egypt—the Ras Banas base, almost directly across the Red Sea from the Saudi oil facility at Yanbu, the Israeli-built Sinai naval facility at Sharm el Sheikh, at the head of the Red Sea, and the two ultramodern Israeli-installed air bases in Eytam and Etzion in the Sinai (bases turned over to Egypt in April 1982). The Ras Banas facility would be an ideal location for the stationing of a mechanized division. Divisional advance elements could be rapidly flown out of Ras Banas aboard transports to any Gulf location, while the division's heavy equipment could be loaded aboard Roll-on/Roll-off vessels for transshipment to the nearest friendly or undefended port. The two Sinai airbases could support the ready brigade of a unit such as the 82nd Airborne Division, available on short notice for contested areas, to be followed up by the rest of the division deployed in Israel.

Meanwhile, Israeli facilities would offer the tightest security of any in the region for American stockpiles of arms, ammunition and fuel. In addition, the country's advanced military bases could provide superb basing for other divisional elements of the Rapid Deployment Force. Israel's armed forces are the most highly-trained and combat-tested in the region. They would not only be able to furnish protection for American logistics lines from the Middle East but could, if necessary, augment the combat capability of the RDF in certain contingencies. Israel's armed forces could play a key role in a confrontation with the Soviets over the Persian Gulf.

Weinberger's continuing reluctance to strengthen U.S.-Israeli politico-military ties, preferring instead attempts to receive the support of the Saudi government in exchange for advanced equipment for Saudi F-15s and AWACs radar-control aircraft, is one more example of strategic blindness. The Saudi regime claims it wants security but refuses to contribute anything tangible toward achieving it. In fact, the Saudis seek to undermine the Camp David Accords, thus far the only framework for peace in the area. By refusing the United States permanent basing rights anywhere on the peninsula, the Saudis and their OPEC allies are placing great demands on already limited U.S. airlift and sealift capabilities. Although increased air and sealift have been requested in the Reagan defense program, continued Saudi intransigence over basing rights will make it extremely difficult for the RDF to have even a marginal ability to deploy to the Gulf. Weinberger's defense plans are based on a long-term build-up of America's strategic and conventional forces. Yet in adopting these, the Administration has failed to use an obvious argument to bolster its case before Congress. Certain weapons systems such as the Nimitz-class carriers (CVNs) and the B-1 bomber (if procured in greater numbers than the 100 now planned) can be of significant value in confronting the Soviets in the Persian Gulf. CVNs are very cost-effective means of safeguarding American interests through the projection of military power in the Persian Gulf, the Gulf of Sidra, the Red Sea, the Indian Ocean and elsewhere. The diplomatic role of the U.S. Navy has been demonstrated time and again, most recently in August 1981 when F-14s off the Carrier Nimitz unilaterally devalued the political claims of Libya's Quaddafi. The B-1's utility as a standoff platform for launching cruise missiles against land targets and Soviet naval forces is undeniable. Operating from bases near South Asia, B-1s could have the sort of political influence now reserved for aircraft carriers. Defense against such a threat, by Soviet-armed clients, would be marginal at best.

In contrast to these simplistic and naive suppositions, a viable political strategy for the Middle East must start with the premise that the sources of tension and conflict are many, complex, and scattered throughout the region. Territorial disputes among Arab states are persistent, while ethnic and religious rivalries and conflicting conservative and radical attitudes toward social change fuel chronic instabilities both within and between them. Inherently unstable Arab states cannot be relied upon for supporting U.S. long-term strategic requirements. It is therefore fallacious to assume that given a *modus vivendi* in the Arab-Israeli conflict, Arab-American relations would necessarily improve. Such a proposition ignores not only the radical nature of Arab nationalism, but also a number of developments that together give the Soviets a historic opportunity for greater influence in the region. In a wider perspective, the unsuccessful American effort to forge with the Arab states a common and long-term alliance (Baghdad Pact), the Suez imbroglio of 1956, Egypt's quest for a leading role in the Pan-Arab movement, Britain's decision to withdraw "East of Suez," French withdrawal from NATO's integrated military structure and from naval bases in Tunisia and Algeria, inter-Arab conflict, the unsolved problem of Cyprus and its role in Greek-Turkish tensions, Arab-Iranian rivalry and conflict in the Gulf, and the highly successful Soviet policy of accommodation with Iran and Turkey—all, to some degree, created new Soviet hopes for achieving old Russian ambitions in the Middle East. All these factors will continue to exist, unrelated to the Arab-Israeli conflict.

The idea that the Arab-Israeli conflict is the central issue in Middle Eastern politics was fundamental to Britain's policy and she used it as a means of consolidating her position. The British hoped to design a coherent regional policy toward the Arabs at the expense of the Palestinian Jews. Much to their consternation, they learned that concessions in Palestine alleviated none of their difficulties in Egypt and Iraq. Endemic unrest in the region, characterized by civil war, military coups, abortive efforts at coalescences and the disintegration of traditional institutions, demonstrate that the more critical issues dividing the Arab world have nothing to do with Israel. These factors promise to keep the region in a state of constant tension.

Illusions continue to underscore the search by the West for an Arab-Israeli "comprehensive settlement" and a "strategic consensus" against the Soviet threat. The latter objective, thought to be conditional on progress in the Arab-Israeli conflict, is wrongly identified as synonomous with the need to satisfy Palestinian Arab aspirations. Unable or unwilling to pose countervailing power to the Soviets in the region, the Carter Administration placed emphasis on the "centrality" of the Palestinian Arab issue as the key to stability in the Persian Gulf. The experience of nearly a decade should have demonstrated that the problems facing the U.S. in the Persian Gulf have no connection with the problem of the Palestinian Arabs. Approaches that treat Islamic ferment and sectarian instability as secondary and Palestinian aspirations as primary represent yet another misreading of the dynamics in the area. Resolution of the Palestinian issue or even the Arab-Israel conflict would not eliminate Arab radicalism, and for the same reason, it would not ensure our access to the oil of the region. Given these conditions, any attempt to accommodate all interests in an overall Arab-Israel settlement is bound to fail. Bringing the Soviet Union into the negotiating process under any guise would create new opportunities for Soviet mischief-making. The Soviets think of the Middle East as their Near South. Termination of the conflict would not eliminate the conditions for Soviet interest and involvement in Iran, Iraq and the other states of the Arabian Peninsula.

The presumption that American resolve can lead to a comprehensive settlement is also in error. It not only assumes that the Soviet capacity to undermine a comprehensive settlement can be checked but it also ignores the built-in limits of American leverage, since such pressure is restricted to Israel alone. Jerusalem's reliance on American arms and economic assistance would not prevent Israel from going it alone, at whatever cost, should its survival appear threatened. Moreover, by exaggerating American leverage on Israel, a vicious cycle is maintained. The more pressure the United States is perceived as being able to apply on Israel, the greater are Arab expectations and Soviet-American tension.

The policy difficulties for the U.S. in the region stem largely from the constant pursuit of incompatible goals—trying to maintain good relations with both conservative and radical Arab regimes. The American obsession with occupying the middle position in regional quarrels blurs any distinction between ally and adversary and undermines the will of friendly regimes to resist radical pressures. Yet to compete with the Soviets in the radical states is self-defeating, since it intensifies both Arab-Israeli tension and radical pressures on conservative states. More significantly cooperation with any Arab state is tied to a politically and strategically prohibitive anti-Israeli line which the Soviets can always easily endorse. Nothing short of capitulation and the abandonment of solemn commitments to Israel would satisfy the Arab states. The fundamental point is that the Soviets are obstructionist. It is their threat to the entire region that obliges America, if only for strategic reasons, to stand alongside Israel. This threat is hardly limited to Israel but extends to Arab states and equally to the non-Arab countries of Iran and Turkey.

A breakthrough in the Arab-Israel conflict will be possible if Saudi Arabia can be persuaded to accept an American security commitment to the region without holding "progress" in the conflict as hostage. With such a course, an option will have been created which would permit Jordan to follow suit. In the present Arab alignment, Jordan cannot be expected to negotiate with Israel as long as Amman is threatened by radical Syria to its north and is intimidated by rejectionist Saudi Arabia to the east. Our diplomacy should aspire to creating incentives for both Jordan and Saudi Arabia to share the American perspective of security in bilateral agreements. Once the concept of bilateral alliances is accepted by the monarchies, the impetus for an Israel-Jordanian peace treaty would follow. Such a course is now possible in consequence of the bilateral Egyptian-Israel peace treaty. In fact, a concerted focus on bilateral relations with each of the states in the region is crucial for safeguarding that treaty. Jordan ought to be obliged to negotiate and accept its responsibilities as the Arab state *in* Palestine. The quest for autonomy should not be allowed to supersede or compromise America's interest in the viability of Israel as a staunch ally. If we look to Israel as a stabilizing force, a deterrent to radical hegemony and one potential military counter to the Soviet Union, we should recognize that the place for meeting Palestinian Arab aspirations is in Jordan. In all this there is no place for the P.L.O.

Nor is there a place for the P.L.O. if Lebanon's sovereignty is to be restored. This might have been achieved on the basis of neutrality under U.S. and Israeli guarantees; a restored, Lebanon would have functioned as a buffer between Arab-Israel, inter-Arab and Soviet-American rivalries. American policy was correct in encouraging the development of a Lebanese political authority that could negotiate and sign a bilateral peace agreement with Israel. The incentive was the return of southern Lebanon to the control of an effective central government. To have linked this objective with the return of Judea and Samania to Jordan however, was foolish in the extreme since Israel within the "green line" would be maximally vulnerable.

As we have seen, no comprehensive policy for the region as a whole is possible. The effort at grouping together proven allies such as Israel and Turkey with Iraq, Saudi Arabia, and Oman in the so-called "strategic consensus" nullifies any effective American diplomacy. Our efforts ought to concentrate, instead, on creating bilateral security pacts on the basis of reciprocal risk and responsibility defined as the capability of each nation to mount credible force and/or willingness to have U.S. ground forces stationed on its soil. The potential security partners are Egypt, Jordan, Oman, Saudi Arabia and Turkey. Of these, Saudi Arabia and Jordan refuse to participate in formal security arrangements. Saudi resistance is due partly to the present U.S. policy which assigns the Saudis a disproportionately high standing as the "linchpin" in the peninsula. That role severely circumscribes American relations with the other political entities in the sub-region. But as a superpower with global interests, the United States requires far greater freedom of action. American contingency planning for securing oil reserves in the Arabian peninsula must be devised independently of local desires and, if necessary, in opposition to local authorities. Arabia and its resources must be protected, but not at the expense of increasing our security dilemma in the Persian Gulf. We must accommodate the reality of unstable Muslim monarchies to the policy demanded by our security. Only by removing any skepticism about our determination and by isolating the states of Syria, Iraq, South Yemen, and Libya can we hope to achieve consensus for an American ground presence in the area.

In the seventies, successive administrations attempted to secure U.S. interests in the Middle East using means other than the commitment of power. It was decided to rely very heavily upon Iran to preserve stability in the sub-region. Later, efforts to achieve a comprehensive settlement of the Arab-Israel conflict reflected the same motivation as the disproportionate reliance that had been placed on Iran. Both policies reflected the anxiety resulting from an awareness of growing vulnerability and a psychological inability to take direct measures in defense of our national interests. The extent of our vulnerability has been laid bare. In one quick stroke, the collapse of the Shah removed the main pillar of American policy in the Persian Gulf. As American power has declined, Soviet power has increased and moved in to fill the vacuum. The invasion of Afghanistan is the latest and most ominous manifestation of Soviet expansionism. At the same time, local rivalries in the Gulf area remain latent; given the steady rise of Soviet power and influence, these rivalries can become more threatening than ever. The vital Western security interest is access to the oil of the Gulf, and this interest must be defended against any threats to it.

U.S. strategy for the Gulf must underline firm and consistent policy, which neither writes off Iran, allowing it to disintegrate, nor flirts with radical Iraq in the guise of seeking a "strategic consensus" for the region. Despite the current turmoil, Iran—like Turkey and Israel—possesses inherent strength. An Iran free of Soviet domination is a worthy goal of U.S. foreign policy in the region. The Carter Administration's negotiating access to "facilities" in Oman, Somalia and Kenya was an inadequate response to the problem of defending the Persian Gulf. The problem lies not in obtaining overflight rights or access to ports and air fields from friendly countries for future contingencies, but rather in the need for sustained action designed to arrest the rapid drift toward regional anarchy and possible war. In the absence of countervailing

American power in the region, it is more likely that Moscow will be tempted to intervene or to exploit the many local forces creating the instability. These threats cannot be deterred by plans for a Rapid Deployment Force. As we have seen, it will take a minimum of five years to establish a military force with a capability to meet its objectives. This may very likely prove to be too late. In the current situation, the very concept of the RDF highlights the fumbling, half-hearted and insufficient measures contemplated. We must deploy, as soon as possible, a substantial permanent ground presence in the region, which would provide forces for rapid movement into threatened areas of the Gulf. This would also serve as a tangible demonstration of American resolve in support of its friends in the region. No other measure can serve a truly deterrent function—one of peace through strength in real terms, not in rhetoric. Initial opposition by those who nevertheless remain almost totally dependent upon American power can be expected to subside once it is clear that the military presence of the United States in the Middle East is strong and enduring.

An active U.S. policy for the Middle East will confront a great unknown: whither Egypt? Cairo is at the crossroads between the Nasserite dream of Arab hegemony and pressures to solve the problem of overpopulation and undercapitalization. If the enormous U.S. investment in resources and its diplomatic effort are to succeed, the U.S. must sustain Egypt's hand in pursuit of its national renewal—not the mirage of Pan-Arabism. Considerations of American security in the region also dictate that emphasis be put on expanding the bilateral Egyptian-Israel treaty into wider relationships regardless of the Palestinian autonomy issue, and it should be reaffirmed that, in accordance with the Camp David accords, the future of the West Bank and Gaza and their inhabitants is to be ultimately resolved between Israel and Jordan, not Egypt. The U.S. must encourage Egypt to provide the protection of Sudan to its south and against Libya to the West. Egypt can draw on the American-Egyptian relationship to provide for regional security primarily in Africa—not in Arabia or the Fertile Crescent (Iraq, Syria, Lebanon and Jordan). The Arabian Peninsula should come under the purview of American responsibility for which Egypt may provide facilities. Egypt can no more be the protector of Arabia than was Iran under the Shah. The policies identified as essential to the defense of the Middle East are mutually reinforcing. When seen and implemented as a whole, they can significantly enhance American power and influence in the region. The goal is to place the Soviets on the strategic defensive and to exploit the vulnerability of their position in the radical states. In contrast to the relatively stronger societal cohesion of Israel, Egypt and Turkey, the ethnic and sectarian fragmentation of the radical states provides an unstable basis for the achievement of long-term Soviet objectives in the area. America's objective should be to maintain this condition by developing unassailable U.S.-Israeli-Turkish power, reinforced by bilateral links to neighboring countries.

While the primary American concern with Soviet aggression is focused on Europe, the U.S. has done little to strengthen the southern flank of NATO. This is particularly pressing need in light of the leftist, drift of the Papandreou government of Greece. Turkey continues to maintain one of the largest and most battle-capable armed forces in the world, yet this force is hampered because the U.S. has been slow to help Turkey modernize its military. Analogously, the Soviet Union has stepped up its air and naval presence on NATO's southern flank. One way to help neutralize this would be to coordinate Israeli air patrols with those of U.S. carrier-based fighter units of the Sixth Fleet. This has not been done, even though it would require only a modest investment in additional standardized communications equipment. The department of Defense agreed during the negotiations on the Memorandum of Understanding (MOU) to hold joint air exercises with Israel, but these were put on hold in the wake of the cancellation of the MOU. The failure to coordinate NATO's southern air defenses with the perimeters Israel already defends as a matter of course means not only that Europe's southern flank is more vulnerable, but also that the proposed airlift, crucial to the operations of the Rapid Deployment Force, would be much more difficult.

Similarly, the routine patrols of the Israeli Navy offer the Sixth Fleet an added, battle-proven enhancement against naval ships operating out of Tartous and Latakia. Again, the U.S. has failed to coordinate its forces with those of Israel, even though such a decision would not require any substantial change in either's extant operations. The Reagan Administration has refused to move toward this obvious and useful position—one in the interest of ourselves and our Arab clients—solely out of concern over potential Arab reaction.

In essence, the Reagan Administration defense plans were stimulated by two realities: first, the neglect experienced during the 1970s; second, Soviet gains both militarily and politically. While the former will only be reversed at great expense, and time, our posture regarding the political component can be improved. While the Administration has made much of confronting Soviet-backed aggression in Central America, and struggles to hold together the European alliance, precious little has been done to undermine the Soviet position in the Middle East. To the contrary, the Reagan Administration sent precisely the wrong signals by accepting Syria's *de facto* incorporation of parts of Lebanon into its own, as well as the Soviet, military sphere; by dallying in the supply of advanced weapons to Morocco in its war against Soviet surrogates; in cultivating Iraq; in refusing to accelerate the breakup of the OPEC Cartel as an object lesson of how the U.S. responds to those who undermine our interests and threaten our security; in emphasizing the need for a comprehensive settlement to the Arab-Israel dispute; and in refusing to exploit the extant polarities in the Arab world and in the third world as a whole. While the U.S. *national* interest would be served by reversing this policy, a select segment of U.S. oil and petrodollar interests would thereby be restricted in the growth of their power. The hold of these interests on many of the reins of the Reagan Administration is intended to protect their *private* gain.

Just as the Carter approach was vitiated by a refusal to define and defend American interests, so the Reagan Administration has failed to require support from friends and to impose costs on adversaries who threaten our positions by their non-cooperation or by aligning with the USSR. The U.S. under the Reagan Administration has spoken at length of Cuban involvement in Central America and East German involvement in Africa and the Middle

East. But nothing substantive has been done to increase the price of such meddling to those two nations serving as Soviet mercenaries. The Cuban presence in Africa continues unrestricted and unopposed; the East German involvement in training guerrillas and organizing "internal security" forces has expanded since this Administration assumed office. Opposing the satellites of one's primary opponent is sound strategy. The Soviets have not been reluctant or restrained in threatening allies of the U.S.—both politically and militarily, in Europe, the Middle East, and elsewhere. The failure of the U.S. to support friends and punish enemies has emboldened the Soviet Union. In this environment, the short shrift given to valuable allies such as Israel and Turkey raises the danger of Soviet miscalculation over the extent to which the Reagan Administration may be willing to retreat before reacting. The dynamic rhetoric of the Reagan Administration, matched by its appeasement and inaction, together endanger the peace of the world as never before.

11

A Strategy
For the Future

What emerges from the foregoing discussion of Reagan Administration policy is the sobering recognition that, rhetoric aside, the current Administration has adjusted itself to plodding along in the well-worn ruts marked out by the previous Administration. As in the past, there is no coherent, effective and long-term strategy for dealing with the Soviet threat, a threat that is serious and becoming increasingly coherent. This chronic deficiency was perhaps acceptable in a world in which the United States alone was capable of exercising overwhelming strategic power. That world however exists no more. Today, such a lack of strategic direction constitutes a liability that can have disastrous consequences for American interests both domestically and abroad. In the following chapter, some thoughts addressing the formulation of an urgently needed forward strategy will be outlined in an effort to identify the challenges that will confront us in the decade ahead, and how to counter them.

A serious discussion of strategy cannot begin without the prior stipulation of the political objectives toward which that strategy should be aimed. Yet it is here, at the very point of departure, that our weakness at strategic conceptualization is most evident, that is, in the formulation of coherent and consistent political objectives. In this regard, the Soviets have a distinct advantage which they have exploited successfully at our expense. The formulation of Soviet political objectives is determined by a consistent ideology based on the idea of the inevitability of change. U.S. political objectives, to the extent that they are explicitly formulated and articulated, are not rooted in any particular ideological orientation but tend rather toward the preservation of the status quo. The Soviet world view is predicated on the ultimate collapse of the capitalist state epitomized by the United States, while the U.S. is committed to ensuring its continued viability. While the Soviet Union strives politically and militarily to accelerate the overthrow of international order, hastening the demise of the capitalist system, the U.S. finds it necessary to assume a defensive posture, reacting to threats to its interests. Consequently, whoever would undertake the task of formulating strategies to defend the status quo starts at a distinct disadvantage relative to those who are pursuing revolutionary change.

Maintenance of the status quo is an anachronism in a world threatened by disregard for the rules of order and stability. The major thrust of U.S. policy since the end of the Second World War has been toward containment of Soviet power and influence, that is, maintenance or restoration of the status quo. However, one has but to compare the extent of Soviet power and influence in 1950 with that of the present to conclude that the policy has not checked Soviet expansion. It is of little comfort to argue that the Soviet advance is not inexorable given their loss of power and influence in China and Egypt and their shifting position in some African states. Such losses do not offset their very substantial gains. The Soviets are not overly disturbed by occasional setbacks. They try again when conditions and the time are right. Included in their world view is the practical notion of "two steps forward, one step back" as the way to achieve ultimate success. In the continued absence of a U.S. policy, incorporating clear and consistent objectives, a policy that is revolutionary in nature (and not conservative and reactive), the pace and nature of the global strategic confrontation will continue to be determined by the Soviets.

Perpetuation of the present approach, primarily defined negatively in terms of checking Soviet aims and in meeting and containing the Soviet threat wherever Soviet adventurism rears its head, is a prescription for losing control over our national destiny. It is, of course, important that Soviet expansionism be contained. It is time to recognize that defeating Soviet goals is not synonymous with promoting American interests. Wedding ourselves to a long-term policy of maintaining the status quo is to accept rather passively the fate that awaits most anachronisms: decline and irrelevance. Indeed, from the Soviet perspective such a policy feeds their self-assurance of ultimate victory since it cedes to them the initiative in altering the status quo at their pleasure, thereby dictating our priorities and in effect controlling our use and expenditure of resources. Our interests demand a more positive and creative approach. We must wrest the initiative from the Soviets by defining national objectives which will assure containment of Soviet totalitarianism as a consequence of their achievement rather than as their sole purpose. To recapture the momentum of history is not an unachievable goal. It requires of the United States a clear and positive sense of what we are about and what we want for the world, coupled with the determination to provide the driving force for realization of those aims.

In essence, then, a forward strategy for the U.S. should reflect two concerns: first and foremost, how the U.S. strengthens itself and its allies and shapes its future: second, how it pursues these goals in a manner that weakens its antagonists, primarily Soviet totalitarianism and its satellites. What follows is not an immutable prescription but, rather, a framework for effectively conducting foreign policy in the current international environment and in shaping that environment in the decades ahead.

First, it should be a goal of our foreign policy to promote democracy abroad, extending to others the benefits that we as a people have derived from it. It is only in a predominantly democratic world order that we can look forward to a world at peace, where nations will not attempt to solve their problems at the expense of others. The American model has proved to have enduring appeal even to peoples subjected to external control and international repression for many years, as evidenced by events in post-Maoist China and most recently in Poland. However, in pursuing such a foreign policy goal, we must be wary of confusing process and substance. We have in the past too often placed inordinate emphasis on promoting the political forms of democracy rather than its social and economic components. The former without the latter establishes nothing but an empty shell, a structure which can have no extended viability in a world in social ferment. We must further recognize that the political systems of the United States and the Western democracies have evolved to their current status over long periods of time in social and economic conditions that are rarely replicated in the Third World or Eastern Europe. A Third World nation cannot become a Western-type democracy overnight. However, to the extent that its people begin to reap democracy's social and economic benefits, no matter how meager by U.S. standards, it will be starting on the road to stability that will permit the emergence of real democratic institutions as well.

As a rule most developing nations tend, for historical reasons to be authoritarian in nature. They have essentially two alternative paths open to them in the present international environment. They may move in the direction of "guided democracies," preserving their more or less authoritarian framework, but progressing in the areas of social and economic democracy; or, they may move in the direction of "people's democracies," becoming, in reality, totalitarian societies, the very negation of democracy as we understand the term. The essence of the Soviet political challenge to the U.S. is over the route these nations will follow now and in the future—to a totalitarian world order dominated by the Soviet Union or a democratic world order ultimately modeled after the U.S. and other Western democracies.

It is now clear that local corruption and economic inequity, rather than authoritarian government, is the primary incubator of the special tumult the USSR strives to exploit. Many peoples in the developing world, whether their political culture is attuned to democratic principles or not, will accept the strictures of centralized power and "guided democracy" so long as the abuse of power is controlled and limited. Corruption and economic mismanagement are an invitation to revolution. In Central America and to a lesser extent, South America, the U.S. is allied with the over-concentration of wealth and power in the hands of the landed elite—an elite organized as oligarchies with only occasional trappings of democracy. Countries which are hostile to calls by the U.S. to democratize their political systems nevertheless are invariably much more sensitive to pressure for the reform of corruption. In the near term, the U.S. does have an obligation to contain Soviet opportunities by supporting friendly states, whether or not they are democratic. Over the intermediate and long term, however, the U.S. by tolerating corruption and repression among its allies does nothing to decrease the number of targets of corruptive opportunity. The Carter Administration's approach was inadequate and timorous: It is insufficient and against our interests to reproach publicly allies for their internal policies while saying nothing of the domestic conduct of Soviet clients. Instead, the U.S., looking to mutual interests with the nation involved should focus remedial pressures to change their internal demeanor quietly and in stages.

The Soviet Union has had dramatic success in the battle for hearts and minds in the developing world because it has seized upon socio-economic inequities as a means of catalyzing anti-Americanism. The U.S. can do much to limit Soviet opportunities by pressuring authoritarian regimes allied with us to control corruption. Democratic, multi-party systems can come later, if at all. Marxist revolts are much less effective when aimed at economically equitable infrastructures. In the long term, in the Third World, nothing is as important to promoting stability and stopping communist-inspired rebellions as the need to eliminate local corruptions, improve economic performance, and correct the maldistribution of economic power.

An American Administration should spell out precisely what it wants in terms of reforms and in what time frame they are to be achieved. The very absence of democratic institutions should facilitate direct pressure on ruling groups to weed out and eliminate outstandingly corrupt officials. Redistribution of land and power in an oligarchy dominated by rich families is harder to achieve, but it is possible that economic sanctions, designed to limit the secure deposit of monies from these countries in the U.S. and Europe could be eminently persuasive. Few oligarchic family power structures today exist without the backstop of Western banks. Pressure here, and upon allied corporations, is apt to bring about the desired effect. The alternative to such an initiative is one Nicaragua after another.

Second, and concomitant with the first point, the U.S. has to reemphasize its support for allies which are democratic and supportive of American interests. The classic failure of such an approach is apparent in the Middle East, where Saudi Arabia has been cossetted while Israel has been devalued.

It inevitably follows from this that the U.S. should be prepared to take measures against countries which undermine our defined interests. It is absurd for the U.S. to sell arms to nations which openly oppose our policies in their region. It is equally foolhardy to support cartels and economic policies that undermine the health of the Western economy. Our policies toward the Middle East and OPEC during the last decade would have been far different were the U.S. determined to make other nations aware that it will not accept economic assaults against its interests without imposing substantial costs on those responsible.

The foregoing assumes a policy which is clearly enunciated and strictly observed. Implementing such an approach will not be easy. Given past experience, many nations which deal with the U.S. would expect that their hostile response to such a proposed stance would in the end elicit American accommodation. This is to be avoided at all costs, for ambivalence is the deadly enemy of effective superpower policy. The Soviet Union has succeeded in instilling in other nations a clear sense of what the USSR might do if crossed; equally clearly the U.S., has instilled a sense of its timidity (except, on occasion, towards our allies). This must be changed. Once the unswerving nature of our commitment to our policy goals is made clear, and our determination to pursue those goals made manifest, domestic and foreign critics alike will come to understand that the historic ambivalence of American policy is indeed a thing of the past.

With direct regard to the Soviet Union, a forward strategy would include a number of mutually supporting components. The ultimate threat posed by the USSR is reflected in recent statements by its military leadership which propound the feasibility of winning a nuclear conflict. A "war-fighting" doctrine is consistent with Soviet rejection of the status quo as an acceptable political or strategic objective. Ideologically convinced of the inevitability of ultimate victory in the historically determined struggle with capitalism, the overriding Soviet objective is to accelerate the dismemberment of the capitalist system with minimum damage to its own empire. The Soviets want to conquer the West and exploit its assets; they do not want to destroy the strategic prize they seek. From the Soviet perspective, massive destruction resulting from a counter-value second strike would serve no valid political purpose. Consequently, a credible U.S. nuclear strategy would call for the ability to survive a Soviet first strike and to reduce the enemy's capacity to launch a retaliatory strike. Affecting such an approach are the military preparations the Soviet Union has made for fighting in a nuclear environment. However, the Soviet preference is to win without fighting if at all possible.

The U.S. should move quickly to convince the Soviet leadership that the assumptions of their strategic planners are ill-founded and that any nuclear engagement with the U.S. will be ruinous to the USSR; that, though the U.S. may not be able to acquire nuclear superiority over the USSR in the near term, it is certain that the U.S. will acquire the capability to respond to any Soviet strike with appropriate weapons. We must move to ensure that our nuclear deterrent does in fact deter, and with the expansion of the battlefield to space along with the multi-billion dollar investments in strategic capability now being made or contemplated, both the U.S. and the USSR need to determine some limit to this seemingly endless spiral that may ultimately bankrupt one or both, without adding anything to the marginal security of either.

The desideratum of U.S. policy should be genuine movement

toward the mutual reduction of nuclear weapons without compromising national security. This could be accomplished by moving simultaneously toward reciprocal reduction of nuclear weapons and assured, increased lethality and survivability of those which remain. Reinforcement of this approach would focus America's strategy on the Soviet Union's primary political point: survival of Soviet military power. Through appropriate means, the U.S. could move to assure the Soviet leadership that in a nuclear attack, the country would seek to destroy Soviet leadership where feasible along with Soviet warmaking capabilities and power projection forces.

In the conventional sphere, there is much that the U.S. can do to restrain the Soviet Union. In addition to pursuing a defined, coherent and predictable political policy, the U.S. can and should convince the USSR of the strength of our intentions by making our conventional military capacity a realistic striking force. To this end, the U.S. must, first and foremost, reestablish universal military service. The American military as presently constituted is simply incapable of fighting and winning a sustained major conflict. In foregoing the draft, the U.S. deprives itself of a critical element in the credibility of its commitments to friend and foe alike. Upon reinstituting the draft, the U.S. should expand the number, depth and readiness of its fighting forces. Too often today, America's military units operate in a state of low readiness and lower capability, hamstrung by severe shortages of trained technicians and sufficient spare parts.

In order to present a credible, conventional deterrent, the U.S. must also move to put men and material in situ, near areas of potential conflict. The USSR understands this strategic requirement, and has during the last decade expanded its access to bases and facilities in the Americas, in Africa, Asia and the Middle East. Consider that the Soviets now have facilities in Cuba, Mozambique, Afghanistan, Angola, Guinea, Libya, Syria, South Yemen, Ethiopia, Vietnam and elsewhere, complete with pre-positioned arsenals capable of sustaining up to five divisions (in the case of Libya) and requiring only the airlift of men (not tanks) in order to swing into action. The Soviets also have refueling and bunkering and support positions in these countries, as well as in India, Bangladesh and

Mauritius. They thus have the capacity to support naval operations in both the Middle East and Asia—operations which emanate from Soviet naval bases in Syria, South Yemen and Ethiopia's Dahlak Archipelago.

The United States can no longer seek bases only where they would be out of harm's way. Instead, we must have bases close to potential areas of conflict and use this presence as leverage for acquiring others. This means bases with support facilities and spare parts already in place, so that U.S. is immediately capable of moving force to the battlefield to deter, and, if necessary, quickly defeat foreseeable enemy forces.

Yet enhancing America's conventional military capacity, while essential, is not sufficient in itself. The USSR is apt to be restrained by a determined show of American power, and will find its opportunities diminished as the political policies of the U.S. gradually decrease the openings for social unrest among our "clients." Ultimately, however, the Soviet Union will pull back in its adventurism only if it feels it cannot sustain such endeavors abroad without destabilizing communist rule within the Soviet empire itself. To wit: if the USSR wants to "Sovietize" Poland (i.e., if it is intent on maintaining totalitarian rule) then the West has a responsibility to "Polish" the USSR (i.e., to assure economic disarray within the Soviet Union).

The U.S. has made but a small start in restricting the flow of trade, technology, and credits to the USSR. A much more comprehensive application of such constraints should become standard policy. The USSR is able to sustain its massive outlays for military adventurism largely because the West has decided to generate the capital for industrial expansion in the Soviet Union and to supply agricultural goods which the Soviet economy cannot provide. Capital starvation should be the first order of business in the West's policies towards the USSR. Capital starvation is certain to hurt the Soviet economy; it will produce inflation and disrupt the central control of GOSPLAN which is essential to the CPSU's domination of daily life.

In combination with this, the U.S. must work to prevent the Soviet Union from using alternative and seemingly innocent-channels to acquire high technology for its capital plant. The Communist Party has been able in part to overcome its managerial inefficiencies and low productivity resulting from its centralized policies through the introduction of labor-saving devices obtained from the West. The U.S. must cut the USSR off from its sources of such succor.

In order to accomplish these goals, it is essential for the U.S. to gain the cooperation of its European allies. It seems apparent that the NATO states, now increasingly "softened," might be less willing to accede to implicit Soviet threats if the lifelihood of nuclear war were reduced (through the aforementioned approach) and if the conventional ability of the NATO forces to defend Western Europe were boosted (again, through the aforementioned reforms and policies). This is apt to be a gradual process, for American policy should aim at cutting the Soviets off technology by technology, rather than country by country. Such gradual disengagement would have greater chances of success. Slower impact on the economies of our allies would assure their fuller cooperation.

A necessary corollary to the denial of high technology to the Soviets is a determined move by the West, the U.S. in particular, to defeat Soviet industrial espionage. It is well-documented that the USSR has been able to acquire illegally a great deal of what it cannot buy on the open market. Industrial security is an enormous undertaking, for it must extend not just to American manufacturers, but to their purchasers, their subcontractors, their foreign subsidiaries and their foreign licensees as well. Yet the near term costs of such a program will prove considerably less than the long term costs to the security of the West.

Should it become necessary for the U.S. to move more directly, it must choose its targets carefully. The KGB's implicit declaration of war on the West, complete with disinformation, gives the West the rationale to reciprocate in kind by intervening directly in Soviet life through the means the USSR has already indicated it fears most: direct broadcast by satellite. The West could prepare such a program, and limit it only in exchange for specific demonstrations of Soviet restraint. Similar pressures could be applied through moves designed to politicize the Soviet Union's Moslem and other national minorities. The USSR must be made aware that it cannot blithely act as agent provocateur in ethnic and political and class conflicts throughout the world and expect to escape similar treatment on the plea that such activity by the West would constitute intolerable interference in its internal affairs. We must extend the concept of linkage to Soviet subversion as well as to overt aggression. A significantly enhanced intelligence apparatus—one as scrupulously cleansed of moles as possible—must be prepared to expose Soviet provocations and meddlings in the affairs of other nations so as to encourage further Soviet restraint.

With regard to the allies of the Soviet Union, it is unquestionable that the USSR would be more circumspect in its foreign adventures if it could not control its client states such as Cuba and East Germany and was unable to rely upon them to execute so many of its policies. Consequently, an important element of a forward strategy should focus on ways of isolating such states as much as possible from their Soviet overlords, in effect to begin the process of dismantlement of the Soviet empire.

In the case of Cuba, which has in effect been forced more tightly into the Soviet grip as a result of its economic strangulation in the Western hemisphere, a more forceful approach by the U.S. may bring about a reduction of revolutionary international behavior—to the detriment of Soviet interests. The credible threat of a U.S. *cordon sanitaire*, subsequent to a buildup of U.S. conventional forces, could induce Cuba to reevaluate its military operations on behalf of other countries. This approach could raise superpower tensions, but the Soviet Union presently is not in a strong position regionally to back Cuba. Appropriate diplomatic preparation for this in the international community—especially among non-aligned countries disgusted with Castro's adventurism—would persuade both Havana and Moscow that any response other than that of a cessation of hemispheric meddling and the standing down of Cuban troops overseas would be inadequate.

In addition to these strategic moves, there is a variety of simple tactical changes which the U.S. can institute to restrain the Soviet Union. The most important affects American negotiating behavior. Over the past decade, the process has been established wherein the two sides make proposals—the Soviet Union's invariably being a non-starter—and then the USSR waits while the U.S. negotiates with itself. The U.S. should adopt the Soviet approach, resolutely holding back from deliberations and focusing attention on the unreality and inequitability of the Soviet position. The American starting point should be not the current specious rationale—that any negotiations are better than none—but rather, the proper rationale—that negotiated agreements must serve American interests, not enhance the "stature" of mythical Soviet "moderates."

The Reagan Administration has made a start in utilizing propaganda against the malefactions of the USSR, particularly in exposing the use of chemical agents and biological poisons by Soviet proxies and Soviet troops in Afghanistan. This sort of pressure needs to be stepped up, with the specific aim of informing the Soviet peoples of the irresponsible actions of their government. Equally important, the U.S. must be prepared to force action in international forums and in the non-aligned movement against such Soviet outrages. The threat of focused, retaliatory actions inhibiting trade and financial support should be persuasive with many Third World governments, and such pressure will probably have to be used only once, if at all.

Analogously, the U.S. must recognize the massive Soviet campaign of defamation against the U.S. for what it is, and move to force the USSR to control the horrendous excesses which have come to characterize Soviet character assassination of the West. Specific linkage of Soviet restraint to the granting of export licenses, for instance, is apt to have some effect with the recognition that results may be three years or more in coming.

In a sense, the overriding American approach to dealings with the USSR must be linkage. The U.S. faces fierce competition with the USSR. Soviet decision-making puts the highest value on risk assessment, and the U.S. must work to encourage the Soviet leadership to appreciate the additional risks that will henceforth accrue from their foreign policies—especially risks which threaten instability within the USSR itself.

As we proceed to think through the requirements of a comprehensive forward strategy, we must evaluate critically the conventional assumptions that have dominated our perceptions of the global role of the U.S. for more than three decades. Of particular importance in this regard is the seemingly unquestionable proposition that our global interests are inextricably tied to the Atlantic community and that NATO is and must remain the cornerstone of U.S. strategic policy. It now seems evident that our virtually exclusive focus on the Atlantic Alliance and Europe as the center stage of world events is becoming increasingly anachronistic, and it has inhibited a dispassionate assessment of the way the world is changing, and how we should respond to those changes.

Perhaps foremost among such changes is the largely unheralded but dramatic increase in the importance of East Asia and the Pacific basin for U.S. interests now and in the decades ahead. One-third of the world's population lives there, six of the most powerful armies (USSR, China, Vietnam, North Korea and Taiwan) makes it the most heavily armed region, and three of the most dynamic economies (Japan, South Korea and Taiwan) are located there. One need hardly be reminded that we have fought two major wars in the region since the end of World War II, and currently maintain heavy commitments of men and materiel in the same area. Of greater significance for the future is the fact that for the past two years our trade with Pacific basin states has exceeded that with Europe for the first time in history. Given that the growth rates of those Pacific nations vastly exceed those of Europe, our international economic interests alone call for a reorientation of our strategic and diplomatic posture to secure those interests for the future.

From the perspective of global politics, the field of major contention has been shifting to Asia and its periphery, spanning the whole continent from the Near East and Persian Gulf to the seas of China and Japan. If then, East Asia's geo-political significance is rising, the challenge is to construct a strategic framework for fostering the continued independence and growth of the nations of the Pacific basin, free from the threat of Soviet hegemony in the region.

Such a strategic framework must be built on prevailing geo-political realities. Thus, while it would seem, at first glance, that the natural focus for such a strategy would be Japan, that country's unwillingness to play a major strategic role in the region suggests that for the foreseeable future she will continue to be a net beneficiary of, rather than a contributor to, Asian security. A bolder but more promising approach would be the upgrading of our politically-neglected ally, the Philippines, to the role of a strategic partner in a new Pacific basin security system. The Philippines, which throughout its modern history has been the one nation in Asia sharing Western values, has persistently made plain its determination to contain Soviet-inspired adventurism in the region, and has demonstrated its capacity to carry out that determination in its own shores. There is already a long record of effective U.S.-Philippines military cooperation, and the Philippines now provides the major indispensible staging area for U.S. forces in the Pacific. There are clear indications that, provided its economy were strengthened, Manila would be ready to assume an expanded politico-strategic role in such a reconstituted security system.

Given the geo-political reality that the maritime route to East Asia for most of the free world starts at the Persian Gulf and its connecting waterways, it is no exaggeration to say that defense of Western vital interest in East Asia begins with the Strait of Hormuz. Accordingly, a bold and innovative forward strategy might envision an enhanced concept of strategic cooperation encompassing both the Philippines on Asia's eastern periphery and Israel at its western gateway. Such a strategic configuration posits a potentially hard capacity to project U.S. and free world power in Asia in a manner that might well transcend in effectiveness and economy anything presently contemplated.

This is not to suggest that the U.S. turn its back on Europe and the Atlantic community. It is rather to emphasize that the power balance in East Asia must be improved if the Soviets are to be denied global hegemony. In pursuing our national interests, we must seek strategic alignment and cooperation with those states willing and able to contribute to a more secure international order. In the Far East as in the Middle East and Europe, it will prove inimical to our long-range interests to structure a strategic framework on a base of security-consuming nations such as many of our NATO allies, Saudi Arabia and Japan. Economic power in the absence of a real defense capability is highly vulnerable and dangerously deceptive as to its ability to contribute to the very security and stability on which it so critically depends.

To meet the strategic challenges of the decade ahead, we must develop a forward strategy built on principles and objectives which are clear and comprehensive, a strategy that will be fully understood by friend and foe alike. Such a strategy must constitute the basis for what we actually do if we are to recapture our credibility, the current loss of which makes the world an even more dangerous place than it need be.

At the most fundamental level, strategic planning must be institutionalized in a manner that provides stability and continuity despite changes in governmental leadership. The grounds for consensus on strategic issues are extensive among both Republicans and Democrats. The differences are primarily in the areas of tactics and timing, not strategy, and the U.S. must institutionalize a means of honing tactics without distorting the underlying vision of purpose and goal.

In essence, the U.S. must do what it has heretofore resisted: it must plan for the long-term as well as the near future. With a sense of long-term goals, we will be *better* disposed, not less disposed, to take advantage of innovations and opportunities which arise from social and technological change. Moreover, the U.S. must now take another initiative which it has resisted in the past: it must exercise much greater control of our actions and image abroad, and that of our citizens and corporations abroad as well—at least to the degree now practiced by our Western allies. Governments, not corporations and not the news media, must make and implement foreign policy. Furthermore, we must disabuse ourselves of the simplistic notion that the business of the U.S. is business, and that what is good for business is necessarily good for the country. This idea is particularly dangerous when extended into the fields of foreign policy and national security—for example where it is implemented by the virtually indiscriminate foreign marketing of high technology weapons systems upon the most specious of strategic rationales. The short range priorities of certain businesses, whether banks, petroleum companies, or manufacturers, must not be the determinants of U.S. policies, the ultimate costs of which will necessarily be borne by the nation at large.

Embarking on the course outlined here will not be easy. It will not happen without extensive debate, front-end costs, or without vociferous nay-sayers. Nor will it be achieved without a concerted, hostile and threatening Soviet reaction. But over a five-to-fifteen-year period, it can begin to show concrete results, and by century's end result in a world more stable and more democratic, a world in which the specter of communist domination is a diminishing light on the horizon of history.

NOTES

CHAPTER 3

1. *New York Times*, March 20, 1981.
2. *Middle East Policy Survey*, June 1981.
3. *Washington Star*, August 5, 1981.
4. *New York Times*, September 6, 1981.
5. *New York Times*, September 11, 1981.
6. *Washington Post, New York Times*, September 12, 1981.
7. *New York Times*, October 2 and October 18, 1981.
8. Wolf Blitzer, *Jerusalem Post*, weekly edition, November 19, 1981.
9. *New York Times*, December 3, 1981.
10. *Middle East Policy Survey*, December 19, 1981.
11. *Washington Post*, December 1, 1981.
12. *Washington Post*, March 25, 1981.
13. *New York Times*, April 9, 1981.
14. *Washington Post*, July 17, 1981.
15. Foreign Broadcast Information Service, August 20, 1981.
16. Aaron D. Rosenbaum, Private notes.
17. *Washington Post*, March 7, 1981.
18. *New York Times*, March 9, 1981.
19. *Jewish Telegraphic Agency Daily Bulletin*, March 27, 1981.
20. *Washington Post*, April 20, 1981.
21. *Washington Star*, June 3, 1981.
22. *Wall Street Journal*, June 29, 1981.
23. *Middle East Policy Survey*, December 4, 1981.
24. *Washington Post*, October 30, 1981.
25. *New York Times*, May 27, 1981.
26. *Washington Star, New York Times*, June 9, 1981.
27. *New York Times*, June 18, 1981.
28. *Middle East Policy Survey*, June 19, 1981.
29. *Middle East Policy Survey*, July 18, 1981.
30. *New York Times*, July 20, 1981.
31. *Washington Post*, July 23, 1981.
32. *Washington Post*, July 23, 1981.
33. *Washington Post*, July 28, 1981.
34. *Washington Post*, August 17, 1981.
35. *New York Times*, September 12, 1981.

36. *Middle East Policy Survey*, September 11, 1981.
37. *New York Times*, October 2, 1981.
38. Aaron D. Rosenbaum, private notes.
39. Aaron D. Rosenbaum, "The AWACS Aftermath," *Moment* magazine, December 1981.
40. Jerusalem Post, November 21, 1981.
41. *Middle East Policy Survey*, December 18, 1981.
42. *Washington Post*, December 15, 1981.
43. *Washington Post*, December 23, 1981.
44. *Middle East Policy Survey*, February 26, 1982, and *Washington Post*, February 15, 1982.
45. *Washington Post*, February 15, 1982.
46. *Washington Post*, February 15, 1982, and *New York Times*, February 16, 1982.
47. *Washington Post*, February 10, 1982.
48. *Washington Post*, February 11, 1982.

CHAPTER 4

1. U.S. Treasury Department, Bureau of Mines, Washington, D.C. July 1982.
2. See Jennifer Seymour Whitaker, ed., *Africa and the United States: Vital Interests* (New York: New York University Press, 1978).
3. See Roger Pearson, ed. *Sino-Soviet Intervention in Africa* (Washington, D.C.; Council on American Affairs, 1977).
4. See Peter Vanneman and Martin James, "The Soviet Intervention in Angola Intentions and Implications," *Strategic Review*, Summer 1976.
5. See Colin Legum and Bill Lee, *Conflict in the Horn of Africa* (New York: Africana Publishing Co., 1977).
6. See A. Kiva, "The Struggle Against the Remnants of Colonialism and Neo-Colonialism," *International Affairs* 3 (Moscow, March 1981).

CHAPTER 5

1. Jeffrey St. John, *The Panama Canal and Soviet Imperialism: War for the World Waterways* (Washington, D.C., The Heritage Foundation 1978).
2. See Admiral Sergei Gorshkov, *Naval Power in Soviet Policy* (Moscow: Voyenizdat, 1979).
3. See statement by Thomas O. Enders, Assistant Secretary for Inter-American Affairs, before the Senate Foreign Relations Committee, April 12, 1983. (*State Department Current Policy Bulletin* no. 476 of April 12, 1983.)
4. The *Washington Times*, January 24, 1984.
5. Timothy Ashby, "Grenada: Soviet Stepping Stone," *U.S. Naval Proceedings*, December 1983.
6. Jiri Valenta, "Soviet Strategy in the Caribbean Basin," *U.S. Naval Proceedings*, May 1982.

CHAPTER 6

1. *The Military Balance 1983–1984* (London: International Institute for Strategic Studies, Autumn 1983), p. 16.
2. David C. Isby, *Weapons And Tactics of the Soviet Army* (London: Jane's Publishing Co. Ltd., 1981), p. 25.
3. *Soviet Military Power*, second ed. (Washington, D.C.: Department of Defense, March 1983), graph, p. 63—labeled "as of 1981"; and *NATO and the Warsaw Pact: Force Comparison* (Brussels, Belgium: North Atlantic Treaty Organization, n.d. [1982] graph, p. 11—labeled "as of 1981.")
4. Isby, pp. 102–103.
5. *NATO and the Warsaw Pact*, p. 27 (including those in the U.K.).
6. *NATO and the Warsaw Pact*, p. 31.
7. *Military Balance 1983–1984* says total Backfires in service is 110, p. 15, *Soviet Military Power* says 40 percent of those in service are deployed in the Far East, p. 53—that equals 66 aircraft. When you add the eight aircraft for the European theater produced in the past six months since *Military Balance* was published, it gives you a total of 74.
8. See C. N. Donnelly, "The Soviet Operational Maneuver Group: A New Challenge for NATO," *International Defense Review*, vol. 15, no. 9, 1982.

CHAPTER 7

1. MX Missile Basing, Office of Technology Assessment, Congress (Washington, D.C.: USGPO, 1981), pp. 45–52.
2. John E. Draim, "Move MX Missiles Out to Sea," *National Review*, December 12, 1980, p. 1527.
3. "Testimony on SUM as a Basing Scheme for the MX and Its Advantages Relative to the Racetrack by Sidney D. Drell before Defense and Military Construction Subcommittees of the Senate Appropriations Committee, May 7, 1980," copy of a typescript document.
4. For a discussion of these aspects, see *ICBM Basing Options: A Summary of Major Studies to Define a Survivable Basing Concept for ICBMs* (Washington, D.C.: Office of the Deputy Under Secretary of Defense for Research and Engineering (Strategic and Space Systems), December 1980), p. 21.
5. For a general discussion of EMP phenomena, see "Nuclear Pulse (1): Awakening to the Chaos Factor," *Science*, vol. 212 (May 29, 1981), pp. 1009–1012.
6. Walter Pincus, " '2 Guys' Hatched Air-Mobile MX Concept," *Washington Post*, August 13, 1981, p. A1.
7. Clarence A. Robinson, Jr., "Weinberger Pushes Strategic Airmobile MX Concept," *Aviation Week & Space Technology*, August 3, 1981, p. 17.
8. "USAF Analysis Attacks Airmobile MX Concept," *Aviation Week & Space Technology*, August 15, 1981, p. 31.
9. See the testimony of Brigadier General Guy Hecker in House, Committee on Appropriations, Subcommittee on Military Construction Appropriations, *Military Construction Appropriations for 1981: Hearings, Part 5: Strategic Programs*, 96th Cong., 2d Sess., 1980, p. 562.

10. See Defense Secretary Weinberger's testimony to the Senate Armed Services Committee on October 5, 1981, reprinted in "The Reagan Administration's Strategic Programme," *Survival*, vol. 24 (January/February 1982), pp. 29–31.

11. "Cost of Hardening Silos for MX Is Put at $7 Billion," *Washington Post*, October 30, 1981, p. A7.

12. See Clarence A. Robinson, Jr. "Pentagon Drops Superhardened Silo Basing," *Aviation Week & Space Technology*, January 11, 1982, pp. 20–21.

13. Ibid., p. 21.

14. Clarence A. Robinson Jr., "Reagan Picks Dense Pack MX Missile Basing Mode," *Aviation Week & Space Technology*, November 29, 1982, pp. 22–25.

15. "Military Preparing Data for MX Basing Study," *Aviation Week & Space Technology*, January 3, 1983, p. 18.

16. *Report of the President's Commission on Strategic Forces*, April 6, 1983.

17. Alton K. March, "New Report on MX Basing Finds Support in Congress," *Aviation Week & Space Technology*, April 18, 1983, pp. 28–29.

18. *MX Missile Basing*, pp. 94–95.

19. Ibid, p. 93.

20. Raymond E. Starsman, *Ballistic Missile Defense and Deceptive Basing: A New Calculus for the Defense of ICBMs* (Washington, D.C.: National Defense University Press, 1981), pp. 29–30.

21. *Ballistic Missile Defense: A Quick-Look Assessment* (Los Alamos, New Mexico: Office of Planning and Analysis, Los Alamos Scientific Laboratory, 1980), pp. 14–22.

CHAPTER 8

1. *Soviet Military Power, p. 30*, United States Military Posture Organization For fiscal year 1984 (Washington, D.C.: Organization of the Joint Chiefs of Staff, 1983), p. 18.

2. *Washington Post*, November 27, 1982.

3. George C. Wilson, "Weinberger Pushes Neutrons for NATO," *Washington Post*, February 11, 1981.

4. For information on the capabilities of the SS-20, see *Soviet Military Power* (Washington, D.C.: Department of Defense, 1981), pp. 26–27.

5. See Jeffrey G. Barlow, "Moscow and the Peace Offensive, *Backgrounder no. 184* (Washington, D.C.: The Heritage Foundation, 1981).

6. Ibid., pp. 16–17.

7. For a discussion of the tactical concepts inherent in the "active defense," see Major Robert A. Doughty, U.S. Army Tactical Doctrine, 1946–1976," Leavenworth Papers No. 1 (Fort Leavenworth, Kansas: Combat Studies Institute, U.S. Army Command and General Staff College, 1979), pp. 40–46.

CHAPTER 9

1. "Washington Roundup: Blackjack Forecast," *Aviation Week & Space Technology*, January 3, 1983, p. 13.

2. *Soviet Military Power*, 2nd Edition (Washington, D.C.: Department of Defense, March 1983).

3. See *Soviet Military Power*.

4. See T. K. Jones, "Civil Defenses" in William R. Van Cleave and W. Scott Thompson, *Strategic Options for the Early Eighties: What Can Be Done?* (National Strategy Information Center, Inc. 1979).

5. See Dr. Angelo Codevilla's damning indictment of the CIA in the *Washington Quarterly*, Summer 1983 (Georgetown Center For Strategic and International Studies, Washington, D.C.).

6. See Steven L. Spiegel, "Israel as a Strategic Asset," *Commentary*, June 1983.

CHAPTER 10

1. See J. C. Wylie, "The Sixth Fleet and American Diplomacy" in J.C. Hurewitz, ed., *Soviet-American Rivalry in the Middle East.*

2. Jeffrey Record, *The Rapid Deployment Force and U.S. Military Intervention in the Persian Gulf* (Cambridge Institute for Foreign Policy Analysis, Inc., 1981), pp. 20–21.

3. *Military Balance* 1983–1984, p. 9.

4. For a discussion of some of the issues involved, see Jeffrey G. Barlow, ed., *Reforming the Military* (Washington, D.C.: The Heritage Foundation, 1981).